HATE THE GAME

HATE THE GAME

ECONOMIC CHEAT CODES FOR LIFE, LOVE, AND WORK

DARYL FAIRWEATHER

The University of Chicago Press
Chicago and London

The University of Chicago Press, Chicago 60637
The University of Chicago Press, Ltd., London
© 2025 by Daryl Rose Fairweather
All rights reserved. No part of this book may be used or reproduced in any manner whatsoever without written permission, except in the case of brief quotations in critical articles and reviews. For more information, contact the University of Chicago Press, 1427 E. 60th St., Chicago, IL 60637.
Published 2025
Printed in the USA

34 33 32 31 30 29 28 27 26 25   1 2 3 4 5

ISBN-13: 978-0-226-83952-3 (cloth)
ISBN-13: 978-0-226-83848-9 (e-book)
DOI: https://doi.org/10.7208/chicago/9780226838489.001.0001

Library of Congress Cataloging-in-Publication Data

Names: Fairweather, Daryl, author.
Title: Hate the game : economic cheat codes for life, love, and work / Daryl Fairweather.
Description: Chicago : The University of Chicago Press, 2025. | Includes bibliographical references and index.
Identifiers: LCCN 2024038398 | ISBN 9780226839523 (cloth) | ISBN 9780226838489 (ebook)
Subjects: LCSH: Game theory—Economic aspects. | Economics—Psychological aspects.
Classification: LCC HB144 .F357 2025 | DDC 650.101/5193—dc23/eng/20240910
LC record available at https://lccn.loc.gov/2024038398

♾ This paper meets the requirements of ANSI/NISO z39.48-1992 (Permanence of Paper).

For all the haters

CONTENTS

A Note from the Author · xiii

Introduction · 1

1

INSIDE GAME, OUTSIDE GAME · 11

Negotiating Power · 11 Graduating into Uncertainty · 17
Comparative Advantage · 20 Game Recap · 22

2

CHOOSING GAMES · 25

Skill versus Luck · 26 Rules and Starting Conditions · 29
Marginal Benefit and Marginal Cost · 37 Cheating · 39
When to Challenge the Rules · 41 The Value of Winning · 44
Changing Goals · 46 Game Recap · 51

3

INFORMATION IS AN ADVANTAGE · 53

Ultimatums · 53 Deception · 57 Fearing the Unknown · 59
Negotiating under Uncertainty · 60 Overthinking · 62
Mitigating Risk · 65 Game Recap · 65

4

DREAMS OF DREAM JOBS · 67

Differentiating Yourself · 67   Selecting the Optimal Employer · 68
Moving for a New Job · 69   Creating the Perfect Resumé · 71
Preparing for a Job Interview · 75   Playing the Interview Game · 76
Curating References · 78   Unanimous Decisions · 79
Game Recap · 80

5

BUYING A HOME · 83

Deciding to Move · 84   Understanding the Housing Market · 86
Creating a Housing Budget · 89   Identifying Needs and Wants · 91
Avoiding Common Mistakes · 93   Bidding on a Home · 98
Game Recap · 101

6

WORKPLACE CONFLICT · 103

Workplace Bullies · 104   Employee Satisfaction · 107
Gender Stereotypes in the Workplace · 109
Evade or Confront? · 111   Identifying Enemies and Allies · 114
Signaling Strength · 115   Game Recap · 118

7

GETTING PROMOTED · 121

The Meritocracy Myth · 121   The Challenges of
Performance Evaluations · 122   Backward Induction: The Secret
Path to Victory · 129   Corporate Hierarchies · 132
Influencing the Kingmakers · 133   The Importance of Allies · 135
Game Recap · 138

8

BALANCING FAMILY AND CAREER · 141

Social Pressures and Gender Norms · 141   Marriage
Is a Game · 144   The Benefits of Commitment · 146
Marriage as a Financial Strategy · 148
Working while Pregnant · 151   Unconscious Bias · 155
Discrimination and the Persistence of Stereotypes · 159
Game Recap · 160

9

KNOWING YOUR WORTH · 163

Reassessing Inside Options · 163   Understanding Reference Points · 166
Higher-Order Beliefs · 169   When to Keep Your Mouth Shut · 170
Signaling Outside Options · 173   Bluffing · 175
Knowing Your Worth · 179   Game Recap · 182

10

OPTIMIZING YOUR LIFE · 185

When Optimizing Isn't an Option · 185   Saving · 187
Investing · 189   Rebalancing Work and Life · 192
Game Recap · 200

11

SELLING A HOME · 203

Assessing Home Values · 204   Preparing to Sell · 205
Setting the Price · 206   Selecting a Buyer · 208
Game Recap · 211

12

A CODE FOR WINNERS · 213

Epilogue · 217

Acknowledgments · 221
Glossary · 223
Notes · 235
Index · 253

Disclaimer: The following book is a work of nonfiction, based on my training as an economist along with my personal and professional experiences. To protect the privacy of certain individuals and to comply with confidentiality agreements, certain names and details have been changed.

A NOTE FROM THE AUTHOR

In 2006, shortly after I graduated from high school and committed to attending the Massachusetts Institute of Technology, I received an envelope in the mail from MIT. The envelope contained an invitation to apply to a summer program tailored to incoming minority students through MIT's Office of Minority Education. I was excited to go to MIT in the fall, but not *before* the fall. I planned to spend my summer days in a bikini on Santa Monica Beach. I planned to spend my summer nights backing it up to Usher, Ludacris, and Lil Jon on the dance floor. But I couldn't tell my dad any of that.

The arrival of this invitation (and my dad's ensuing discovery of it) made passing on the invitation impossible. I was going to that summer program. As I was leaving for the airport, my dad handed me a book. "You should read this," he said. "One of the authors graduated from MIT." The book was *Freakonomics*. The author my dad was referring to was Steven Levitt, who did his PhD in economics at MIT and had become famous for doing the kind of work promised in the book's subtitle: *A Rogue Economist Explores the Hidden Side of Everything.*

I read the book during the long flight from LA to Boston, and by the time the plane landed, I was sure I would be an economist. Before reading *Freakonomics*, I had assumed economics was about money or the stock market. But Levitt and his coauthor, Stephen Dubner, showed something different and more important: that economics is the study of how people make decisions under uncertainty and how all those little decisions made by all of us collectively constitute the economy. Levitt and Dubner didn't just make economics matter—they showed how economics offered a way of understanding the world from an elevated point of view. I wanted more of that.

A few days later, my father called me to check on how MIT was treating me. I told him things were going well—I was making friends and keeping up with my studies. And, exciting news: I had figured out my major. Economics.

My dad pushed back. "MIT is known for science and engineering," he said, using what I recognized as the voice he used in his job as a public prosecutor for the city. "You should be majoring in science or engineering."

I reminded him that he was the one who gave me *Freakonomics*, and that its author went to MIT for graduate school. MIT was tied at number 1 for having the best economics department in the world. This was a good decision! But he wasn't hearing it.

We hung up after that, but no more than ten minutes later, I got a call from my grandmother, my dad's mother. My dad knew that my Grandma Norma was my role model, so this was a calculated move. Norma Merrick Sklarek was the first Black woman to be a licensed architect in New York state, the first Black woman to be licensed in California, the first Black woman to receive an architecture degree from Columbia University, and the first Black woman to be inducted into the American Institute of Architects. Her projects included the original Terminal 1 of LAX, the United States Embassy in Tokyo, and the Mall of America.

Because of my Grandma Norma, I've always known that there were no limits to what I could achieve in my career—and, as a corollary, what I was expected to achieve.

My grandmother reiterated my dad's arguments, and added one of her own that I was not expecting: she told me that engineers make better husbands than businessmen. According to her, businessmen are self-centered. They care about money and status, so I should major in engineering so I could meet a better spouse—one who wasn't an economist.

My grandmother was full of contradictions. She had been divorced three times and married five times, and here she was giving me marriage advice. (I guess she did have a lot of experience.) I wondered how someone so ahead of her time could be so behind the times. What she understood better than I did, and what I couldn't appreciate then, is that marrying the wrong person could derail my career before it started.

My dad called me back a few minutes later. "Listen. I just want to say one more thing, and then I'll stop," he began. "You should consider the fact that engineering is objective. If you do it well, no one can dispute that. You will experience less prejudice when there is less subjectivity." Here I recognized that he was speaking from experience, and on a topic we'd discussed before. In the courtroom, he had to deal with biased judges and juries all the time. He was pushing me to the hard sciences to shield me from the challenges of other people.

He may have been on to something. But it was too late, as my identity was already wrapped up in becoming an economist. Economists seemed like prophets. They knew the secrets xvi A NOTE FROM THE AUTHOR

behind why people act the way they do and why the world is the way it is. I wanted that power.

※ ※ ※

If it weren't for *Freakonomics* and Steven Levitt, I never would have decided to be an economist. Levitt and Dubner's book showed me and millions of other people how to use economics to see the world in a different way.

It would also be one of the last times an economist was successful in doing such a thing. After *Freakonomics* was published in 2005, economists became overly concerned with impressing one another instead of impressing ideas onto the public. Economists stopped being prophets and instead became hermits, self-indulgently pursuing research without any intentions of sharing it with the outside world. This, to me, seemed like a less interesting version of the job.

After MIT, I went to graduate school at the University of Chicago, where Levitt became my PhD thesis chair. I spent more time talking about my research with him than any other professor. I took his graduate course and was his teaching assistant for his undergraduate class. My research was highly inspired by his. But I ended up leaving academia after earning my PhD because it became clear that academia didn't need or want another Steven Levitt. And perhaps economics didn't want or need to be of use to people, either.

I wanted to do research that people outside the ivory tower found useful. In the late 2010s, Big Tech was figuring out that economics was an incredibly useful pairing with the big data they had been collecting. So that's where I went: first to a famously giant tech company and later Redfin, where I am now the chief economist.

At Redfin, I study the housing market and its relationship to the broader economy. I research these topics so that renters, homebuyers, and home sellers can make better, more informed decisions about handling the most significant part of their budgets. Buying a home is the most important financial decision most people will ever make, so I take the responsibility of delivering useful and accurate research seriously. With this book, I want to offer a guide to how these tools of economics can help everyday people not only find a home but win in any game in life. It will teach you strategies that work when negotiating your home's price or your salary, finding a partner or letting a prospective partner walk away. The methods I teach here are rooted in economics and game theory, backed up with empirical real-world evidence. (I am a PhD-trained economist, after all.)

So please, compare me to Steven Levitt. But know that it's an incomplete comparison. If we were movie directors instead of authors, it would be like comparing Jordan Peele to John Carpenter. Levitt is my favorite economist, and Carpenter is Peele's favorite director. There would be no *Get Out* without *Halloween*, the same way that there would be no *Hate the Game* without *Freakonomics*. But apart from a few homages, the two masterpieces share no similarities. *Get Out* is nothing like *Halloween*. The two films are poles apart regarding plot, character, tone, and theme. And that's because John Carpenter could have never made *Get Out*. Jordan Peele's experience as a biracial Black man gives him a perspective that John Carpenter cannot access. So, if you are going to compare me to Steven Levitt, make sure to compare me to Jordan Peele too. And throw in Beyoncé while you're at it. (I'll get to her later.)

INTRODUCTION

When I started my career, I had no idea how to go from being a diligent student to an accomplished career woman. In school, the rules of the game and the path to success were clearly laid: attend lectures, study diligently, submit assignments on time, and excel on exams. But the real world doesn't work like that. There was no manual to consult and no set of rules to follow. I had to figure it out on my own, with no guarantee that hard work would translate to success. This amounted to a game: a competitive exercise against myself or others, with a given set of rules and an outcome determined by strategy and skill.

This approach is critical because, in today's world, it takes more than just hope and hard work to get ahead. It requires a strategic approach because victory is becoming more elusive. In 2022, the income of people in the top 10% of earners was 13 times higher than those in the bottom 10%.[1] The rewards for winning in this economy are exorbitant, while the odds of ascendancy are slight.

If achieving financial success is like a game, it's like that level in Donkey Kong where you have to jump from platform to

2   INTRODUCTION

platform as they fall beneath you. Looking down will give you vertigo. And, if you stand still and ignore the fact that the platforms are plummeting, you'll go down too. But if you keep your eye on your goal and move strategically, you can make it to the top with ease. The hard part is identifying a strategy amidst the chaos.

As I attempted to navigate the early stages of my career, I sought advice from books like *Lean In* and *Never Split the Difference*, but they proved to be less useful than what I had learned in my economics courses. While these works provided some entertaining insights, they didn't seem to reflect my specific situation: they treated success as a natural result of engagement, as if boldness and brashness were the keys to victory.

In my experience (and experience of many others, I believe), it is simply not always the case. One area where this was particularly evident was in the advice around negotiating salary. I had studied the economic principles that underpin negotiation outcomes. And I knew that broad rules of thumb could not compare to an in-depth understanding of how negotiation games work.

For example, *Lean In* encourages women to ask for a raise, citing statistics that show that those who ask are more likely to receive raises than those who don't. While this may be true in some cases, game theory tells us that confidence alone isn't always enough to sway a negotiation. If the person across the table has better options than giving you a raise, no amount of confidence or determination will change their mind. In these cases, it's better to focus on finding a better job with a more generous employer.

Similarly, both *Lean In* and *Never Split the Difference* advise negotiators to specify a target salary when negotiating a raise. While this approach may work in some situations, my knowledge of game theory informs me that it's often better to leave your personal target unstated if your negotiating opponent has a higher target in mind. In these cases, it is better to remain silent than to set a reference point.

So, I stopped reading career books for advice and resigned myself to reading them for what they truly were: memoirs and personal essays written by authors who didn't understand the economic context that led to their successes.

In behavioral economics and statistics, there is a concept called *survivorship bias.* Survivorship bias is the tendency to focus on successful outcomes or "winners" in a particular field while ignoring or dismissing those that did not make it through a selection process. This bias can cause a skewed perception of what factors lead to success. For example, Sheryl Sandberg is undoubtedly a winner in her field, but focusing on her story of success and trying to reproduce it can give us a skewed perception. The main message of *Lean In* is that the primary thing holding women back is confidence, because that's what she thinks made the difference in her success. But she doesn't know whether that's what holds her readers back.

A lot of us have plenty of confidence and still struggle to advance because of the obstacles in our way. Those obstacles mean we don't live in a perfect meritocracy where success is primarily the result of talent or hard work instead of class or wealth. How could our economy possibly be meritocratic when white Americans are 28 times more likely to become millionaires than Black Americans?[2] Women may have an easier time securing elite levels of wealth, but this typically happens through marriage. Among households in the top 1% of incomes, 19 out of 20 times it is a high-earning man, not a high-earning woman, who obtained those elite earnings for the family.[3] If you happen to belong to a disadvantaged group—whether it be due to your gender, race, or other difference—you're likely facing obstacles that the winners of this economy never encountered.

Even though I am not white or a man, I am not immune to survivorship bias either. Had I not succeeded in my career, I wouldn't be in a position to write this book. There are systemic reasons why you don't see many books on economics authored by Black women doctorates. I am an outlier. In recognizing that, I can look for an understanding of how that happened—how *I* happened. That exercise, set against the innumerable things economics can tell us about the world, produces lessons for anyone, regardless of their economic or social circumstances.

※　※　※

My career began at an unlucky moment in economic history: the beginning of the Great Recession. In 2009, as an undergraduate college student working as a research assistant at the Federal Reserve Bank of Boston, I conducted surveys of homeowners who were facing economic ruin. I heard the urgency and desperation in their voices as they pleaded for assistance.

This experience highlighted to me the large and lasting impact a recession can have on a person's life. Of course, none of these homeowners was responsible for causing the foreclosure crisis. Yet, a single regrettable decision—borrowing to buy a home before the market crashed—had drastically altered the courses of their lives.

I feared that one regrettable decision might change the trajectory of my own life, too. My generation, the Millennials, had a statistical 50–50 shot at being better off than our parents.[4] Compare that to kids born in the 1950s, who had an 80% shot of being better off than their parents, and the inequities across generations look stark. Millennials like me were being pushed into college under the guise that it would guarantee financial security. But during the Great Recession, many unemployed college graduates could not find any work that implemented their education. (Plenty of others still find themselves under the weight of student loans—another thing foisted on Millennials and Gen Z.)

I coped with this economic dread by fixating on achieving career success. And to obtain that success, I was willing to do whatever was asked of me. If a boss said, "Jump," I would say, "How high?" (It wasn't until later in my career that I gained the courage to ask, "Why do you want me to jump?" And "How does jumping help me achieve my goals?" More on this approach later.)

The Federal Reserve was also the first employer to ask me to take a drug test—a fraught moment for most anyone living and working in the 21st century, but especially for a kid in college. I remember walking into a room that looked like a nurse's office on the ground floor of the Boston Fed building. I entered the bathroom stall that was missing a door, urinated in a cup, and handed it to the lab tech, who watched to make sure I didn't switch my sample for someone else's. Afterward, I felt gross and violated.

I submitted to the drug test, but it made me wonder how far I would have been willing to go for a job. How much more of myself would I have been willing to give up? They had asked for urine, but what if they had asked for a blood sample, a DNA test, or pictures of my feet? At what point would I have finally said enough is enough?

In economics, this concept is called *surplus*. The concept of economic surplus refers to the net gain that a person or group reaps from a business transaction. In theoretical terms, it's the difference between the total value or benefit received in doing something and the total cost or sacrifice incurred in the process. By hiring me, the Boston Fed gained economic surplus: a smart kid willing to work hard out of economic anxiety and the inexperience inherent to being in her first real job. To the Fed, my value as a research assistant exceeded my $12 per hour pay. I gained economic surplus too: I got more out of the internship than I had to put in. The effort I put into the job involved waking up early, walking a mile to the train station, working for three hours, and returning to campus for my classes. That effort cost less than what I gained from the job: $12 per hour, research skills, and the most valuable part of all—a line of experience on my résumé that could advance my career.

Understanding the concept of economic surplus helped me overcome my vexation about the drug test (and the 12 bucks an hour) because I could rationalize that the internship was worth more than my urine (and my unease about when I'd last smoked some weed). However, back then I was still naive about the broader economic implications of occupational drug testing. I understand now that drug tests function as gatekeepers, preventing specific people from advancing professionally.

Economics and game theory provide tools to optimize decisions in an unfair economy that is filled with gatekeepers and other barriers. The goal of this book is to unlock that gate-kept economic knowledge, which in turn can be deployed in most any situation—work, home, anywhere—to maximize gains and outcomes.

Why economics? Because economic thinking comprises the tools to tease out causality from correlation—cause and effect from mere coincidence—and to discern a lucky circumstance from a career decision that matters. Every lesson in this book is supported by studies from renowned economists and behaviorists spread across decades. So, you can trust that this isn't just a recollection of stories from my career. Whether from my personal life, pop culture, or the natural world, each story is about winning or losing a game. Games, I show, are the episodes that make up contemporary life. Some games are individual, some are competitive, and some are cooperative. Nevertheless, they all follow the rules of game theory.

Game theory is a branch of mathematics and economics that studies how people make strategic decisions when success depends on the decisions of others. It examines how people or groups interact, taking into account their preferences, strategies, and likely outcomes. Traditional game theory assumes rationality and selfishness drive people's strategic choices. *Behavioral game theory* attempts to account for the psychological factors that lead people to act irrationally. *Evolutionary game theory* applies the concepts of traditional game theory to the survival of animals. For instance, in a flock of birds, each bird competes with the others for food and mates, but the success of any one bird depends on the flock's collective survival. Similarly, professional success is about survival of the fittest, but an individual's prosperity is predicated on the overall well-being of the economy.

Trying to make sense of the economy and your place in it can be disorienting. But it is possible to reorient yourself. In the same way a bird can sense Earth's magnetic field and its own position in relation to the sun and the stars, once you understand economics, you will be able to sense the economic forces at play. This will empower you to see the path from wherever you are in your career to where you want to be.

I unlock this economic knowledge by distilling it down to game theory principles with a few recurring concepts:

- Most challenges in life can be viewed as games—where the outcome of each game is determined by strategy and decision-making by the players.
- Within a game, players can make strategic choices that improve their chances of success.

8 INTRODUCTION

- Players can opt out of playing any game, and are justified in that choice when their chances of success are better elsewhere.
- Most games are designed by, and for, the winners.
- Every player can, and must, decide for themself what games are worth playing.
- Learning the rules that govern games is the key to success.

Chapter 1 covers the fundamentals of economics and game theory. It explains how negotiations impact different aspects of our lives such as employee wages, the prices of goods, and even the success or failure of romantic relationships. It explores why low-wage entry-level workers are at an inherent disadvantage during negotiations. It teaches how the options available to players in and outside a negotiation largely determine whether a negotiation is won or lost.

Chapter 2 explores the significance of starting conditions in a game and how certain players might have an advantage over others. The chapter introduces strategies to help players determine if they are at an advantage or disadvantage. It also teaches economic concepts that can help players overcome their disadvantages. The chapter concludes by discussing how to decide whether to quit a game or pursue a new one. This chapter will be especially useful for readers who are about to start a new career or are considering a change in their existing career.

Chapter 3 investigates the importance of information when playing games. It explores how information can be an advantage to players. It introduces strategies for making decisions when a player lacks information about the rules of a game or the circumstances of other players. This chapter will be of particular interest to readers who are early in their careers and lack experience.

Chapter 4 explores how applying for a job is like a game. It offers strategies for increasing the odds that a job applicant will advance through each stage of the application process, from securing an interview to securing a job offer. It explores the tension between the goals of securing a job offer and determining whether the job is a good match.

Chapter 5 explores how deciding where and how to live is like a high-stakes game, and how those high stakes come with high emotions. It teaches lessons from behavioral economics that will help first-time home buyers overcome their emotions and biases to win their ideal home without overpaying. It dives into the tradeoffs between renting and buying and explores why housing has become so unaffordable.

Chapter 6 is about workplace conflict. It investigates the causes of conflict, and how scarcity leads to competition. It teaches how to tell whether a workplace is especially prone to conflict, and how to decide whether to confront workplace rivals or leave for a less confrontational work environment.

Chapter 7 explores how promotions and performance evaluations are types of games. It uncovers the way employers use games to motivate employees to work more or harder. It teaches how to work backward and use influence to win a promotion.

Chapter 8 delves into marriage, family, and career, and how winning in one area may hurt a person's chances of success in other areas. It explores conventional and unconventional marriages, demonstrating how marital decisions related to the division of labor and family priorities impact the earnings of each partner. It illustrates the ways that mothers and parents who take time off for child rearing are at a disadvantage in the workplace.

Chapter 9 returns to negotiation games. It teaches how a player may use their opponent's assumptions to their advantage when deciding whether to make the opening offer during a negotiation. It explores how perceptions of class and race shape assumptions. It also emphasizes the importance of a player knowing their worth when it comes to negotiating.

Chapter 10 explores the difference between external rewards and internal rewards. It teaches how to make decisions about spending, saving, and work-life balance that align with personal values about what it means to be successful.

Chapter 11 returns to the housing game. It investigates how the scarcity of homes has caused increasingly high home values. It explores how cities are failing to provide affordable housing to the detriment of their residents.

The book concludes with an example of a policy change in chapter 12 that could be implemented that would make the economy a more fair, prosperous, and better game to play.

The rules of the economy are unfair, but that doesn't mean you can't win. My goal is to empower you to develop a strategy that works for your specific situation and values, so you can find your own path to the top. That way, when someone tells you to jump, you can decide for yourself how high—if you jump at all.

Now: let's play.

1
INSIDE GAME, OUTSIDE GAME

According to the Nobel Prize–winning economist Milton Friedman, one of the great benefits of living in a free society with a free market is the ability to choose.[1] If an employee doesn't like their job, they can quit. If a tenant doesn't like their rent, they can move. And if a spouse doesn't like their marriage, they can get a divorce. Quitting, or even just threatening to quit, is a power move.

Friedman's work was less mindful of the role of power in an economy—that is, not everyone in a free-market economy has equal choice, and that's because of unequal power. This is apparent within workplaces, rental agreements, and households. When negotiating for a better wage, rent, or allocation of responsibilities, it's important to understand where power resides.

NEGOTIATING POWER

For any negotiation to work, both parties must accept the terms of the negotiation agreement. In game theory, a negotiation refers to a situation in which two or more parties engage in discussions, interactions, or strategic choices with the aim of reaching a mutually acceptable agreement. If either player in a negotiation game decides to walk away rather than compromise on an agreement, the negotiation fails. Therefore, the person most willing to walk away holds power over the person desperate to make the negotiation work. The player with the most negotiating power is best able to influence the terms, conditions, and outcomes of the negotiation game.

Romantic relationships can be thought of as extended negotiation games between two partners competing to get the best deal in the relationship. Within a romantic relationship, the inside option represents the potential terms of the relationship: who does the chores, who pays the bills, and sometimes even who gets to mess around on the side. On the other hand, the outside options represent everything each partner would have if the relationship broke down. For example, if each partner were single, they would do their own chores and pay their own bills. Or, they could date new people. However, they wouldn't have each other's love, support, or company.

In the 2001 romantic comedy *Two Can Play That Game*, Vivica A. Fox portrays a successful career woman who knows how to wield negotiating power. When she catches her boyfriend, portrayed by Morris Chestnut, dancing flirtatiously with another woman at the club, she restrains herself from an emotional outburst. Instead, Fox plays it cool and shows Chestnut that he risks losing her to one of the many men she has lying in wait. Fox's antics peak when she fakes car trouble to pick up a handsome stranger and brings him to a party that Chestnut is attending. She purposely drops a condom in front of Chestnut to make him think she plans to have a one-night stand with the stranger. Through these manipulations, Fox regains the upper hand in her relationship and ultimately wins back Chestnut's loyalty.

You can think of the surplus for inside and outside options as two weights on opposite sides of a scale: both partners need the inside option to outweigh the outside option for the relationship, the negotiation, to work. The relationship is stable when each partner is better off remaining in the relationship. It's what economists call a *Nash equilibrium*.

A Nash equilibrium occurs when a game is in a stable state where no player has an incentive to deviate from their chosen strategy (given the choices of other players.) However, the Nash equilibrium is not necessarily the best outcome. A relationship can be stable and still be unhappy. Each person may have a common interest in wanting to be in a relationship and still irrationally hurt their happiness by bickering or engaging in other destructive behaviors. When Chestnut flirts with another

FIGURE 1.1. In a Nash Equilibrium, both sides of a game are optimized: each player benefits most from not deviating from where they are.

FIGURE 1.2. Inside options don't have to be weighted equally to still be best for both players.

woman, he is changing the terms of his relationship with Fox. In doing so, he removes weight from the inside option side of Fox's scale. As a result, Chestnut cut into the surplus she received from the relationship. However, he left just enough weight for the scale to still be tipped toward her keeping the relationship.

Fox could have screamed at her boyfriend or destroyed his possessions to reduce his surplus out of revenge. However, that would only have worsened Chestnut's inside option, and he would have had even less motivation to stay in the relationship. So instead, Fox aptly chose to focus on improving her options outside the relationship to make Chestnut fear she might leave him. That way, Chestnut would work harder to try to keep her.

This strategy worked because Chestnut wanted to be with Fox over being single and having the opportunity to date other women. Chestnut loved Fox, so none of those other women could replace her.

For a successful negotiation, both players must decide to engage in talks instead of walking away. Both players must have something to gain from negotiating, meaning their inside option beats their outside option. That's true of negotiations between romantic partners, a buyer and seller, or an employee and boss.

※ ※ ※

In January 2022, the real estate firm Redfin reported that 70% of customer offers to purchase a home faced competition from other bids—the highest level of competition on record. In Spokane, Washington, an astounding 83% of Redfin customer offers faced competing bids, making it the most competitive housing market in the country. Brynn Rea, a Redfin real estate agent in Spokane, remarked at the time, "One of my listings just had 45 showings in five days and received 14 offers. Another received 12 offers and sold for $120,000 over the list price of

$525,000." Homebuyers have no negotiating power when competition is as fierce as this: sellers can simply move on to the next best bid.[2]

But by August 2022, the rate of bidding wars had plummeted to 45%. In just a few months, the pool of potential buyers had shrunk significantly due to the fastest increase in mortgage rates in history. With most offers facing no competition, buyers regained negotiating power. When sellers received multiple offers, each one became interchangeable. However, sellers became more willing to negotiate when they received only one or zero offers. Tzahi Arbeli, a Redfin agent in Las Vegas, noted that "the housing market has changed very quickly in buyers' favor" in the summer of 2022. "Not only have prices fallen in recent months, but sellers see the market cooling, and they're more open to negotiating prices, giving concessions, and paying closing costs. They may even accept an offer that's $20,000 below the asking price and pay for repairs the buyer found during an inspection." As sellers' outside options dwindled, their willingness to negotiate increased.[3]

When the Spokane home was sold, buyers outnumbered sellers, which gave the seller negotiating power in the game of selling their home. That same game was taking place all around the country. In total, the number of buyers demanding homes exceeded the supply of homes for sale. When *demand*, which is the willingness of buyers to make purchases at a particular price, exceeds supply, prices go up.

And when *supply*, which is the willingness of sellers to accept a purchase at a particular price, exceeds demand, prices go down. For example, the Las Vegas home sold at a time when there were fewer buyers than sellers on the market. This gave negotiating power to the buyer, who could win the house for less than the listed price.

Negotiating power dynamics in the job market works the same way as in the housing and dating markets. The better the employer's outside options are, the worse the worker's inside options will be. When employers think of employees as replaceable, there's little a worker can do to improve their job conditions. The employer can exploit and mistreat its workers. A worker can threaten to quit, but the employer won't care. The employer doesn't love or need its workers; they are replaceable. Flaunting outside options won't work to improve an employee's inside options when that employee can be replaced. It would be like submitting a $400,000 offer on a home with competing bids over $500,000. It's a waste of time.

According to research published in *Economics Letters*, workers with a higher likelihood of quitting can negotiate better offers than workers with a higher likelihood of being laid off. The researchers identified the workers most likely to quit and most likely to be laid off based on the worker's level of experience, time in the role, education, job complexity, and job type within a dataset of employees and employers in the Netherlands. The results confirmed that workers willing to quit can negotiate higher wages. However, when the employer is inclined to end the negotiation by laying off the worker, the employer has more negotiating power, and the worker receives (or maintains) lower wages.[4]

According to another study, one published in the *Journal of Labor Economics*, when a worker's outside options improve, the lower-wage workers are the ones most likely to quit. However, in that same circumstance, higher-wage workers negotiate better pay for their inside option while staying in the same job. The researchers studied people who worked two jobs in the state of Washington and experienced a change in the earnings at their second job. So, for example, if an office assistant at Amazon headquarters also worked part time as an Uber driver, the researchers looked for changes in the Uber wages. The researchers then measured how that change impacted the earnings in the assistant position. Lower-wage workers were more likely to quit their primary job when wages at their secondary job improved. But this wasn't the case for higher-wage workers at the same company. Think of a senior cybersecurity engineer who moonlights as a consultant: when the higher-wage worker's secondary job wages increased, the worker could negotiate a higher salary at their primary job.[5]

So the more likely you are to be laid off and the lower your rank in the workplace, the less likely you are to successfully negotiate a higher wage when your outside options improve. All you can do is assess whether you are better off accepting your inside options as they are or taking your newly improved outside option.

GRADUATING INTO UNCERTAINTY

I was a junior in college when the housing market collapse turned into the financial crisis, which then became the Great Recession. All of this unfolded after I'd already secured a summer analyst position within the financial industry, with the investment bank Morgan Stanley. Many of my classmates had summer jobs in the financial industry as well, and their positions disappeared as financial firms like Lehman Brothers, Bear Stearns, and Merrill Lynch either closed shop entirely or cut workers. Lehman Brothers filed for bankruptcy in 2008; Bear Stearns was sold to JPMorgan Chase; and Merrill Lynch was sold to Bank of America. But Morgan Stanley survived. And so did my summer gig.

The internship gave me a valuable advantage in my career simply by virtue of existing on my résumé. Economics research published in the *Journal of Human Resources* found that university students who participated in internships went on to earn 6% higher incomes on average. The researchers examined a real-world example in Germany, in which a university introduced, and then eliminated, a mandatory internship program. The before-and-after effects of this change allowed the researchers to isolate the impact of internships and rule out other factors, such as academic performance or internal motivation. The results showed that students entering weak job markets saw the most significant benefit from interning.[6]

Interning was critical for me because, in 2010, I would graduate into the weakest job market since the Great Depression. The United States unemployment rate was 9.6%, more than double the unemployment rate when I graduated from high school in 2006. So you can understand my fixation on finding gainful employment during my college years—including the summer break during the financial crisis.

My timing in hitting the job market was unlucky. According to research published in the *American Economic Journal*, college students who graduate during a recession suffer persistent earnings declines lasting ten years. Recession graduates start their careers working for organizations that pay less and then slowly job-hop toward better employers. The study found that graduates from more privileged backgrounds suffer less from graduating during a recession because they move on to better employers more rapidly. Meanwhile, graduates from less privileged backgrounds tend to stay stuck with low-paying employers.[7]

The researchers compared pairs of students with the same major and grades. The difference was that one student graduated before the recession, the other during the recession. The students who graduated during the recession earned 9% less in their first year of employment and 4.5% less in the fifth year; not until the tenth year did the earnings gap fade to zero. This means students graduating into a recession would need to secure an extra internship or two to earn as much as students graduating in more prosperous economic times.

Lucky for me, Morgan Stanley survived the financial collapse and my internship offer was still good. However, the investment bank was cleaning house, executing layoffs, and reducing compensation. Overnight, securing a full-time offer from an investment bank became a much more competitive and much less lucrative opportunity. I had competed against thousands of applicants to get one of the hundred summer analyst positions at Morgan Stanley. I felt lucky to have it in that economy. Morgan Stanley went out of their way to recruit underrepresented minority students like myself, and I was grateful to be selected. I craved the security of receiving a job offer before graduation day so I wouldn't have to anxiously wonder what was next. I didn't think much about what the internship would actually entail.

The job was much more tedious than I expected. Even though the internship selection process was highly competitive, anyone who earned a B in high school algebra could have handled the tasks. The internship did not require the higher-level calculus I learned how to deploy in my MIT coursework. In fact, Morgan Stanley taught us all the necessary skills on the job. At the start of the summer, Morgan Stanley had all of us interns crowd into a makeshift lecture hall for a weeklong course teaching us the hundreds of Excel spreadsheet keyboard commands we would deploy endlessly. In effect, the program gave Morgan Stanley an airtight system to ensure they always had a steady flow of incoming talent to fill their employment needs. As an individual intern among hundreds, I could see how replaceable I was.

COMPARATIVE ADVANTAGE

Because the work of an analyst required little analytical ability, the only way I could distinguish myself from the other interns was to grind longer. This would demonstrate just how much of myself I was willing to give to my job. But I couldn't compete in that regard. Even though I was at my desk from 8 in the morning to 8 at night every weekday, the other interns arrived at the office before me and stayed longer. One day, as I was eating lunch in the company cafeteria with my colleagues, one of the interns from Harvard bragged about his dedication to his work, claiming he was working so much he had slept only five hours in the last two days. I was fighting a losing battle.

At first, I felt like a loser for underperforming. I felt lazy for not trying as hard as the other interns. But I cannot function on less than seven hours of sleep. In economics, a person or group of people have a *comparative advantage* if they can offer a service or product at a lower opportunity cost than anyone else. *Opportunity cost*, in a sense, is how much you value your outside option—how you value the activities you're being kept from.

From an employer's perspective, it's preferable to have employees with weak outside options, as they will work harder to hold on to their inside options. An employee with solid outside options will quit as soon as the going gets tough because, well, they have better options. At Morgan Stanley, it seemed like the other interns valued their outside options (including sleep) less than I did, which gave them a comparative advantage. They didn't seem to mind missing out on rest or mental stimulation. That lower opportunity cost meant the other interns could be more productive at the internship because the internship was the best use of their time. I wasn't sure if that was true for me.

In economics, leisure is typically defined as an individual's time not engaged in work. Leisure time is often used for enjoyable or fulfilling activities, such as socializing with friends and family, engaging in hobbies or interests, or relaxing. Leisure is always an available outside option to working. So, the more a person values leisure, the fewer hours they will want to work.

Placing a high value on leisure is not the same as laziness. Work can be stressful, and too much stress can affect health and productivity. A systematic review of the medical literature found that job stress elevates the heart rate and lowers heart rate variability. People with elevated heart rate are more likely to die of heart disease. And research suggests people with lower heart rate variability are less able to regulate their emotions and struggle focusing.[8]

Research published in the *European Journal of Health Economics* found that in one year, about one in 100 French workers suffered from illnesses exacerbated by workplace stress. Workplace stressors included intense pressure to perform tasks at high speed or on deadline and a lack of ability to act independently. Workplace stressors cause employees to miss work or stop working entirely. These employees often require expensive medical care. The researchers estimated that workplace stress costs France billions of dollars each year.[9]

As a healthy 21-year-old, I could see how years of sleepless nights from overwork might damage me, even if it wasn't going to put my life at immediate risk. My managing director looked old enough to be my grandfather but was only middle aged. His fitness apparently came second to his job. His money allowed him to send his kids to Manhattan's most expensive private schools and go on luxurious vacations. But money couldn't buy him health. Putting my nose to the grindstone might increase my financial success; however, it was no guarantee, and it wasn't worth the physical and mental health risks.

So the finance lifestyle was not for me. Each week, the under-represented minority interns were invited to a different exclusive event. There were gourmet dinners at fancy restaurants, lunches at the executive dining room, and open-bar happy hours for those old enough. But this access was temporary. The intern from Harvard was more willing to work hard to sustain these perks. He valued the lifestyle and class identity that was offered to us. Good for him for knowing what he wanted and going after it.

The questions for me remained: What did I want? What was my best outside option? I knew I liked economics, and the long, monotonous days at my internship felt like a form of punishment compared to the intellectual stimulation of staying in school. I enjoyed studying, reading, and problem-solving, so returning to graduate school seemed like a logical choice that would play to my comparative advantages. Plus, the recession meant fewer job opportunities were available, so returning to school would allow me to weather the storm and come out on the other side with better job prospects. Lisa B. Kahn of the Yale School of Management found in her research that students are more likely to attend graduate school if they finish college during a recession, so I was playing to statistical type in that regard.[10] Going for my PhD in economics would take me away from the labor market for half a decade. However, a PhD would qualify me for better job opportunities than the ones I could get with only an undergraduate degree.

The outside option was my best option. I spent the rest of my internship with a GRE prep website tab open on my computer at all times.

GAME RECAP

The next time you find yourself in an undesirable relationship, whether it be an employment relationship or a romantic one, take a step back and identify the options that are available to you and your opponent/partner. Then you can assess whether you have the power to negotiate better terms within your relationship, or whether you're better off walking away.

Identify your inside option and best outside option. A negotiation is a specific kind of game where two players attempt to split a figurative pie. Each player must agree on the split; if they don't, the negotiation falls apart and neither player gets any pie. The inside option is the share you receive of the current pie. The outside options are buying a pie from someone else, making your own pie, or eating something else. Your economic surplus from the pie is how much better your slice of pie is than your best outside option. Figure out how much pie you'll get from the relationship and how much you could get outside the relationship.

Identify your opponent's inside option and best outside option. Put yourself in the shoes of your negotiating opponent. What alternatives do they have to your relationship? Does your romantic partner think of you as irreplaceable? Does your employer think of you as an interchangeable cog?

Determine whether you have the power to negotiate better terms within the relationship. If your romantic partner would rather leave you than treat you better, negotiating won't work. If your employer would rather replace you than give you a raise, negotiating won't work.

Commit to your best option. Once you assess whether you can negotiate a better inside option, compare it to your outside option. If your outside option is better than what you can negotiate inside the relationship, end it. At Morgan Stanley, I knew there was no way for me to get a bigger slice of pie since they had had hundreds of other interns willing to give up way more pie. So the only way to improve my economic surplus was to take my best outside option: graduate school.

2
CHOOSING GAMES

Some games are easier to win for certain players. These players hold advantages that give them a better chance at victory from the start. When deciding whether to pursue one career path or another, an important step is to determine how likely success would be in each path.

When I told my dad that I wanted to be an economist, he warned me that I would be disadvantaged because of my gender and my race. The fact that less than 14% of economics professors are women and less than 4% are Black supported that notion.[1]

However, if having a disadvantage is unfair, there is no such thing as a fair game. The only kind of perfectly fair games, where all players have an equal chance at winning, are games of pure chance, like the casino game roulette, the card game War, or the board game Candy Land.

Knowing that I would be at a disadvantage, I still wanted to be an economist. I wanted to be like my favorite economist author, Steven Levitt, and I was on my way to his institution, the University of Chicago. Having just graduated from MIT, I was confident my skills would outweigh my disadvantages.

SKILL VERSUS LUCK

Not all advantages are inherently unfair. The game of chess, with its origins dating back more than a thousand years, is the prototypical strategic game. In some of its earlier iterations, dice were employed.[2] However, as this element of luck was removed, chess became a game of skill favored by intellectuals seeking external validation of their superior mental abilities. In chess, it is intended that the most skilled player emerges victorious. However, at least one advantage unrelated to skill remains: the advantage of the white player.

The white player takes the first move in chess, granting them a tempo advantage. Tempo refers to the speed at which a player can execute a strategy. The player with a faster tempo holds an edge over their opponent, as they can implement their strategy in fewer turns, thereby taking a quicker path to checkmate. Most players gain or lose tempo in the opening game. For instance, by taking an aggressive opening such as the Queen's Gambit or the King's Indian Defense, a player can force their opponent into an impulsive reaction. A wrong move made in haste loses tempo for the opponent. The white player, with the first-mover advantage, is better able to execute such an aggressive opening.

However, in chess, the gains from skill typically matter more than taking the first turn. And when a player takes two turns to make a move that could have been completed in one, it is like gifting their opponent tempo; the white player's advantage can be lost, whereas the benefits of skill will persist and, in some cases, overtake other advantages. In practice, most players—even computer players—will make a mistake that loses tempo, as it is impossible to predict every possible circumstance. This means the first-player advantage often has little impact on the outcome of a game unless players are evenly matched. In elite tournament games featuring evenly matched players, the white player wins 62% of games that do not end in a draw.[3]

So, is chess worth playing with the black disadvantage? It depends on your level of skill in the game. If your opponent is more skilled and holds the white advantage, your chances of victory may be slim. On the other hand, suppose you outplay your opponent significantly. In that case, the disadvantage of moving second may be a minor factor, as your opponent will likely make a mistake that hurts their tempo and nullifies their first-mover advantage.

Of course, the choice to play a game hinges on more than just the probability of victory. This decision also depends on your enjoyment of the game, your potential for learning, and the availability of alternative games.

Skill can inoculate players from the unfairness of a given game. But untangling these two dynamics is fraught. Players have limited control over how skilled they are and even how skilled they can become. This is true in competitive chess and in life.

In life, a lot of advantage is predetermined by unfair circumstances. For example, it's a matter of luck whether a person is born to wealthy parents, parents who value education, or parents who pass on advantageous traits like intelligence or skin color.

Research published in the *Journal of Political Economy* found a causal relationship between parents' wealth and children's wealth. By looking at Korean children adopted by Norwegian parents, the researchers identified the impact of being raised by a wealthy parent separate from the genetic factors passed down from parent to biological child. Adoptees raised by wealthy parents were more likely to be similarly rich in adulthood. For example, for every additional $10,000 the parents had in wealth, an adopted child could expect an additional $2,470 of wealth in adulthood.[4]

In another study, the economists Kerwin Charles and Erik Hurst found that for every 10% increase in parental wealth, child wealth in adulthood can be expected to increase by 4%. And that's before taking into account bequests upon the parent's death. In addition, the researchers found that homeowner and business owner parents were the most likely to have children who would become wealthy adults; their children grew up to become home-owners and business owners, just like their parents.[5]

Other research has found that, along with wealth, parents can pass down other traits that give their kids advantages. Econo-mists at USC, Johns Hopkins, and the University of Wisconsin have found that a large amount of individual wealth can be tied to characteristics an individual was born with—characteristics that can be seen across a large sample of people's DNA. The researchers used a series of genetic markers, called a polygenic score, known to be associated with years of education, and cross-checked it against individuals' wealth at retirement. Where the presence of these genetic markers increased, so did the inci-dence of individuals' wealth. In other words, if you took 100 ran-dom people and look at their Ancestry.com or 23andMe genetic test results, you could predict with good accuracy who has the most wealth.[6]

If we believe that fortune is predetermined at least in part by our genetic code, this might be cause for disillusion. But the results of this study probably wouldn't hold on a truly random sample of people—and thus in a diverse field like a job market. The researchers looked only at individuals with European ances-try. (Here they were constrained by the nature of genetics: the supposed "genes for educational attainment" wouldn't be the same for people of African, Asian, or any other non-European ancestral groups.)

Genetics produce unfairness in social ways because of the social connotations of a given inherited trait—especially skin color. Here the genetic combination associated with dark skin may impede a person's ability to attain advanced education not because of a lack of intelligence, but due to societal discrimination. And the severity of the discrimination depends on the norms and values of a society, not the genetics themselves. For example, sociologists at Virginia Tech found that Black Americans with lighter skin had a higher socioeconomic class compared to dark-skinned Black Americans. Light-skinned Black Americans also had spouses of higher socioeconomic class. Furthermore, they possessed less awareness of the issues that Black people faced. Research published in the *Journal of Human Resources* found that lighter skinned Black workers earned more than their darker-skinned counterparts. According to the study, the wage gap between light-skinned Black workers and white workers was about half as large as the gap between dark-skinned Black workers and white workers.[7]

Intrinsic factors give players advantages or disadvantages that have nothing to do with the good or bad choices a player makes. And that's true whether an innate characteristic makes a person a better player, like intelligence, or whether it gives a person an easier path to success, like skin color. Furthermore, an innate factor may provide an advantage in one game while presenting a disadvantage in another.

RULES AND STARTING CONDITIONS

A personal characteristic can be advantageous or disadvantageous depending on the game being played. For example, in chess, without the rule stating that white always moves first, there would be no white advantage. And in a society without colorism, there would be no advantage to being light skinned.

In games, *starting conditions* refer to the initial set of rules, circumstances, skills, resources, and difficulties that players face. They define the environment in which players interact. Innate characteristics are one type of starting condition, but there are many other circumstances and strokes of luck that impact a player's chances of victory. If a particular type of player consistently emerges victorious in a game, it is due to the game's starting conditions granting that type of player an advantage.

According to *the law of large numbers* in probability and statistics, as a sample size increases, the average of the sample approaches the average of the entire population. This is because the sample becomes increasingly representative of the population. So in chess, if the white player wins more frequently than the black player in a large number of chess games, the white player statistically holds an advantage.

Chess players might know from experience that the person playing white has an advantage. But testing that belief for its accuracy is still a scientific process. This process of comparing the probability of living in a world where a fact is true (a world in which the white player has an advantage) to the probability that a fact is false (a world in which the white player has no advantage) is known as *hypothesis testing*.

Statisticians refer to the world in which a fact is false as the *null hypothesis*. The null hypothesis represents the conditions and assumptions that would be consistent with the hypothesis being false. To test a hypothesis, statisticians calculate the probability that we would see data like the kind we observe if the null hypothesis were actually true. When testing whether a fact is true, they estimate how likely it is that the fact is false.

For example, we can test a hypothesis that the white player

has an advantage in chess games by observing games and recording data on the color of winners and losers. If the probability is less than 5% that a white player with no advantage wins a certain, observed number of games, most statisticians will reject the null hypothesis, and say they are more than 95% confident in their hypothesis that the white player does indeed have an advantage.

The number of games required to confirm whether a player holds an advantage depends on the size of the advantage and the level of confidence the statistician is aiming for. For example, if, in 100 evenly matched chess games (excluding draws), white wins 62 times or more, we can be 99% confident that white holds some advantage.[8] The source of the advantage may be unclear, but the existence of an edge can be established confidently. On the other hand, if white wins only six out of ten games, we can be only 62% confident that white holds the advantage.[9] The more games witnessed (or played), the greater the confidence we can have about the existence or absence of an advantage. However, absolute confidence is impossible, as it would require that *every* game that has been played, or could ever be played, be observed.

※ ※ ※

There were no Black winners in the first 22 seasons of the CBS hit reality game show *Big Brother*. Out of 301 contestants, 11% were Black. If race played no role in determining the winner, there should have been only an 8% chance that no Black players would have won in 22 seasons.[10] Therefore, there was a 92% chance Black players had a disadvantage in *Big Brother*.

However, in season 23, following the murder of George Floyd and subsequent protests, the highest number of Black contestants in any season of *Big Brother* was cast by CBS. Six out of 16 contestants identified as Black. Statistics tell us that if the Black players had no advantage or disadvantage over non-Black players, only two of the Black contestants should have made it to the final six. However, *all six* Black contestants made it that far in the game; every non-Black contestant was eliminated prior. Statistically, there was only a 0.01% chance of this occurring if Black players had no advantage or disadvantage over non-Black players.[11]

But if the game's rules didn't change, how did the game flip from Black contestants having a statistical disadvantage to Black contestants absolutely dominating the game? The starting conditions changed. This greater number of Black players allowed the formation of a strong Black alliance. *Big Brother* is a social game where players vote each week on which contestant to eliminate. A strong alliance is the best advantage a *Big Brother* contestant can have.

Recall that the level of advantage a player has in a game depends not only on the traits a player possesses, but also on the starting conditions of the game. Being Black in the game of *Big Brother* was a disadvantage only when there were few other Black players at the start of the game. However, being Black flipped to an advantage when there were many Black players at the start.

In the early seasons of *Big Brother,* Black contestants often found it difficult to forge alliances with white players. Even when they could form such alliances, Black contestants were often the first to be voted out when the alliance eventually turned in on itself. However, when there were more Black contestants in the game at the start, they were able to create a powerful alliance based on their solidarity. Every player in the Black alliance knew they were better off sticking together (the inside option) than turning on one another (the outside option). As a result, this alliance became the strongest in *Big Brother*'s history, with every member making it to the final six.

Economists have noticed a similar phenomenon regarding gender diversity in graduate school. Researchers at Kansas State University and the Ohio State University studied how the proportion of women in STEM (science, technology, engineering, and math) doctoral programs changed the likelihood of students successfully obtaining a PhD. According to the study, women who started doctoral programs without any other women in their cohort were 12 percentage points less likely than men to graduate within six years. Most women left during the first year of enrollment, and women without any female peers were 7 percentage points more likely to drop out in year 1. The first female classmate mattered the most, but each additional woman further increased the likelihood that women successfully obtained a PhD. The more women in the program at the start, the more likely women were to persist in their studies.[12]

When I started graduate school in 2010 at the University of Chicago's department of economics, I was one of eight women in a class of 39. Men outnumbered women nearly five to one. When I received a PhD four years later, I was the first Black woman to do so—a period dating all the way back to when the University of Chicago's Economics Department awarded its first doctoral degree, in 1894.[13]

I don't bring up my firstness out of pride. I think the Economics Department should be embarrassed that the first—and, depending on when you are reading this, only—Black woman they deemed worthy of a PhD was my light-skinned, wavy-haired, half-white self. In fairness to the University of Chicago, they weren't unique in this regard: elite institutions granting PhDs in economics have not, for most of their histories, granted PhDs to Black people. In 2021, only 13 PhDs were awarded to Black Americans out of the 1,248 degrees awarded, and only four of them went to Black American women.[14]

Even though I was a racial minority within a gender minority at UChicago, there was at least global diversity. Most of my classmates were international students: only 14 out of 39 were US citizens. During the first few weeks, when we all got to know each other and before the graded coursework began, I didn't feel different.

But that quickly changed. After our first lecture on price theory, the teaching assistant explained how the homework assignments would be graded: we could work in study groups as long as the study group was no bigger than five students. And the teaching assistant cautioned us against doing the homework alone. The assignments were intended to be challenging, even for a handful of doctoral students putting their heads together.

After class, I asked one of the students I had bonded with (over us both being Californians) if he wanted to be in a study group with me. He told me he had already joined a study group with four other white American male classmates.

I was disappointed.

There were ten white American men in my cohort. So statistically, there should have been only a 0.2% chance of his study group being all white, American, and men if study partners were picked independent of gender, race, and nationality.[15] I wanted to believe it was just a coincidence, but that was unlikely.

Unfortunately, my experience seemed to be part of a larger pattern. Researchers at Colorado State University and California State University, San Bernardino, found that men perceived women to have lower abilities in the classroom. This was despite the fact that women outperformed men in undergraduate physical and life sciences courses. Instead, men perceived that women had lower academic abilities. Men in the classroom were less likely to choose women as study partners, to ask women for help, to view a woman as the most knowledgeable in class, and to view women as among the best students in the class. And yet, in reality, women in the study received better grades than the men.[16]

As I looked around the classroom at the groups of students forming, I started to panic. I had falsely assumed that graduate school would be like chess, a game based almost entirely on individual skill. Suddenly it looked more like *Big Brother*: a game based on making the right social alliances, where being in the minority was a disadvantage. My classmates somehow knew ahead of time about the team-based homework, yet no one had asked me to join them. Soon, thankfully, another one of my classmates asked me to be in his study group with two other women.

I felt lucky to join their group. One study conducted at the University of Amsterdam found that students performed better in their classes when their study groups contained a higher share of women. When students were randomly assigned to study groups, both male and female students benefited academically from having more women in their study group.[17]

My new study partner invited the group over to his apartment for Guitar Hero and drinks to celebrate our study group's formation. I figured drumming would help relieve the stress from graduate school. So, I showed up promptly, eager to practice my skills on the toy drum kit included with Guitar Hero. As I began banging away to "Seven Nation Army," my study partner poured himself a drink and sat on the couch behind me. I'm not sure how many times I restarted the song to achieve a higher score, but when I finally took a break to grab my first drink, I realized he was already *drunk*.

"I'm so screwed," he sighed.

"What are you talking about?" I asked. Classes hadn't started yet. *Screwed* seemed unlikely, or at least premature.

"*No . . .*" he cried. "It's Emma! I like her so much!" Emma was another member of our study group.

"Emma is engaged!" I yelled.

"I know. I know. She's just so perfect. Beautiful. Smart. Funny . . . I-I, I need to tell her how I feel."

"No, you *don't!*" I shouted. "If you tell her how you feel, she'll quit the study group. Don't make her do that. It's not her fault you have a crush!"

According to research from social psychologists at Cornell University, initiators of unrequited romantic advances are unaware of the challenging position this puts their targets in. Targets of unwanted advances report feeling uncomfortable and unsure of how to proceed, professionally and personally. The researchers surveyed graduate students in STEM fields. They found that women were more than twice as likely to report having been the target of unrequited advances, with 33% of women being a target versus 14% of men. As part of the study, participants roleplayed stories describing unwanted romantic advances. The person playing the initiator role consistently underestimated the discomfort of the person playing the target. So when it comes to fending off unwanted romantic advances, women are at a startling disadvantage.[18]

"I would never force Emma to quit the study group," he offered. "I would quit the study group if she rejects me."

"What's the difference?" I asked. Either way, our study group was busted. If he quit, it would be three women left on our own, while everyone else had five people—and thus five brains—in their group. We would be the ones who were screwed.

He let out a moan and buried his face in the couch cushion.

"Okay, okay," he relented.

Even though our study group felt unstable, we completed our assignments and learned the material. Eventually, our four-person group added a fifth member when a student dealing with visa issues arrived.

I started my first year of graduate school knowing it would be difficult and that my race and gender would make me a double minority. Still, I didn't understand how being in the minority would make graduate school all the more difficult.

It's easy to second-guess yourself when you feel like you're at a disadvantage. Even if you're 95% certain that there is racism, sexism, ageism, or other prejudices at play, there is still that pesky 5% chance that says what you are experiencing is just a coincidence. It's also enough for naysayers to insist discrimination isn't discrimination, or that you just don't have the skills to succeed. Even if the behavior of others doesn't rise to the level of being objective discrimination, everything is data: tracking these factors can help you understand your odds of success and whether you need to alter your strategy.

MARGINAL BENEFIT AND MARGINAL COST

My grades in graduate school started off weak: I received a D in my first quarter of econometrics. Thankfully, those grades didn't matter. All that mattered was the core examination—a three-day test covering the entirety of the material taught in the first year. Failing it meant I would have to either repeat the first year or leave the doctoral program.

The core exam was terrifying. *How could I possibly memorize all the material I learned in the last nine months? Where should I even begin? Do I go back to the beginning and cover every topic? Do I focus on the subjects that I know the least well?* But then I thought to apply what I was taught in my economics courses: marginal cost and marginal benefit.

Marginal cost is the extra cost that comes with making a choice or action. It's not the same as the total cost, which is the amount you spend (or exert) for a given thing. For example, the total cost of studying for the test was pretty much fixed at a brutal number: I was going to spend 50 hours a week studying for one month. The marginal costs differed based on which topics I chose to study and in what order. A subject I knew well would take me a couple of hours to review, but a subject I hadn't grasped would take me multiple days. If I spent too long trying to master the difficult material, I might run out of time for reviewing the easier material. I needed to also consider the marginal benefits.

The *marginal benefit* is the additional benefit or usefulness gained from making a choice—here, the choice of what to study, in what order, and in what amount. The total benefit would be whatever score I ultimately got on the test. However, the marginal benefits came from deciding what topics to cover and in what order.

To maximize my chances of getting a passing grade, I needed to study efficiently. The most efficient way to study would be to prioritize the subjects that were most likely to show up on the test. Failing to learn those topics would hurt my test score the most on the margin. By the same token, mastering those topics would help my test score the most on the margin.

The teaching assistants provided all the old tests dating back decades as study materials, so I coded and categorized each question that appeared on past tests into subject areas. I counted about 50 topics that could show up on the test. I then calculated the frequency of each subject. For example, the concept of backward induction showed up on the core exam in about 90% of years, and there was a question related to hypothesis testing only 20% of the time. So I focused my effort on the most frequent topics—I studied the subjects that appeared on the exam more than 50% of the time until I felt confident in my understanding of them. After mastering those subjects, I moved sequentially through the topics covered 40%, 30%, and less than 20% of the time. That way, I put the most effort toward the subjects that would most significantly move the needle on my likelihood of passing the exam. And if I ran out of study time, I would miss only those topics with a low chance of appearing on the exam.

This strategy can apply to any goal, whether passing a test, completing a work assignment, or finding a romantic partner. It's easy to become paralyzed when deciding what steps to take to reach a goal. Time and resources are always limited, so prioritize the actions with the highest marginal benefits and the lowest marginal costs. Organizing your potential actions in this manner can give you a clear path that you will feel confident in.

CHEATING

When the results of the core exam were posted later that summer, I was delighted to see my student ID among the two-thirds of students who passed all three tests. When classes started, I discovered that only one other woman had fully passed the core exam and enrolled in second-year coursework. Even by the skewed gender ranks of an economics program, this was shockingly low: there should have been only a 2% chance of so few women progressing if women were as likely as men to proceed in the graduate program.[19] It was impossible to know exactly why an improbably low share of women passed, but there was clearly some intangible disadvantage at play.

A few weeks later, I heard a rumor that one of our classmates had cheated on the core exam by hiding notes in the bathroom. At first, I was surprised, but with the stakes of the exam so high, I understood his desperation. Research published in *College Teaching* reviewed empirical evidence from various studies on academic dishonesty. The study found that a common reason for cheating was that the benefits outweighed the costs.[20]

My benefits from cheating would have been low. Secret bathroom notes wouldn't have helped me do better on the test, because my long-term memory is much better than my short-term memory. The opportunity cost of cheating was high for me too. As the only Black woman, I felt I had to be a perfect representative for my group. Plus, I didn't want to deprive myself of knowledge. I wanted to know if I could pass on my merit. People could look at me and assume I got to the University of Chicago based on affirmative action, but the core exam was graded blindly. It was an objective indication that I deserved to be there. The costs of cheating outweighed the benefits for me. I could start my second year of graduate school free from impostor syndrome.

Some players may cheat—that's true in every game. And some game designs make the marginal benefits of cheating high and the marginal costs low. In these games, cheating is common.

Still, not all players will decide to cheat in a game. Some players face smaller marginal benefits or bigger marginal costs. For some players, the marginal benefits of cheating outweigh the marginal costs. For instance, a student confident they can pass a test without cheating would have a low incentive to cheat. Similarly, a person with strong moral values would find cheating unappealing because it goes against their principles. Additionally, someone who is the sole representative of their race, gender, or other identity group may feel that the costs of cheating are too high, as it could negatively impact the perception of others in their identity group.

When deciding whether or not to play a game, assess the marginal benefits and costs of cheating—not only for yourself, but also for your opponents. Not cheating, even if others do, can often be the smartest play.

WHEN TO CHALLENGE THE RULES

In my second year of graduate school, I signed up for Steven Levitt's class on empirical research. During the first class, Levitt talked about the importance of narrative when describing data—how people have difficulty contextualizing facts and figures without it being part of a story they can relate to. He ended the class by telling us that if we wanted his feedback on any research ideas, we should wait outside his office because he rarely responds to emails.

I did have a research idea, and Levitt was my first choice for mentorship, so I did as he suggested and camped outside his office between my classes. As I waited, I thought about the last time I met with Levitt.

It was during the preview weekend for prospective graduate students. I was deciding between attending University of California, Berkeley, or the University of Chicago. While UC Berkeley is an excellent school, the University of Chicago is world renowned for economics. However, UChicago was the more challenging program, with more students flunking out or quitting. On the other hand, UChicago had the professors I most wanted to study under.

In that first meeting, Levitt told me I should come to UChicago because it would be so difficult and miserable that it would make me want to quit academia—a good thing, he said, because academia is difficult and miserable. This could have been a red flag, but all I heard was that Steven Levitt thought *I* should come to UChicago to study economics, and that was all I wanted to hear. Plus, his point made logical sense. I shouldn't waste tempo failing slowly; it's better to fail quickly and move on.

Levitt wandered into his office, and as I waved to him, he gestured for me to follow him. He began snacking on a bag of pistachios, slowly shelling them one by one. He offered me some, but I declined. I was too nervous, face to face with my economics idol, to eat.

"Thanks for meeting with me. I have a research idea that I would love your feedback on," I said.

"Sure, sure," Levitt said. "Remind me, is this your second or third year?"

It was my second year.

"Did you pass the core exam?" he asked, shelling another pistachio. "It's okay if you didn't. Plenty of students fail on their first try."

"I passed."

"Oh! That's great." Levitt said it as if he was happy to get an answer he wasn't expecting. "Many women don't pass on the first try, but they usually go on to be better researchers than the men."

Overall, female economists were gaining recognition in their field, and Levitt's views on their capabilities were consistent with the trend. For example, one study published in *Econometrica* looked at the selection process for a prestigious organization of economists called the Fellows of the Econometric Society. The study used data on the published work and citations of over 40,000 economists from the early 1900s to the present day. They found that historically, women were less likely to be chosen as Fellows than men with similar qualifications. However, this changed in recent years—now, women are more likely to be selected as fellows than men with equivalent qualifications. The researchers concluded that this tilt toward women occurred because the selection process rules changed to consider more women as candidates.[21]

Here I asked: "Doesn't that mean the core exam is doing a poor job measuring women's propensity to be successful?"

Levitt dismissed the idea of an issue with the test. And he alluded to how difficult it would be to convince other professors in the Economics Department that a test which was graded anonymously could be biased.

The test may have been unbiased when examined out of context. Still, from my perspective, it was clear that the system statistically disadvantaged women. If what Levitt said was true, then the test underestimated the economic research ability of women relative to men. Therefore, the test filtered out women who would have been just as good, if not better, at economic research than some of the men who passed. There were a few ways the testing system could have been improved, in my view— for example, addressing the underrepresentation of women, changing the rules for forming study groups, and setting standards for academic integrity. For a place and program as sought-after as the University of Chicago Economics Department, those didn't seem to be urgent matters.

There are two main ways to encourage an institution to change its policies: voice your concerns as a participant in the institution, or exit the institution in protest. According to research published in the *Journal of Political Economy*, the optimal strategy among activist investors attempting to change a company depends on the share of investors who are also activists. According to the researchers' model, voicing concerns is the best strategy if most of the other investors share the sentiments of social responsibility. Under this strategy, investors can successfully vote for policy changes. However, if most investors don't feel social responsibility, exiting is more effective. Under this strategy, the company risks losing investors unless changes are made.[22]

44 TWO

I didn't expect the leaders of the Economics Department to enact policies based on my views on diversity or inclusion. After all, their positions of leadership were, in effect, the status quo I was challenging. So, I decided to focus on my research and hoped that one day my accomplishments would give me the kind of professional status that persuades people to see things from my viewpoint.

Changing the rules of a game is typically possible only after you have already won. However, this doesn't happen all that often: a winner is unlikely to perceive the rules as unfair, because that would tarnish their own success. Most people don't want to believe they have benefited from unfair advantages. That's why it's so important to pay attention to the probabilities. When choosing games, you can use those probabilities to assess whether a game will be fair to you. And, if you are in a position of power with the ability to change the rules, looking at the statistics can help you overcome the urge to believe that merit alone determines success.

THE VALUE OF WINNING

In simplified economics models, individuals decide which games are worth playing based on their utility function—an abstraction of the mind; the thing that determines what a person wants. *Utility* is how much value a person gets from doing something, whether that be dining at a fancy restaurant or playing a game of chess. A person's utility function isn't inherently knowable—not to outsiders, not to supercomputers, and not even to that person themself. Everyone figures out what they want—what their utility function is like—based on experience and intuition. The more enriched your experience and intuition, the more confidently you can decide what games to play to get what you want.

Utility functions are easier to understand when observing other animals, which are primarily concerned with staying alive

CHOOSING GAMES 45

and reproducing rather than dealing with more complex desires. According to optimal foraging theory, the animals that have the most effective strategies for finding food will be the ones that can survive and reproduce. Over time, a species of animals will approach the optimal environmental strategy.

For instance, consider a hawk that has the option of preying on an injured mouse or a healthy rabbit. The injured mouse might be an easier catch, but it provides a smaller amount of food. On the other hand, the healthy rabbit requires more energy to hunt, and there's a chance it could escape—but it provides a larger amount of food. The hawk must decide whether to pursue the mouse or the rabbit. It weighs the reward, the cost, and the risk of failure. The decision to chase the mouse or the rabbit is just as important to the hawk's survival as its skill at catching prey.

The choice of what game to play is more complicated for humans. We have to decide which rewards are worth pursuing. Some rewards hold monetary value, and some are symbolic trophies. Their values are often subjective. I assume all hawks prefer to dine on a healthy rabbit over an injured mouse. But try getting two people to agree on what the best meal is, let alone what constitutes the best career, family life, or games worth playing—it's complicated.

Some games are worth playing for the prize. For example, a lottery game is worth playing for the jackpot. Similarly, an employee trying to win a promotion is motivated by the prize of a better title or a pay increase.

Some games are worth playing because they are enjoyable. For example, the point of playing the Hokey Pokey is to have fun. There are rules to the Hokey Pokey, but there are no winners. No trophy is awarded to the person who best follows along with the musical instructions. Having fun is the only reward.

And some games are worth playing because of what is learned along the way. Player traits aren't fixed. But, through learning, whether in the classroom, on the job, or in a game, a person can gain skills that alter their traits.

Economists call this the accumulation of *human capital*, which is just jargon for knowledge that increases productivity. It's the knowledge that gives an advantage in future games. For example, I wasn't born understanding economics and game theory. I learned it in school, and then I applied it in my work, in my life, and in the games that I play. With practice, I honed my economics skills, which have made me a more productive person and a superior player.

The fact that experience alters skills makes choosing what game to play more complicated. The outcome isn't just win or lose. It's often: win or lose, and either way learn something along the way. How much you learn and how that might increase your odds of winning future games should be considered when choosing what game to play.

Not all games allow players to learn. For example, it doesn't matter how many spins a gambler takes at a roulette wheel—they aren't going to learn how to be a better roulette player because that game is based entirely on luck. Perhaps, after a hundred spins, they might discover that the law of large numbers guarantees them they will lose money in the long run, but that's about it.

However, failure can turn a chess player into a better chess player. Seeing how an opponent plays can teach a player what moves not to make in the next game.

CHANGING GOALS

Whether I won or lost at the academic game, I was learning along the way. The knowledge I gained in graduate school would help me navigate my career, finances, and personal relationships.

In my third year of graduate school, I worked relentlessly to pursue my goal of being a top academic economist—the kind of economist who becomes a university professor and conducts research. Every waking hour of my life, I was either sitting at my computer searching for interesting datasets, analyzing those datasets, roaming the library for research inspiration on the bookshelves, or daydreaming about how to piece everything I was doing into a research project for my doctoral thesis. Finally, I settled on a research project.

It was on a topic near to my heart: I analyzed data from California and Texas before and after their respective bans on affirmative action. And what I found was that college students did better in school when they went to college with more students of the same race as them. This effect was more prominent for college students who, when growing up, did not interact with many students of a different race from them. For example, a Black college student who went to a predominantly Black high school was more likely to drop out of college if the college was overwhelmingly white.

The morning of my thesis proposal, I was so nervous I couldn't eat. I tried, but I couldn't keep anything down. As I stood there in front of my academic advisers—Levitt, Richard Thaler (*Nudge* author and Nobel Prize winner), Kerwin Charles (who later became dean at Yale School of Management), and Edward Lazear (former chairman of the White House Council of Economic Advisers)—I felt like a baby bird spreading my wings for the first time.

And then the reality set in: maybe I couldn't fly. My advisers told me they found my research compelling, but it was too different from the kind of research that would get published in a top journal. They said my methods needed to be more rigorous. My research was good enough to earn me a PhD, but it wasn't enough to put me on a path toward an academic career as impressive as theirs.

Levitt, after delivering that disappointing feedback, asked me how I was taking it. I told him, "I'll be okay. I've been meaning to practice detachment." I had just finished reading a book about Buddhism that made me question my attachment to academia and, in turn, offered me a roadmap to serenity. But Levitt gave me a look like he did not think I was going to be okay.

Because I didn't have a clear reason for being in academia, I had absorbed the values of the people around me. I originally went to graduate school to avoid the weak labor market of the recession while furthering my knowledge of economics, a topic I loved. But once I got to graduate school, I started to forget why I was there in the first place. My professors seemed to think that the signifiers of success included publishing in top journals and earning tenure. Most of my graduate student peers held the same values. So, without much thought, I followed the social norms around me. I absorbed the value system of my peers and set out on the singular goal of producing research that could be published in a top journal.

Economics professors at Stanford University proposed a dynamic theory of *endogenous preference formation*. In plain terms, it was a model to describe how people's internal values develop over time and how they inform the goals people pursue and the games they play. In the model, preferences are not fixed; they are shaped within the economic system itself. Preferences are formed as a result of individuals' experiences and their environment—individuals adopt worldviews that shape their judgments about their experiences. The economic theorists who wrote the study argued that their model explains the "sour grapes" phenomenon.[23]

In *Aesop's Fables,* a hungry fox tries to jump up and reach grapes hanging from a vine, but falls short. The grapes are too high. At the same time that the fox resigns himself to failure, he declares the grapes aren't ripe, and he doesn't like sour grapes. The fox is plainly being petty, but the basic idea of the story is that anyone can choose whether to desire something. Anyone can detach from a goal by deciding a goal is no longer worthy of being pursued—that the grapes are too sour to merit the effort.

Before my advisers delivered their feedback, producing a top research paper was the only game I was playing. But deep down, I knew I had a warped perception of my utility function. And maybe I shouldn't be playing the academic game at all. Perhaps I had become overly attached to *that game.* Detachment, Buddhists say, is the release from desire. It's like taking an eraser to what you think your utility function is and trying to figure it out again from scratch. I needed to step back and examine more carefully what games I really wanted to play.

I gave myself a deadline: I would give my research my all for one more year. And, if I could not develop a better research project than the one I was already working on, I would finish my thesis, graduate, and leave academia behind. At some point, just like the fox, I had to resign to stop jumping and accept that the research I had already done was the best I could do, the highest I could jump.

The same problem of when to stop comes up in dating. Of course, most people want a romantic partner who is the best possible match. But how do you know when you have found that person? What is the point at which you stop looking and put a ring on the very nice person in front of you? Mathematicians have estimated that the best approach—the one that maximizes effort, minimizes waste, and produces the best probability of success—is to make a decision after you have dated 37% of your potential partners. The numbers indicate that it's the best sample size with the best odds of success—go with the next match that beats the best option among the first 37%.[24] But how do you know how many potential partners you might have? I certainly didn't know how many potential research project ideas I could come up with. If my advisers had given me a grade on my research proposal, it would have been a B. And I needed to know if I could produce grade-A work consistently.

If I didn't have a grade-A research project after one year of trying, what were the odds I would come up with a grade-A research project if I kept on? If I was the kind of student that got As at least half of the time, I should have had at least a 75% probability of getting an A after two tries. If I was the kind of student who got only Bs, I would have had a 0% chance of getting an A no matter how many times I tried.

The only evidence I had so far about my research ability was my one B. If I initially assumed there was a 50% chance I was incapable of getting As, that one B increased the probability to 67%. If I received another B on my second try, that probability would increase to 80%. So I decided in that scenario, I would give up. Otherwise, I might end up chasing that A for years and years. After one year of giving my total effort to research, my original project was still the best I could come up with. So, I decided to go forward with my grade-B research project. That way, I could graduate and move on from academia to the next game.

I recognize it was shallow of me to want to be an academic only if I could be a top academic—a researcher who comes up with grade-A research projects most years. It was shallow in part because that value system wasn't my own. If I kept playing the academic game, I would be turning away from the opportunity to play new games. I was satisfied with what I had accomplished. I learned skills and gained advantages I didn't have before starting graduate school. I acquired knowledge of economics, behavioral economics, and game theory, which would prove extremely useful in my career.

But ultimately, I had to walk away from playing the academic game to play a new game: the corporate game. I didn't know whether I would have a better chance of winning. I didn't know exactly what working in the corporate world would be like. Still, I figured I had the skills to succeed and could always change the game I was playing once again if necessary.

There is no shame in changing goals, especially after you realize that the prize isn't valuable or attainable. At the beginning of your career, you likely don't have much information about what goals will be fulfilling to you. And if you've learned something along the way, that's a nice consolation prize.

GAME RECAP

The next time you decide what direction to take for your career (or another part of your life), follow these steps to determine whether to continue playing your current game or start a new one.

Identify your level of advantage. Do you have a better shot at winning the status quo game or a new game? Do your traits collectively serve as an advantage or disadvantage in each game? Does the new game have favorable starting conditions?

Identify opportunities to gain skills. During each game, is there an opportunity to learn? You might be at a disadvantage going into a new adventure game, but over time you'll learn by doing. Is there more learning to be done in the status quo game? If not, at least in the new adventure, whether you succeed or fail, you'll have new experiences and add proficiency in new skills.

Give yourself a time limit. Reflect on how long you've been playing the status quo game and how likely you are to reach success moving forward. Identify goalposts to stay motivated. If you don't accomplish your goals within your self-defined time frame, let go and move on to a new game. That way you won't get stuck playing a losing game.

Determine which game you would rather win. Decide which win is more valuable to you. And if you have yet to learn your values, trying out a new adventure will help you learn more about yourself.

Ask yourself: Are you afraid of change? Even though new games are scary because of the fear of the unknown, new games are more often than not the better choice than the status quo game. The fact that you shudder slightly at the thought of trying something new should tell you that fear of the unknown gives you what psychologists call *status quo bias*, which is the tendency to prefer the current state of affairs and to resist change. Behavioral economists and psychologists have demonstrated in multiple experiments that status quo bias prevents subjects from making rational economic decisions.[25] Think of it this way: if you keep playing a losing game because that's what's familiar, you automatically forfeit every other game you could play instead.

3
INFORMATION IS AN ADVANTAGE

There are all different types of advantages in games. A player advantage is innate; a comparative advantage is situational. But an informational advantage, or what economists call *asymmetric information*, can be the most consequential. For example, when buying a car, the first-time buyer who knows nothing about cars will be at a disadvantage compared to the car dealer who knows exactly how much each vehicle on the lot is worth. The dealer has the informational advantage.

For the buyer, this disadvantage is tricky. To overcome it, a player must figure out what their opponent might know and whether their opponent might be hiding something. They must imagine the world through their opponent's eyes, which requires empathy.

ULTIMATUMS

The player with worse information is often the loser of negotiation games. If a player mistakenly believes that their opponent's outside option is worse than their inside option, they might issue an ultimatum that is doomed to fail. When a player with bad information declares: "Take this deal or I walk," that player may be shocked to see their opponent reject their ultimatum and regret being so disagreeable. The opponent, it turns out, had outside options.

In 1999, Destiny's Child achieved their first number 1 hit in the US with the R&B track "Bills, Bills, Bills." The four members of Destiny's Child—Beyoncé Knowles, Kelly Rowland, LaTavia Roberson, and LeToya Luckett—had been performing together for nearly a decade, and now fans and critics recognized their talent. But the media focused mainly on Beyoncé instead of the group. She was the one who appeared on television and was featured in magazines.

Mathew Knowles, Beyoncé's father, managed the group, which LaTavia and LeToya concluded was the reason Beyoncé received preferential treatment. A few months after Destiny's Child reached the top of the charts, LaTavia and LeToya issued an ultimatum to the group: it was either them or Mathew.

Behavioral economists have studied the nature of ultimatums in laboratory settings. In the ultimatum game, two players negotiate over a sum of money to be shared.[1] The first player makes a take-it-or-leave-it offer, and the second player chooses to accept or reject the offer. If the second player accepts, the money is split as the first player initially proposed. However, if the second player rejects it, that, in effect, destroys the prize: both players get nothing.

From a purely rational perspective, the second player should always accept the offer from the first player as long as the first player offers them more than 0% in the split. That's because the inside option of accepting the offer is always better than the outside option of rejecting the offer—something is better than nothing. But in lab experiments, researchers have found that second players can be petty: they engage in *negative reciprocity*, reciprocating an action that has negatively impacted them with an equivalent action that hurts their opponent.[2]

In this game, the first player typically understands these dynamics and makes a reasonably high offer. Most first players offer around 40% of the pie, which is almost always accepted by the second player. But, when the first player makes an insultingly low offer, less than 20%, the second player almost always rejects the offer.

Even though the second player gets zero dollars in their outside option when they reject the offer, they still sometimes choose zero dollars over at least some money. That's because people care about more than just money—for example, some people care about justice more than a couple of dollars. So if a player can figure out what their opponent cares about and what their opponent values, a player can determine what offers their opponent will accept and reject.

LaTavia and LeToya were unhappy that Beyoncé was receiving almost all the attention. The rest of the women were seen as mere backup singers. In an ultimatum, they threatened to destroy Destiny's Child unless Beyoncé fired her father. Their ultimatum ultimately failed. LaTavia and LeToya mistakenly assumed that Destiny's Child could survive only with them as members. But Mathew didn't see it that way, and he promptly dismissed LaTavia and LeToya from the group.

From LaTavia's and LeToya's point of view, if half the group wanted new management, the current manager should be let go. So they chose a moment when the group had the most to lose and threatened to derail its momentum just as it began gaining traction. However, Mathew was unwilling to give up his role as manager under any circumstances. He had worked hard for years to help the group succeed, even quit his high-paying corporate job and sold his six-bedroom home to finance the group's music lessons, performances, and travel.

He didn't do all of that for the group. The group was a means to an end. That end was turning Beyoncé into a Diana Ross–

or Michael Jackson–caliber superstar. Both artists started in groups, but eventually, the Supremes turned into Diana Ross and the Supremes, and then just Diana Ross. The Jackson 5 turned into the Jacksons, and then just Michael Jackson.

In the music industry, a small number of superstars receive the lion's share of attention, radio play, music purchases, and digital streams. According to the economist Alan B. Krueger, the top 1% of musicians earn 60% of concert revenues, and the top 5% make 85% of concert revenues.[3] This is because interest in an artist can spread like a virus, with each additional fan spreading their love of the musician, which leads to exponential growth in popularity. As a result, minor differences in the likelihood of a listener becoming a fan of a musician at the beginning of their career can lead to immense differences in the number of fans an artist will have.

This phenomenon can be seen in any industry that relies on popularity. For example, executives at Penguin Random House report that the top 4% of books account for 60% of the publisher's profits.[4] Similarly, in terms of overall wealth, the top 1% of the population own 32% of the wealth in the United States.[5] Because popularity matters in many industries, this phenomenon of a small number of people becoming much more successful than the average person matters for wealth accumulation in general. Beyoncé was breaking out as the star of Destiny's Child. Her fan base ballooned faster than the other group members'. So, it was practically inevitable that Beyoncé's fame would skyrocket and leave the other women in the dust by comparison.

Mathew Knowles seemingly understood this. Since Beyoncé was the star, the other group members could come and go. The fans were coming to see Beyoncé. Not LaTavia. Not LeToya. When one player has relevant information that the other player does not have, there is asymmetric information. LaTavia and LeToya were unaware that Mathew placed so little value on maintaining continuity for the members of Destiny's Child. They didn't understand that Mathew saw them as replaceable. Perhaps this information asymmetry was due to their naivete. Regardless, LeToya and Latavia did not have or could not process all the information, which is why their negotiation failed.

Asymmetric information provides an advantage in negotiation games. When one player has more or better information, that player gains negotiating power and influence over the outcome. The economist George Akerlof won a Nobel Prize in part for showing that car dealers have better negotiating power than car buyers when the dealer knows more information about the condition of the car than the buyer. According to Akerlof, buyers can't distinguish good cars (peaches) from bad cars (lemons). When trying to determine the fair price for a vehicle, a buyer may fall somewhere between the value of a lemon and a peach, as they cannot accurately assess the car's quality. Since a dealer would only sell a peach for its high value, they instead sell lemons to unsuspecting buyers. The dealer holds on to high-quality automobiles for more discerning buyers.[6]

Suppose Akerlof applied his "lemons" model to Destiny's Child. He would probably agree that Mathew gave LaTavia and LeToya a lemon management experience and reserved his best, peachiest work for his daughter, Beyoncé.

DECEPTION

When a player withholds information or lies to mislead their opponent, there is risk involved. This is because their opponent may eventually catch on to the deception if they are paying attention. For example, savvy car buyers will call on an expert to inspect a car's quality. Eventually, car buyers will buy only from trustworthy car dealers.

Animals have a knack for figuring out when they are being lied to. Like many birds, blue jays communicate through their birdcalls, using them to announce their location, attract a mate, or warn of predators. However, blue jays have also been known to deceive others with their songs. For example, they may mimic the sounds of red-tailed hawks to scare away other birds and protect their territory. If a blue jay finds another bird at a bird feeder, it may let out a threatening hawk sound to frighten the other bird away and claim the seed for itself. But the blue jay cannot always deceive others. Eventually, the other birds will learn to ignore the hawk imitations and assume it is just another false alarm.[7]

According to researchers at Kennesaw State University, the frequency with which a species, such as the blue jay, deceives others depends on the gullibility of the species they are attempting to deceive.[8] If the other birds never realize that the blue jays are lying, the blue jays will continue to deceive them. However, suppose the other birds start to ignore the blue jays' false alarms. In that case, the blue jays will alternate between lying and telling the truth. That way, the other birds can never be sure whether the sound they hear is from a real hawk.

For LaTavia and LeToya, the high-stakes task of reading Mathew would have been an extraordinary challenge based on their early successes as a group. He told them he would turn Destiny's Child into a successful music group, and he did. But those successes produced a space in which discerning truth from non-truth—hawk versus blue jay—was fraught.

※ ※ ※

Embarrassingly, I had my own LaTavia and LeToya moment in my career. In 2015, in my first job out of graduate school, I worked as a litigation consultant for a small firm in San Diego.

At the time, I didn't know what I wanted out of a career, but I took the job because I wanted to be close to the beach and my family in Southern California. With a salary of about $200,000 a year, I figured I could at least live it up in my time outside the office, even if I didn't enjoy my time in the office.

FEARING THE UNKNOWN

The inclination to focus on the known over the unknown is what behavioral economists call *ambiguity aversion*, or *uncertainty aversion*. For example, if given the option to choose between two bets, most people choose the bet where they know the odds, even if those odds are unfavorable.[9]

A famous experiment in behavioral economics demonstrates that people prefer to know the odds even when the odds aren't consequential. Subjects were told they could earn $1 if they pulled a red ball out of a bag. They had the option to pull the red ball from a bag with half red balls and half black balls, or pull from a second bag with an unknown red-to-black ratio. The second bag might have been 100% red, 100% black, or some mixture. Without knowing anything, the odds of pulling red from the second bag are *equal* to the odds of pulling black. There is no reason to believe there are more black balls than red or vice versa. Yet, people overwhelmingly preferred to draw from the first bag, where the odds were known, even though it didn't increase their likelihood of success. Unknown risks are scarier than known risks, even when the odds of success are the same.[10]

I had yet to decide what kind of career I wanted, so instead of focusing on unknown aspects of the job, like company culture, opportunities for growth, or work-life balance, I focused on the knowns, like salary and location. I should have asked these questions during the job interview. I didn't, and I made it worse by neglecting to seek insight from former employees or review sites like Glassdoor.

But I was focused on simply *getting* the job offer rather than thinking about whether the job was right for me. The unknowns were scary, so I ignored them—to my own detriment.

NEGOTIATING UNDER UNCERTAINTY

When accepting a job offer, limited information about the nature of the job is available; this is to some degree inevitable. However, spending time in the job can provide a better understanding of how valuable the inside option—staying in that job—is to both the employee and the employer. Workers can use this knowledge to negotiate a higher salary or better job responsibilities. Or they can leave.

During the first year at my consulting job, I learned that the job conditions were worse than I had hoped. The job constantly blended into the time I thought I would have to myself. I would be sitting on the beach, on a Saturday, with a pit in my stomach that I might miss a work email. The job also demanded a level of perfectionism I did not possess.

My coworkers had much better attention to detail than I did, which put me at a comparative disadvantage. But it was worse than that: the perfectionist culture seeped into every aspect of the job. This made my flaws more debilitating than necessary. For example, the CEO once rebuked me for sending an email to a client that didn't meet company standards because I forgot to begin the message with: "Good morning, I hope you are doing well."

Despite my error-prone ways, I kept getting more responsibilities. It was my job to assess the economic value of intellectual property, which requires creativity plus analysis. During my second year on the job, I was already managing a project involving a Fortune 500 company. The team member who was supposed to be comanaging the project with me had just given notice. His impending departure put all the pressure on me, and it felt like more than I should be expected to handle.

I didn't want the extra responsibility. But instead of quitting, I thought, *Maybe I won't begrudge my job if I were compensated better.* So I went to the CEO and asked for a 20% raise. In my mind, I deserved the additional 20% on the grounds that I was taking on so much more than my original job description entailed. I expected the CEO to negotiate down to 10%, and that would be enough to make me feel like he recognized my hard work.

Instead, the CEO said no. As his face turned to stone, he told me it was company policy to give out raises only at the end of the year.

That excuse made no sense. He was the CEO. He made the policy. If he cared about keeping me, he would have thrown me a bone, at least.

At that moment, I had a flashback to my first extended interaction with this CEO. Two weeks in, he took me out to lunch to welcome me to the company. Although I was still ramping up, I was already proving to be a high performer. My manager would give me a task that he expected to take all day, and I would complete it in a couple of hours. At lunch, the CEO told me how excited he was to have me join because I was such a "workhorse." *Workhorse* . . . that expression stuck with me. It seemed like a backhanded compliment, or a dehumanizing microaggression.

When he rejected my attempt at negotiating a pay increase, I broke through the information asymmetry. I could see for the first time what he meant by *workhorse*: a workhorse gets the job done and doesn't complain. A workhorse doesn't get uppity and ask for a raise. The act of asking for a raise proved that I wasn't the workhorse he thought I was; therefore, I wasn't the kind of employee he valued.

I completely misunderstood the CEO's objectives. I mistakenly thought his primary goal was to impress the client. I knew the client would be concerned about seeing me leave after the other project's economist left. But now I understood the CEO cared first and foremost about having complete control over his employees. *That* was the missing piece of information I couldn't see, even though it was in front of my face the whole time.

The hard part about negotiating under uncertainty is that you don't know what you don't know. I thought I had better information about my value as an employee, but I was wrong. So, of course, my attempt at negotiation failed.

In retrospect, though, I didn't want a raise. I just didn't have the nerve to quit, because I was afraid I would be walking away from a good job. But it wasn't a good job; it was a toxic job. The job was a lemon. My uncertainty aversion was getting the best of me.

During a negotiation game or any game in life, it's natural to try to avoid uncertainty. But this is typically detrimental. Wading into uncertainty allows for information-gathering, which in turn is how advantages are sown. This allows for better, or at least more informed, choices.

OVERTHINKING

Information provides advantages. But there is a cost to gathering information. Thinking too hard for too long will cause headaches. Yes, educated guesses are better than uneducated ones. However, there is no perfect guess without perfect information. But perfect information regarding a decision is rare, at best: some knowledge will always be hidden from view. So a good-enough guess will usually have to suffice.

INFORMATION IS AN ADVANTAGE   63

Take what's known as the beauty contest game. During the Great Depression, a newspaper game challenged readers to select the most beautiful face out of a selection of 100 photographs; the photo that received the most votes from players would be judged most beautiful. This created a strange dynamic between game and player: the players had to render their play based on how they thought the game would proceed based on the strategies other players would use.

Pretend you are playing the beauty contest game: to make an easy guess, you could simply select the face you personally find the most attractive. This guessing strategy naively assumes all players share your same beauty standards. A more informed guess would be based on the most common standard of beauty among other players. However, this assumes that all other players make the easy guess. An even more educated guess would be based on what other players believe the most common standard of beauty is, even if they are wrong. For example, most players may find brunettes the most attractive. Still, they may falsely believe that blonde hair is the most common beauty ideal. It is difficult to know how other players will guess. Will they guess their personal preference, brunette, or the perceived collective beauty standard, blonde?

So, it's unclear in this game whether the best guess would be a photograph of a blonde or a brunette. Figuring out the best guess can become complicated fast and may not necessarily lead to a more accurate guess. At a certain point, excessive thinking about the game may not increase your likelihood of guessing correctly. There are diminishing returns to overthinking.

In economics, the *law of diminishing marginal returns* predicts that there is such a thing as doing too much. In fact, doing the most is rarely optimal. There is usually some optimal point of effort where the incremental benefit of doing more is less than

64 THREE

the incremental cost. You can think about a problem all day and not come up with a better solution than what you thought of in the first twenty minutes.

The behavioral economist Rosemarie Nagel attempted to determine the optimal level of thinking in a modified version of the beauty contest game. In this version, players selected a number between 0 and 100. The player who chose a number closest to two-thirds of the average won. Nagel found that the typical (median) choice was around 33, indicating that most people believed their opponents would randomly choose a number.[11] If most people thought this way, the average answer would be about 50, making 33 the optimal guess. However, if everyone else guesses 33, the winning solution would actually be 22. And then, if you start to think too hard and conclude that the winning answer should be two-thirds of 22, it would result in a worse guess.

Playing such games, then, requires finding a balance and accepting that even the best guess may be incorrect. Assuming that everyone else is blindly picking a number at random is too simplistic. However, assuming that everyone else thinks as hard or harder than you is too complex. Find a happy medium and accept that even your best guess might be wrong.

This advice applies to the stock market. Picking a company stock is just like the beauty contest game. The goal is not to select the stock you like the best. Instead, the goal is to select the stock everyone else will want next because that's the stock primed to go up in value.

Trying to figure out the stock that everyone else will want in the future becomes a headache quickly. Some games, like the stock market, can become too complicated for accurate predictions. In those cases, success is determined by luck.

MITIGATING RISK

The northern jacana, a black and yellow wading bird found in the tropical wetlands of the Americas, engages in a diversification strategy when reproducing. The female does not put all her eggs in one nest. That would be too risky, considering that a crocodile may come upon it and devour all her offspring. Instead, she lays many eggs with many mates in many nests. That way, she has the best chance of having offspring survive.[12]

According to economists, the best way to invest is to not overthink it. Diversify instead of buying individual stocks. Diversify across both space and time. The northern jacana doesn't lay eggs in just one year, but every year. That way, if there is a drought or a famine in one nesting season, she may still produce successful offspring in her lifetime. Similarly, make a habit of investing every year.

GAME RECAP

The next time you play a game against an opponent, try to see things from your opponent's perspective. Take an educated guess about what information they have that you don't, and try to predict what moves they will make.

Identify your opponent's objective. Don't be like LaTavia, LeToya, or me and go into a negotiation without understanding what your opponent actually wants.

Identify whether your opponent is lying to you or withholding information. Your opponent might mislead you about their objective, so don't take what they say at face value. Instead, consider whether your opponent benefits from misleading you, and be skeptical. If you're worried your car dealer is trying to sell you a lemon, have a trusted expert inspect the car on your behalf. If you fear your employer is misleading you about opportunities for a raise or a promotion, look at Glassdoor reviews or ask other employees their opinion.

Realize that there is a limit to your knowledge. It's impossible to know everything, so at a certain point, you must take a risk and make your move. An educated guess is better than a blind guess. And when you don't know what the best guess is, guess multiple times if you can; diversify.

4
DREAMS OF DREAM JOBS

There are two approaches to finding a job. One strategy is to apply to dozens of jobs with the same résumé. This scattershot approach can work well when you're at the beginning of your career, looking for a job that doesn't require specific skills or experience. However, once you do have experience on your résumé, a better approach is more nuanced: target the ideal job and hunt it like you're an apex predator.

DIFFERENTIATING YOURSELF

When my résumé was blank, I was what economists call an *undifferentiated product.* An undifferentiated product has no unique or distinguishing features or characteristics. Undifferentiated products usually command lower prices than differentiated ones because an undifferentiated product is replaceable.

Based on my résumé, an employer couldn't distinguish me from the thousands of other applicants trying to secure an entry-level position; we were all interchangeable. So at that point in my career, all I could do was apply broadly and hope an employer would randomly select me from the pile. Here I had to act like an omnivorous animal, turning over every log and eating whatever I could find. A job seeker can't afford to be picky when they lack differentiation as a job candidate. Only after they have gained unique skills and experience can they be selective.

Once I finished my PhD and worked two years as a consultant, I had something unique to offer, and I gained the ability to hunt selectively. Instead of being a job omnivore, I could be that apex predator. But I needed to select a target carefully because I would put all my energy into only one hunt.

SELECTING THE OPTIMAL EMPLOYER

After my negotiation with the "workhorse" boss failed, I immediately started looking for a new employer. My inside option of staying at the same job was worse than I had realized. There was no future for me there.

Before I could play the "get hired" game, I had to identify my dream job. I needed to find my best outside option, or perhaps take an educated guess. So as soon as my negotiation with my CEO failed, my job became finding a better job. I didn't want to lose any tempo sulking about my failure. I called up a friend from graduate school who had bounced around a couple of companies to give me his perspective on the pros and cons of different work environments.

I had avoided asking these questions of myself and others when applying for the consulting job. In the experience that followed, I learned what I didn't know then: just how critical work culture is. This failure in my last position gave me greater insight into what I valued in a job. Other things I now knew about myself that went on the list: I hated being micromanaged. I hated the strict deadlines that were preceded by 80-hour work weeks. I hated that my contributions went unappreciated. I hated that my shortcomings mattered more than my strengths. I hated that I couldn't work from home during the weekdays, but I was expected to work on weekends from wherever I might be. I wanted to find an outside option superior in all those dimensions.

My friend, who was working then at one of the biggest tech companies in the world, told me that his experience was nothing like that. At this company, people were expected to work autonomously without much direction. People usually set their own deadlines. Most people didn't pay attention to how many hours you worked or whether those hours were spent at your desk. Efficiency mattered more than perfection (or perfectionism). And the leadership cared about results above all else.

I'd found my game.

MOVING FOR A NEW JOB

There was one problem, though: I was in San Diego, and this Big Tech company was in Seattle. That kind of geographic mismatch between job seekers and job opportunities is a core friction of labor markets—though it has been improved some, with the rise of remote work. But for low-wage workers especially, geographic mismatch can contribute to unemployment and a lack of advancement because options in a given geographic market can be limited. I was lucky that I had the financial means to move. In fact, my moving expenses would be covered if I were offered the job. That perk was given to their high-paid employees only.

But even if I was willing to move, and with the good fortune of having means to do so, I faced another challenge: I wouldn't move for a job without my husband, Adam. If he didn't want to move to Seattle with me, this Big Tech company I was after wasn't an option at all.

The economist Alan Benson at the University of Minnesota theorized that in labor markets, men tend to be drawn to occupations that are geographically clustered—specific jobs in specific places—whereas women tend to pursue occupations that are geographically dispersed, thereby allowing them to move. The implication is that, after marriage, the wife will be able to follow her husband to wherever his job necessitates. For example, there are only so many places in the United States where a nuclear engineer can find employment; the country doesn't have that many nuclear reactors, so the jobs are necessarily centered on the few places where they exist. Similarly, jobs for actors are clustered in Los Angeles and New York. A schoolteacher, however, can find employment in any city or town. Benson found empirical evidence that a nuclear engineer husband is more likely to marry and stay married to a woman with a geographically dispersed occupation, like a teacher, than a woman with a geographically concentrated occupation, like an actress. That's because the teacher can relocate more easily and prioritize her husband's career more effortlessly than an actress could. When the husband and wife have careers that don't overlap in geography, they will eventually face a dilemma when deciding where to live and which career to prioritize.[1]

When my husband and I first started dating, he was studying nuclear engineering, and I was studying economics. This set us up for a structural challenge: both our careers were likely to be geographically concentrated, so it would be difficult for us to find employment in the same city. In recognition of this inevitable challenge, we made an agreement early in our relationship: we decided that my career would be the primary career in our relationship. We wanted kids, and we wanted our kids to have at least one parent available at home. Adam had grown up without a father. He wanted to give his children the experience he wished he had—the experience of having a present and caring father who put his children first. I wanted to be a mom, but I also wanted a career. I wanted to be like my grandmother. (But my grandmother had five husbands in her lifetime; I wanted only one.)

For the inside option of our marriage to work, I wanted a partner who wouldn't bail on me. Someone who would support me. Someone who would move thousands of miles across the country if it was the best move for us in our game.

Based on both our needs and wants, it made the most sense for me to focus on my career and for Adam to focus on our home life. (Some years and two kids later, he says being a stay-at-home dad isn't all that different from being a nuclear engineer: the key is to avoid meltdowns.)

In a cooperative game, players work together to accomplish a common goal. As a result, players all win together or all lose together. I have seen marriages fall apart because each partner played an individual game instead of a cooperative game. A cooperative partnership like a marriage can last years, with both players playing individually as long as each partner's goals are mostly aligned. But when goals diverge, a time will come when the best move for one partner is not the best move for the other partner, and if the two partners can't align on what's best for them as a cooperative, the relationship ends. Lucky for me, Adam and I have always played the same game with the same objectives together.

CREATING THE PERFECT RÉSUMÉ

Now that I had identified the Seattle tech job as the one I wanted, I needed to present myself to the company in a way that would maximize my chances of getting an offer. When applying for a job, the applicant has an advantage in having more information about themselves than their potential employer. The employer will try to learn more about the applicant through their résumé, a phone screening, an onsite interview, and references. But, perhaps counterintuitively, it's the applicant who is in control. The applicant can choose what information to reveal and how to present it. The applicant selects the presentation to best convince the employer to offer them the job over other candidates. This game is about strategically sharing information.

The bowerbirds of Australasia are known for their elaborate courtship rituals, which involve the construction of intricate structures by male bowerbirds. These bower structures are made of twigs and decorated with flower petals and sparkling trinkets. They resemble small shrines, standing about a foot tall, and are adorned with eye-catching touches such as berry juice or charcoal paint. These bowers showcase the male bowerbird's creativity and attention to detail and are meant to impress potential mates.[2]

The bowerbirds don't stop at creating an objectively impressive structure—they use optical illusions to make their artistry more impressive than it actually is. The male bird arranges objects covering the structure's entryway, such that the small objects are at the front and the large objects are at the back. This makes the small objects look bigger than they actually are.[3]

The bird's designs are intentional. When researchers messed with the bowerbird's design by putting the large objects at the front and the small objects at the back, the bowerbird corrected the arrangement of objects.[4] In another experiment, researchers used motion-sensitive digital video recorders to observe the building patterns of males in their natural environment.[5] The birds that created the most compelling optical illusions were most likely to successfully attract a mate.

When applying for a job, be like the bowerbird. The bowerbird puts effort into collecting the most desirable trinkets, but he doesn't stop there. He makes sure to arrange the collection in the most flattering way possible. Likewise, when applying for a job, put your accomplishments on display in the most appealing way possible.

I wanted to design my résumé to be optimally appealing to the tech company, creating the illusion that I was the ideal job applicant. I studied their job postings for economists to see what the company wanted from that role. Along with what my friend had told me about the job, I took an educated guess at what the company's objectives were in this hiring game. Based on that educated guess, I could signal to the company that I was the winning candidate.

The job postings included the phrases *statistics methodology*, *big data*, and *business problems* throughout, so I made sure to insert those phrases into my résumé. The job posting also called for an *experienced economist*. So, I presented my internships next to my full-time position to create the optical illusion that my internships gave me as much experience as my one full-time position. After updating the content of my résumé, I focused on erasing any evidence of my error-prone ways: I double-checked it for spelling and formatting errors, and then I had my husband triple-check it.

In an experiment, professional recruiters evaluated three fabricated résumés for economic researchers. The résumés were randomly selected to contain either no spelling mistakes or one, two, or five spelling mistakes. The more spelling errors a résumé contained, the less likely the recruiter was to deem the candidate worthy of an interview. Two mistakes reduced the likelihood of an interview by 7 percentage points; five spelling mistakes reduced the probability of an interview by 18 percentage points.

The recruiters assumed the candidates who had spelling errors in their résumés had worse interpersonal skills, were less conscientious, and were not as bright as the candidates who had error-free résumés. (They may have been wrong: dysgraphia, a writing disorder associated with spelling errors and illegible handwriting, is correlated with above-average intelligence in children.)[6]

The recruiters exhibited *negativity bias*. Negativity bias causes people to focus on negative information more than positive information.[7] A résumé might contain positive information like a strong job history or an impressive college grade-point average. However, it takes only a few spelling errors to negate all the positives. I didn't want the recruiter to fixate on my spelling errors and miss my accomplishments. I wanted to create the illusion that I was perfect in every dimension.

My next decision was how to put my name on my résumé. My full name is Daryl Rose Fairweather. My mother named me Daryl, a gender-neutral name, on purpose. As a freelance journalist in the 1980s, she felt like her work was rejected because of her feminine name, Kathleen. In the 1980s, when I was born, Daryl was a gender-neutral name, exemplified by two famous Daryls: Daryl Hannah was one of the biggest movie stars in Hollywood after she starred opposite Tom Hanks in the romantic comedy *Splash*; Darryl Strawberry was a famous athlete as a right fielder for the New York Mets. In 1988, when I was born, 43 out of a million baby girls were named Daryl.[8] But by the 2010s, the popularity of the name Daryl among baby girls shrank to less than five out of one million.

Namsor, a name-checking technology based on 7.5 billion name records, estimates that "Daryl Fairweather" is most likely a Black American man, like Darryl Strawberry, with 48% confidence about the Black American part and 86% confidence about me being a man. "Daryl Rose Fairweather," on the other hand, is most likely a white woman, like Daryl Hannah. The app is 41% confident that "Daryl Rose Fairweather" is white and 54% confident that I'm a woman. So, in deciding whether to put my middle name on my résumé, my choice was effectively to present as a Black man or white woman, when in reality, I am a biracial woman.

In the early 2000s, researchers at the National Bureau of Economic Research conducted a study in which they sent fake résumés to real job recruiters.[9] These résumés had randomly assigned names associated with Black or white and male or female identities. The study found that résumés with Black male names had a 67% chance of being selected, compared to the 92% success rate for résumés with names that were perceived as white and female. White male names and white female names both had a 92% success rate, while Black female names had a 61% success rate, slightly lower than Black male names. I included my middle name, Rose, on my résumé.

PREPARING FOR A JOB INTERVIEW

Within a day or two, I received an email from a recruiter to participate in a phone screening. In this short phone interview, the recruiter would ask questions about my experience to determine if I should be brought onsite for a full day.

I was nervous about the phone screening and already felt attached to the idea of working for the tech company. However, I knew I couldn't let my anxiety or desperation show through. Instead, I needed to come off as warm and friendly so the recruiter would think more highly of me overall. Psychologists have characterized this as what they call the *halo effect*: the attribution of one positive aspect of a person to their entire personality. For example, the halo effect predicts that people are likely to think a person with a great fashion sense is also good at solving crosswords. Of course, the two qualities are unrelated. However, the halo effect will make a person see everything about someone in a more positive light. In one experiment, researchers from the University of Michigan had subjects watch video lectures. In the video, one lecturer acted cold and distant, and the other instructor acted warm and friendly. The subjects who watched the warm and friendly instructor rated his appearance, mannerisms, and speech as more appealing than the cold and distant instructor.[10]

In a follow-up study, psychologists replicated the original halo effect experiment. But this time the researchers warned subjects about the nature of the study in advance. Despite this warning, and even with some study participants knowing about the halo effect that was being studied, the halo effect was still observed in people's responses. Being interpersonally warm garnered people all kinds of other favor.[11]

I tried to come off as enthusiastic and friendly during the interview. It worked. I received an invitation for an onsite interview at Seattle's headquarters.

PLAYING THE INTERVIEW GAME

At the onsite interview, I would be playing two simultaneous games. In game A, my objective was to win a job offer. In game B, my objective was to learn as much about the job as possible. That way, I could assess the value of winning game A—in particular, whether I wanted to accept the job if it was offered. I didn't want to work in another toxic environment, but toxicity is subjective: one person's toxic trash is another woman's treasure. Game A was more straightforward than game B, so I had to overcome my uncertainty aversion and dedicate equal effort to game B.

As I packed for the trip, I carefully curated a head-to-toe look. I hoped that flattering my appearance would give me an advantage in game A. The halo effect associated with beauty has been studied by the University of Texas economist Daniel Hamermesh. He found in his research that attractive people earn 3–4% more than average-looking people. As you may recall, an internship is estimated to increase lifetime earnings by 6%. Being attractive, according to research, is nearly as valuable as having actual work experience.[12]

To improve my chances of winning game A, I called my tech-job friend again and asked him for advice. He clued me in. He said I should be prepared to answer analytical questions, and that I would have to take a coding test. I should look up the company's leadership principles, memorize them, and think of two examples from my life that exemplify each leadership principle.

This was excellent direction. Companies are usually transparent about what they value (or, at least, what they think they value). Those values are taught to recruiters, who in turn use them to determine company fit with applicants. If a company says they value teamwork, discuss the times you worked well on a team during your interview. If a company says they value independent thinking, talk about the times you disrupted an instance of groupthink. Arrange your experiences so they look the most impressive from your potential employer's perspective, even if it is a bit of an illusion.

At the all-day onsite interview, I was evaluated by four different employees, with a break for lunch and a coding exam. For each interview, I prepared monologues on each leadership principle. At the end of each interview, I had the opportunity to ask questions, which was when I launched into game B.

The anxiety I experienced working in my consulting job was the thing I wanted to avoid most in my next position—and accordingly, it was the red flag I was on the lookout for in my conversations. If anyone interviewing me had work-related anxiety, I wanted to hear about it. So I asked the same question in each interview: "What gives you anxiety about your job?"

One answer stood out. The first interviewer said that the competitive workplace culture gave her anxiety. She explained that the leaders believed in survival of the fittest. They pitted product managers against one another by assigning them virtually identical products, such that only one manager's product would succeed. That anxiety sounded agonizing, but as an economist, not a product manager, I hoped that problem wouldn't be relevant to my role. Her answer was a yellow flag.

During lunch, I had a chance to relax. Another economist, who was not evaluating me, accompanied me, and we had a casual chat about our favorite board games. At the end of the lunch, he warned me to remember to clean the data at the start of my coding test, which was next on my schedule. In economic analysis, the presence of outlier data points can skew an analysis; *data cleaning*, then, means fixing or removing incorrect, corrupted, or misformatted data within a dataset to avoid bad or misleading results. In the dataset there would be obvious outliers that most people forget to check; I probably would have. So his hint was crucial. The halo effect of having a pleasant conversation must have made him want to see me get a job offer.

CURATING REFERENCES

After my onsite interview, the recruiter asked me to provide two references. I thought about the colleagues at my consulting job, who I feared would say some of the things I'd say about myself: that I made careless mistakes; that I mentally and emotionally shut down when required to work longer than nine hours in one day; and that I would leave them to shoulder the burden because I couldn't cope with the anxiety of it all. But then I remembered that I needed only *two* references, and I could think of at least two people I left with a positive impression. I didn't have to give an unbiased sample of colleagues. Instead, I could select colleagues who would be the most likely to say positive things about me. I was a bowerbird: I was trying to present the most attractive portrayal of myself, even if that portrayal wasn't wholly accurate.

It didn't matter that many of my coworkers at the consulting firm would give me a negative review. I only needed two of them to vouch for my performance.

UNANIMOUS DECISIONS

By contrast, among my interviewers at my new job opportunity, I needed every single one of them to like me enough to give me a positive review. The week after my onsite interview, all my evaluators would meet and discuss their impressions of me and then vote on whether I should be hired. If just one person felt strongly that I wouldn't be a good fit for the role, that would be enough to make me lose out. Luckily, though, unanimous juries are relatively easy to achieve, even though the requirement for 100% agreement seems tough to meet.

In a voting game, voters do not necessarily cast their ballots according to their true preferences but instead vote strategically to achieve a specific outcome. Game theorists have studied strategic voting in the context of court trials. According to Princeton University and Northwestern University economists, the requirement for unanimous decisions among juries often results in false convictions.[13] In a jury trial, each juror wants to convict the guilty and acquit the innocent, but under strategic voting, they may not necessarily vote that way. That's because when a unanimous vote is required for a "guilty" conviction, there is only one scenario in which a juror's vote matters: when that juror is the sole "not guilty" vote. Because a unanimous "guilty" vote is required in order to convict. It doesn't matter whether one or two jurors vote "not guilty"—either way, there isn't a unanimous decision. Only when everyone else is voting guilty can a juror's vote change the outcome from unanimous to non-unanimous, from convict to acquit.

But if everyone else is voting guilty, it would seem pretty likely that the defendant is, in fact, guilty. Why else would every other juror agree on guilt? So the "not guilty" voter may start to doubt themself—like, maybe they spaced out during a key testimony and missed the part that made every other juror vote to convict. This kind of impostor syndrome can cause groupthink among jurors.

Job-candidate evaluations work the same way. The only time a vote to not hire someone would be consequential is if every other evaluator votes to hire. And if that's the case, voting *not* to hire means going against the group and possibly angering the group. So unless one of the interviewers really disliked me, they would likely vote to hire me.

A few days later, while I was running an errand with my husband, the recruiter called with the good news that I had gotten the job. All my interviewers had unanimously agreed to make me an offer. I was elated.

GAME RECAP

The next time you are seeking out new employment opportunities, follow these steps:

Identify your outside options. Research what job opportunities exist and which may be your best option. Do some soul-searching about what you value in a job: the pay, the work culture, and the work-life balance you most desire. Ask for informational interviews with the people in your network who have experienced the kinds of jobs you are interested in.

Identify what your potential employer wants out of a job applicant. Study the job posting and the employer's website. Identify the experiences and values that the employer seeks.

Present yourself as the ideal candidate. Drop keywords in your résumé that appear on the job posting and the employer's website. Elevate the parts of your résumé that speak to what the employer seeks.

Be aware of recruiter bias. Remove any pieces of your résumé that might trigger negativity bias in the recruiter, like spelling or formatting errors. Likewise, don't reveal information about your race, national origin, gender, parenthood, religion, disability, age, or sexual orientation that might hurt your chances. Economic research indicates that recruiters hold biases in all those areas.[14]

Take advantage of the halo effect. Be enthusiastic and friendly to everyone who can help you get the job offer you want. This includes employees who aren't explicitly part of your interview process.

Be selective when naming references. Ask for references only from people who like you. If a coworker or manager doesn't have an enthusiastically positive opinion of you, don't list them as a reference.

5
BUYING A HOME

Buying a home is a high-stakes game, often with hundreds of thousands of dollars on the line. Making a wrong decision can lead to foreclosure and bankruptcy; making the right decision can generate wealth that is passed down for generations. For many people, buying a home is the most important financial decision they will make in their lifetime. Yet, first-time homebuyers often have little experience and limited education on the process. Unfortunately, this can lead homebuyers to make costly and preventable errors.

In the best cases, homeownership presents all kinds of financial benefits. Owning a home allows for long-term wealth accumulation, since property values typically rise over time. Additionally, mortgage payments can be viewed as a type of forced savings, enabling investment in an asset that will be worth more in the future. Homeownership also provides tax benefits, such as deductions for mortgage interest and property taxes. Finally, homeownership promotes stability and security, removing concerns about rent increases or lease terminations.

However, homeownership is not necessary nor optimal for many people. Owning a home is like laying down roots; however, those roots can feel like chains if you aren't ready to commit to staying put. Renting is typically a better option for those who don't plan on staying in one place for more than a few years. Plus, you can still accumulate wealth by other means. Property values tend to rise over time—but so does the stock market's value. In fact, the stock market has historically outperformed the housing market.[1] You could also put your money toward paying down debt or starting a business instead of putting it toward buying a home.

But when people *are* ready to settle down, they're still confronted with all the usual dilemmas: whether to buy a home; where to buy a home; what kind of home to buy; and how much to spend. These decisions are all more manageable using the lessons of economics—specifically, behavioral economics.

DECIDING TO MOVE

Taking the tech-job offer meant leaving San Diego for Seattle after I had already invested time, money, and effort into buying a home there. Selling that home felt like I was admitting I made a mistake buying it in the first place. But whether or not it *was* a mistake was irrelevant: all that mattered was whether my family and I would be better off moving to Seattle going forward.

When deciding whether or not to make a significant change like a move, it can be tempting to focus on the past—to believe that decisions about the future can make up for past mistakes. Economists call this cognitive bias the *sunk-cost fallacy*. The sunk-cost fallacy describes people's propensity to continue with an endeavor after devoting time, money, effort, or all the above, regardless of whether the costs outweigh the benefits moving forward. In other words: treat the past as past. Nothing done today can change what happened yesterday. Therefore, what happened yesterday should have nothing to do with the decisions you make today.

A skilled chess player can evaluate a game board at any moment to determine the best move forward. The chess player doesn't need to know what happened leading up to that point. For example, if the black king's rook is missing, it doesn't matter if the black player lost their king's rook on turn 10 or turn 20. The relevant information is captured on the board at the present moment.

It didn't matter that I bought the house only a year before and would lose money after paying real estate fees and taxes. The only thing that mattered was whether my happiness and earnings potential would be better moving forward if I left San Diego behind to work in Seattle. I bought the San Diego home in the first place because I needed a house big enough for me, my husband, and my mom, who had health problems at the time. Although my mother's health problems were a tribulation, the intergenerational living arrangement we came up with is what allowed me to buy my first home. Without the money from selling my mother's condo, I wouldn't have had the 20% down payment for a home for several more years, at least.

But in retrospect, it had also been too early for me to buy a home. I wasn't ready to settle down and start laying roots. I didn't appreciate how those roots would turn to chains that had to be broken. Maybe if I had introspected more about my career, I wouldn't have purchased that home.

None of that could be changed. I could only improve the future. So I put those self-critical feelings to the side because they were hurting, not helping, my ability to make positive change. If I had listened to my irrational negative internal monologue and stayed in San Diego, I would have stayed unhappy and stuck, a victim of the sunk-cost fallacy.

Moving to Seattle to work for the tech company was better than my inside option of continuing my status quo as a consultant in San Diego. Despite initially thinking I would enjoy living in San Diego, the city's poor public transportation, heavy traffic, and lack of walkability ultimately detracted from my enjoyment of the lovely weather and beaches. Additionally, the job market for economists in San Diego was weak compared to Seattle's thriving tech industry. So, I decided to sell my home in San Diego and pursue my new opportunity in Seattle. While living in San Diego did not turn out as expected, I learned about my values concerning where I wanted to live.

UNDERSTANDING THE HOUSING MARKET

Intergenerational wealth and intergenerational living (both things that came with my mom) gave me an advantage as a first-time homebuyer. This is not typical. For many Americans, housing costs have risen beyond something that is achievable. According to Redfin research, as of 2022, a homebuyer must earn $107,000 a year to afford a midprice American home. In expensive West Coast cities, the income required to afford a midprice home is notably higher: $205,000 for Seattle, $213,000 for San Diego, and $363,000 for San Jose.[2]

Home prices have become so unaffordable because of strong demand for homes combined with low supply. Many more people would like to buy a home than there are homes available to buy. As a result, the United States is short almost four million homes, according to a 2020 study from Freddie Mac.[3] To make matters worse, the US isn't building quickly enough to catch up to demand: fewer homes were built in the 2010s than in any decade dating back to the 1960s.[4] Time and time again, local governments have prioritized the wants of existing homeowners who benefit from higher property values over the needs of renters and first-time homebuyers.

NIMBY, or "not in my backyard," refers to homeowners who oppose new housing construction and other development projects, including high-density affordable housing. One example is the California-based organization Catalysts for Local Control, which seeks to block laws that would specifically facilitate the building of affordable housing.[5] This group offers resources to homeowners who want to sue the state to prevent affordable housing development.[6] Formal and informal groups of homeowners like this block housing all over the country. The commonality among these homeowners seems to be psychological resistance to change: they don't know what it would mean to have greater housing concentration where they live, and they're unwilling to find out. However, it is difficult to disentangle resistance to change from the historical opposition to integration. It is typically white, upper-class homeowners who oppose development projects, including those that would house a more economically and racially diverse population.

Because the US doesn't have enough housing, home prices roughly reflect what well-off people are prepared to spend. In simplified terms, if there are 10,000 homes for sale in a city but 40,000 families are looking to buy a home, only the wealthiest quarter of families will succeed; the houses that are available will be priced with these families' budgets in mind. Without resources like cash and credit, the other three-quarters lose when trying to compete.

To make matters worse, many people, myself included, start out with more resources. My own family's story of economic mobility started with my great-grandfather, Walter Merrick,

88   FIVE

who immigrated from Trinidad to the US to attend Howard University's medical school in 1915. He became a physician in Harlem and used his earnings to buy a brownstone townhome in the formerly redlined Brooklyn neighborhood of Bed-Stuy in 1931. At the time, banks wouldn't make loans for housing in neighborhoods deemed risky because of their racial makeup, so Black homebuyers, like my great-grandfather, had to rely on the pooled resources of their families and communities. Bed-Stuy was and largely remains a Black community, which means that for generations, residents of Bed-Stuy have faced barriers to accumulating wealth through homeownership. My aunt still owns the Bed-Stuy home, and I lived there rent free while I interned in Manhattan. In other words, the homeownership status of my ancestors still benefits me, nearly a hundred years later.

Most homeowners have parents and grandparents who were homeowners.[7] First-generation homeowners, meanwhile, face considerable hurdles to acquiring wealth compared to families with a history of homeownership. This means that the policies that excluded Black people from homeownership have effects that still persist. It explains why, as of 2020, just 45% of Black families own a home, compared to 74% of white families.[8]

All of this is to say: you should not feel bad if you can't yet afford to buy a home. If you didn't come from a legacy of homeownership, you are at a considerable disadvantage. As a rule of thumb, you want to spend, at most, 30% of your pretax income on housing. But in practice, this is often not the case: 46% of renter households in the US spend more than this amount.[9] These households are what housing economists call *rent burdened*. They spend so much on rent that they don't have money left to cover their food, healthcare, or childcare costs.[10]

Spending only 30% of your income on rent is absurdly out of reach for most renters in high-cost cities. That said, it's just a rule of thumb. There are many more considerations a renter should take into account.

CREATING A HOUSING BUDGET

Here's how to figure out what you can manage for housing: First, determine how much you currently spend on categories like housing, transit, utilities, paying down debt, entertainment, food, medical needs, clothing, savings, and other big spending categories. You can use websites like Credit Karma to connect your credit card, bank accounts, and other financial accounts in one place to analyze trends. Once you know how much you spend on each category per month, consider how your budget will change after you rent or buy your next home. Examine the amount you spend on each category and estimate how your expenses may change after moving.

Try to be as honest with yourself as you can. For example, while living in San Diego, I spent $200 to $300 a month on gasoline. But, since Seattle had much better public transit and my employer provided a complimentary bus pass worth $40 per month, my family got rid of one of our two cars; I started taking the bus to work, and our gas expenses went down to only $50 per month. This freed up hundreds of dollars in our monthly budget that we could put toward either housing, savings, or something fun.

On top of that, my long-term earnings potential was higher in Seattle than in San Diego. I was initially making less at my Big Tech job than I did as a consultant. However, I foresaw I had a better chance of getting promoted than in my old job. That made me feel more comfortable stretching my budget in the near term because I was confident I would earn more in the long run.

Both factors helped me justify spending $4,000 a month to rent a home in Seattle when I first moved there in 2016, which

90 FIVE

amounted to about 30% of my pre–tax base salary. I wasn't the only tech worker moving into Seattle with the lure of a high salary. Seattle's population grew by 19% in the 2010s—the most out of any major city.[11] If I wasn't willing to spend that much on rent, someone else would. Still, spending that much on rent felt outrageous. As a graduate student in Chicago in 2010, I paid only $800 per month. But back then, that was 40% of my monthly stipend. Now that I was earning much more, I could spend more on rent without exceeding the 30% rule of thumb.

Figuring out a reasonable renting budget was a different mental exercise than figuring out a budget to buy a home. That's because I was on the hook for paying my rent only for the term of my lease, but I would be on the hook for my mortgage until I sold the home or paid it off in full.

The difference between buying and renting a home depends mainly on how your housing costs will change over time. Assuming that housing costs will continue to rise on average, you can expect your rent to go up most years unless you move into a more affordable home. By contrast, if you have a fixed-rate mortgage, your monthly mortgage payment will change only if you refinance your loan. This means that when budgeting for housing costs, it can make sense to spend more on your mortgage than what you were spending on rent. For example, it can make rational sense to buy a home based on what your income and needs will be five, ten, or fifteen years down the line. That's because a person in their 30s can expect to earn more money in their 40s.[12] And a 40-year-old raising multiple kids will need a bigger home than a 30-year-old without children.

Budgeting for rent is more straightforward than budgeting to buy a home because you need to worry only about meeting your short-term needs. But renters should also pay attention to long-term needs, like saving for a financial goal such as retirement or eventual homeownership. One added benefit of home-ownership is the automatic savings. Over time, as you pay down your mortgage and your home's value increases, your wealth will increase too.

IDENTIFYING NEEDS AND WANTS

As I set out to find a new home in my new city, I knew I needed to approach the process carefully. I wanted to avoid getting caught up in the competitive pressure of beating out other buyers and making rash decisions that I might later regret. So I decided to divide my search into two phases. In the first phase, I would take my time getting to know the city and its various neighborhoods by renting a home. This would allow me to get a feel for what I wanted and needed in a home before making any offers. And in the second phase, once I had a clear sense of my preferences, I would begin making offers on properties that met my criteria. By taking this approach, I hoped to avoid the pitfalls of hasty decision-making and make an intelligent, informed choice.

For about five months, I spent a great deal of time exploring the different neighborhoods and assessing their pros and cons. I also made a point of going on several in-person home tours to familiarize myself with the various styles of homes available in the city. From historic Queen Anne homes dating back to the 19th century to midcentury modern homes from Seattle's post–World War II boom to modern new construction, there were plenty of options to choose from.

Each style had its unique set of pros and cons, and it was up to me to weigh the costs and benefits of each home. Queen Anne homes, for example, were often on the smaller side. Midcentury modern homes might require significant updates to their electrical and plumbing systems. On the other hand, new homes came with a higher price tag. It was a lot to consider.

The most significant tradeoff to be made when choosing a home is location versus home size. I initially thought of a short commute and a large home as must-haves, but given my budget, I had to sacrifice on the length of my commute. Many homebuyers make this same compromise. According to a Redfin survey, 89% of homebuyers would rather purchase a single-family home with a backyard than a unit in a triplex with a shorter commute. Additionally, having plenty of living space was ranked as the most important criterion more often than any other factor.[13]

As you browse homes in search of the perfect one that fits within your budget, you will invariably come across some that you love that are either out of your price range or outside your desired location. If the types of home you want are too expensive, there are a few options to consider. One option is to rent for a while and save for your dream home. Alternatively, consider purchasing a unit in a multifamily building rather than a single-family home, or you could look for a home in a less expensive neighborhood. Even if you buy a home that isn't exactly what you want, it can still have a secondary benefit of allowing you to accumulate wealth to eventually move to your dream home.

※ ※ ※

As we continued our search for the perfect home, we focused our efforts on West Seattle, a neighborhood located on a peninsula across the sound from downtown. The commute to office headquarters by bus would take about 30 minutes each way. But I could use the commute time to get some work done using the complimentary Wi-Fi. This was a decent tradeoff, given that homes in West Seattle were priced around $100,000 less than homes closer to the office headquarters.

In addition to the more affordable prices, we also liked the vibe. West Seattle had once been its own city; it still maintained a distinct identity as a more laid-back and free-spirited alternative to the rest of Seattle.

Other neighborhood features a homebuyer may consider, beyond just vibes, are walkability, access to transit, nature, shops and restaurants, air quality, and school quality (if you have or plan to have children). As we worked with our real estate agent, we developed a list of requirements for our new home, including a private area for my mother with her own bathroom, space for future children, and a yard for our dogs. We also created a wish list of desirable features, such as a spacious kitchen, a walkable neighborhood, and high-quality schools. Finally, we made a list of items we didn't want, including a pool, heavy traffic, and a homeowners' association.

AVOIDING COMMON MISTAKES

Once I progressed to phase 2 and began viewing properties and making offers, I became hyperconscious of how my emotions might influence my decision-making. Common mistakes made by homebuyers include becoming too attached to a particular home, fixating on the list price instead of the market value, following the herd, and letting fatigue cloud judgment.

You must try to avoid falling in love too quickly with a home. Once you start picturing your future in a home, it could become challenging for you to walk away, especially if you get into a fierce bidding war. Dismiss any and all thoughts about hosting holidays or your children playing in the backyard. Yes, it is a good idea to consider whether the home will suit you in the future, but if you become too attached to that future, you're working against yourself. People value a home more if they already feel like they own it. The *endowment effect* is a term used by behavioral economists to describe this phenomenon.

The behavioral economist Jack Knetsch observed the endowment effect in lab experiments.[14] He found that people's willingness to sell an item they own was lower than their willingness to buy an item they did not own, even when the subjects knew ownership was assigned randomly. In one experiment, test subjects were given either a lottery ticket or cash. Most people opted to keep whatever form of compensation they had received first, and at random, instead of trading it for the other option. The people with the lottery tickets in their hands felt an unexplainable pull toward retaining the ticket. However, the people who had the cash in their hands were less interested in the lottery. Maybe it's superstition. For whatever reason, people tend to get attached to the bird in their hand, even when there might be two in the bush. That attachment could lead you to make an aggressive offer on a home you feel like you own when there might be a better option available.

It may also be the case that how you feel about the home today may differ from how you will feel about the home in the future. For example, that swimming pool may seem like an oasis on a hot summer day but could feel like an eyesore come winter. Focusing too much on the present while ignoring the future is what behavioral economists call the *present bias.* For example, a study from the National Bureau of Economic Research found that homebuyers overvalue homes with swimming pools and central air conditioning when bidding on a home during the summer. By looking at repeat sales of homes, the researchers were able to compare the price of a home sold in the summer versus the winter while controlling for housing market conditions. When a house with a pool was sold in the summer, it typically went for a price 0.4 percentage points, or about $1,600, more than when it sold in the winter. Most homeowners own their home for over a decade. Therefore, homebuyers should consider the long term. But those touring homes during a hot summer day are evidently more focused on the features of a home they could utilize in the present moment. If a swimming pool is a want, not a need, don't prioritize it over your future needs, like your retirement savings.[15]

List prices can also be misleading. In a hot market, sellers may advertise their homes for significantly less than what buyers are ready to pay in order to spark a bidding war—which could net a sale price well above market value. Under this strategy, the seller entices more buyers to play the bidding game by making it seem like a buyer could get a below-market price. This amounts to a bait-and-switch: what seems like a deal results in an overpay because of savvy pricing and a knowledge of buyer behavior.

The economist Edward Lazear studied the *bait-and-switch* marketing phenomenon whereby a store manager advertises a fake low price for an item to draw more shoppers into the store. Lazear found that this strategy is typically employed when there is an abundance of shoppers looking for low-priced items and searching for deals is costly. A competitive housing market, like the one I faced in Seattle in the spring of 2017, fits this description.[16]

As a buyer, don't take the bait. Don't anchor your expectations on the listed price. The *anchoring effect* refers to a person's tendency to focus on the first piece of information they hear while making decisions. In a famous lab experiment by Daniel Kahneman and Amos Tversky, research subjects spun a wheel of fortune with numbers from 0 to 100. The participants were then asked to guess the share of African countries that were members of the UN. Even though the wheel spin clearly had nothing to do with the correct answer, participants whose spin landed on a lower number were more likely to guess a low number for the trivia question. Participants whose wheel spin landed on a high number were more likely to guess a high number.[17] The number the needle of the wheel landed on was completely irrelevant, yet the research subjects still used it as an anchor for their guesses.

The list price of a home may contain some helpful information about what the seller believes its value is. However, ultimately the value of the house is set by the market. Don't let the list price anchor your bid if the price isn't justified.

If you need to, take a break. Losing bidding war after bidding war—which happens a lot—can foster fatigue and impatience. This can cause people to give up too soon or to purchase a home they later regret. *Decision fatigue* is the mental tiredness people feel after a lengthy decision-making process.

Researchers have found that the quality of decisions deteriorates when an individual is weary and in need of rest. For example, a study published in *Health Economics* found that orthopedic surgeons made worse recommendations toward the end of their shifts. Doctors were less likely to recommend surgery for patients who would have benefited just as much from surgery as patients seen earlier in the surgeon's shift.[18] Similar to the doctors, consumers are likely to make worse decisions when fatigued.

Avoid following the herd; think in terms of yourself and your life. If others are ready to bid high, you could be tempted to do the same and stretch your budget. When a person does what others are doing instead of thinking independently, this is what behavioral economists call *herding behavior.* This phenomenon can lead to bubbles in the housing market or the stock market and was one of the culprits for the subprime mortgage crisis of 2008.[19] In the early 2000s, nearly everyone believed home prices would only go up. Detractors were proven wrong for years as prices continued climbing to new heights. But eventually, prices did come down—quite dramatically—and everyone who bet on endless price growth lost and took the economy down with them. In short: you never know what will happen with the economy or home values. The best way to avoid getting caught up in speculation bubbles is to not speculate in the first place. To play it safe, make offers appropriate only to your personal financial circumstances.

After spending a few weeks touring various homes in the area, I came across a property that immediately caught my eye. It had everything my family was looking for. However, there was a red flag: the home had been on the market for nearly a year without any offers.

Despite my initial excitement about the property, I worried that the home was overpriced. Upon further inspection, I noticed that the house had a few quirks that might have turned off other buyers. For example, it was located across the street from a strip mall and had a strange layout. Even though I liked the home, I wanted to avoid paying more than other buyers might think it was worth. So I decided to keep looking for a property that offered similar features at a more reasonable price.

That calculation makes home buying trickier than other financial decisions. When you rent, you only have to worry about yourself. You don't have to think so much about what future residents would be willing to pay—that's your landlord's problem. But when buying a home, you have no choice but to concern yourself with resale value. Because life is unpredictable, there is always the chance you might not stay in the home long term, and you don't want to pay more than what you can resell it for.

There is tension in this advice: that a homebuyer must avoid herding behavior by thinking for themself while simultaneously considering how other people might value homes in the future.

The way to walk the middle path is detached observation—recognize the behavior patterns of others without letting it unduly bias your decision-making.

About a month later, we found a home that seemed too good to be true. It checked off all our must-haves, including ample space, and it was close to public transit. Plus it had a view of Puget Sound and the Olympic Mountains. However, the home was seventy years old, so we would need to update the electrical, plumbing, and heating. Since we were renting elsewhere, we could delay moving to get this work done.

BIDDING ON A HOME

Things go wrong after you buy a home. Thinking that these problems won't end up costing you significant time and money is what behavioral economists call *optimism bias*: the tendency to overestimate the likelihood of favorable outcomes and underestimate the likelihood of unfavorable outcomes. The challenge, then, is to consider the risks and whether they are worth the reward.

As I prepared to make an offer to buy a home, I thought back to the hundreds of homeowners going through foreclosure that I interviewed while interning at the Boston Fed. They experienced bad luck on top of bad luck—deaths, divorces, medical emergencies, job loss, and a global recession. Any of those things could happen to me. In an unlikely but not impossible scenario, they could all happen simultaneously.

This put a pit in my stomach. I thought about backing out of buying a home altogether. But continuing to rent had its own risks as well. I was paying more in rent than what my mortgage would be. Because of Seattle's hot tech-job market, many young professionals were moving in and needed housing. Even though the home I was renting was worth only $800,000, I was paying rent that equated to the mortgage for a million-dollar home at the time. And none of that money was building equity.

I calculated how much I was currently spending on housing, utilities, taxes, transportation, entertainment, retirement savings, and miscellaneous expenses. Then I estimated how each of these categories would change if I owned the home I was making an offer on. My housing, utilities, and tax expenses would all change. I would get a tax benefit from the mortgage tax deduction. I would be upgrading the heat and cooling for the home, which would cost me tens of thousands of dollars up front, but would save me money in the long run. So overall, my expenses would go *down* if I bought a home priced less than a million dollars. In the spring of 2017, the midprice single-family home in the city of Seattle sold for $850,000. So far, so good.

With all the repairs the house needed, I determined the maximum amount I could afford to pay was $950,000. I liked this particular home more than any other home on the market priced below $950,000, so I reasoned that this amount must be my value for the home. But I still had a nagging feeling that I was overextending myself and overpaying.

What if the roof sprang a leak? And what if, because I had already spent my savings repairing the plumbing, electrical, heating, and cooling, I didn't have any money left to repair the roof? I would have to go into credit card debt, which I always try to avoid because of the high interest rates. That debt would be stressful and expensive, but it wouldn't be the end of the world. If I had more bad luck, like losing my job, I figured I could easily find work in Seattle, where tech jobs were plentiful. I estimated that in these scenarios, I would still be able to afford my mortgage and could avoid selling at a loss. The scenarios where I could as a fail-safe sell my home at a profit weren't catastrophic, just inconvenient.

I could have kept going down the list of unlikely catastrophes. Instead, I focused on the unlikeliness of the scenario rather than the pain of the scenario. This helped me get out of my head and back to the task at hand. In economics, *expected utility theory* hypothesizes that individuals weigh uncertain outcomes according to their likelihood and the net benefit of each outcome. I shuddered at the thought of a bad scenario, like being laid off during a severe recession and housing-market downturn. However, according to expected utility theory, I should weigh that feeling against the likelihood of that scenario, which I reasoned to be a once-in-a-century event. In all likelihood, my job was safe, the economy was fine, and the value of homes would keep going up.

I downgraded my value of buying the home by $10,000 to make myself feel safer about the risk I was taking. But even with all that future planning, I missed the scenario where a global pandemic would turn my job into a remote position. This unforeseeable event would completely change my value of my home.

The home was listed at $840,000. I submitted my bid on the home for that amount. When you're deciding whether to bid above or below the asking price, look up how competitive the housing market is in the neighborhood and how the home compares to what else is on the market. You can do this research on sites like Redfin, or you can ask your agent. If the market is cool, it's advisable to come in low. However, if the market is hot, the seller may completely ignore your offer if it's below the asking price.

Even though I offered $840,000, I was ready to pay more. I calculated I would go as high as $940,000 in a bidding war. I set that amount ahead of time so I wouldn't get caught up in herd behavior and bid more than what I calculated to be reasonable. I patiently waited for my real estate agent to tell me whether I had won the house or whether I would need to outbid a competing buyer.

While waiting, I felt conflicted about whether winning would be a gift or a curse. The *winner's curse* occurs when bidders in an auction lack information about the value of an item. Each bidder takes a guess at the item's value, and the winner necessarily makes the most inaccurately high guess. Maybe my information about the home was inaccurate. Perhaps I lacked knowledge about whether the neighborhood was going up in value, or maybe I lacked information about the difficulty and cost of repairs.

Later that day, my agent called me to deliver the good news: we won the home for $840,000, the listed price. No one else even submitted a bid. Now that I had bought a home, I was ready to settle in. I was over the initial ramping-up period at the tech job and settling into a work rhythm too. But that rhythm was about to be disrupted.

GAME RECAP

The next time you're moving into a new home to rent or buy, follow these steps:

When debating whether to make a move at all, check your thinking for the sunk-cost fallacy. When deciding whether to move or stay, consider only present and future factors, never the past.

Set a budget. Understand that housing is expensive, especially in coastal metros like Seattle. Assess your current spending habits and how they might change after moving. When renting, you only need to plan for the short term, but when buying, you should consider long-term risks and how your earnings and spending patterns may change over time.

Determine the qualities in a home that you need versus what you want. You will likely have to make tradeoffs during your search for a home. Decide what you need versus what you want ahead of time, and hold yourself to your budget. Thinking through this ahead of time will help you stay level-headed.

Check your thinking for cognitive biases. Avoid falling in love with and becoming attached to any individual home. Put your future needs over your present wants. Avoid fixating on the list price and instead assess the home's market value. Take a break if you feel yourself becoming fatigued. Think for yourself instead of following the herd.

Plan for different future scenarios. Think through the worst-case and best-case outcomes and assess each scenario's likelihood. Then, make a decision that will make you happy in the most likely scenarios. But still make plans for emergencies. Building up savings is an excellent way to stay prepared.

6
WORKPLACE CONFLICT

In the best cases, coworkers work together to achieve common goals within a company or organization. However, that doesn't happen very often—colleagues can have their own agendas and priorities that lead to conflicts.

Competition takes place when players have something to gain from seeing their opponent lose. In a *competitive game*, players act in their self-interest, and the outcome for one player occurs at the expense of others. This is unlike a *cooperative game*, where players work together to achieve a mutual goal.

Competitive games are difficult to avoid because not playing isn't really an option: choosing passivity is the same as forfeiting. For example, when a snake invades a robin's nest, the robin can't opt out of that confrontation without sacrificing her eggs. Her offspring's survival depends on her successfully scaring away her adversary, the snake. The snake's defeat is the robin's victory, and vice versa. There is a scarcity of success.

Scarcity is present in most games in some form. For example, there are often more job seekers than positions in the job market. There are often more buyers in the housing market than

homes for sale. In college admissions, there are often more qualified applicants than the school has spots for students. These are
all semicompetitive games where one player's success is indirectly related to another player's demise.

WORKPLACE BULLIES

One example of a game with limited resources is the hawk–
dove game. In it, two players square off to gain a reward and
have the choice to either act like bullies (hawks) or pushovers
(doves). When a player chooses hawk, they attack the other
player—causing them harm and stealing the reward. When a
player chooses dove, they ask nicely if the other player would
like to share the reward. When both players choose hawk, they
both end up hurt, with only a 50–50 coin toss determining who
gets the reward. That's assuming both players are equally strong.

If one player is stronger than the other, the stronger player
is more likely to win when both behave like hawks. When both
players choose to act like doves, they don't suffer any harm and
split the prize. When one player chooses hawk and the other
chooses dove, the hawk gets all the reward and the dove just
gets hurt.

In an ideal world, players would be able to see beyond their
own individual strategy to do what's best for all players—that is,
everyone would always act like a dove. But when everyone else
acts like a dove, it is easy to get away with being a hawk, so players will always be tempted to act like hawks.

Scientists have observed the hawk–dove game play out in real
life in the monsoon forests of Northern Australia. But instead
of hawks and doves, there are finches. The Gouldian finch is a
little bird with a vibrant coat of feathers that includes a mustard-
yellow belly, a sapphire-blue tail, an apple-green cape, and a

purple breastplate. The birds are a sight to behold, and their appearance alone makes them notable. But what's most interesting about the Gouldian finch is how its appearance relates to its behavior: male Gouldian finches with red heads are more prone to starting fights, while those with black heads tend to avoid conflict. However, there is a trade-off to being a redheaded male—the aggressive redheads are bad dads.[1]

Even though bully birds may exploit pushover birds to gain food or territory, pushover birds are actually more common in nature. When the bullies start to dominate a flock, the group suffers because the bullies run out of pushovers to victimize. At this point, the bullies often waste their energy fighting with each other rather than caring for their offspring. This infighting among the bullies allows the pushover birds to make a comeback. Pushover birds that avoid conflict often raise more offspring than bully birds, which leads to a shift in the demographics of the flock toward more pushovers. Eventually, the flock reaches a balance where pushover birds outnumber the bully birds.

The relative number of bullies to pushovers depends on the availability of resources to the flock. When a flock has plenty of food and territory, the cost of bullying is low; bullies abound because they can afford to waste their energy on useless fighting. However, habitat destruction and climate change threatens the environment and food sources of Gouldian finches, which could lead to the extinction of the redheaded bullies. Only flocks that, by chance, lack the genes for bullying can survive when resources are so scarce. This is an example of evolutionary game theory at work. When a strategy is advantageous for an individual but disadvantageous to the flock's survival, selfish individuals can survive until the entire flock's survival is at stake.

The workplace can sometimes resemble a flock of Gouldian finches, with some offices being overrun by bullies and others having few or none. The prevalence of bullies in a given workplace is determined by the cost of bullying. For Gouldian finches, the cost of being a bully is fewer offspring, which can lead to the extinction of the flock when resources are scarce. In the workplace, the cost of bullying depends on the company culture. If bullying goes unpunished—or, even worse, if it is actively encouraged—the number of bullies in the workplace will be high. When the number of bullies in the workplace is too high, it can harm productivity and profits, ultimately hindering the company's success.

I heard during my interview for my new tech job that the company culture was based on a "survival of the fittest" ideology. But as evidenced by the Gouldian finches, survival of the fittest isn't always conducive to the best social outcomes: competition can be counterproductive to a group's prosperity. It can lead to unnecessary infighting that makes it harder for everyone to succeed.

Shortly after I had settled into my new home, I found myself in a competitive game with two of my colleagues. It all started during the quarterly review of my team's progress toward goals. The senior vice president of our department sat in on this meeting, and we all wanted to impress him. While we were reviewing the employee-satisfaction survey results for each office around the globe, the senior vice president interrupted and told a story about his recent visit to Delhi.

A worker at the Delhi office pulled the senior vice president aside to tell him that many of the employees assigned to work overtime were unsatisfied and underperforming. The senior vice president let us know he took this issue seriously and was considering doing away with the mandatory overtime assigned by lottery. So, the senior vice president asked me to research whether the employee's anecdote was supported by data. It was exciting—the first time a research request came directly to me from a senior executive. I reached out to the Delhi staffing analyst to get the IDs of the overtime employees so I could construct the data for analysis.

EMPLOYEE SATISFACTION

The way an employee feels about their job is subjective. It depends more on what the employee wants from the job than the job itself. However, even though employee satisfaction is subjective, it can still have significant consequences. If employees hate their jobs, they might discourage others from joining the company, complain online or to the press, or be less motivated and less productive.

My analysis of employee satisfaction showed that the overtime employees had higher satisfaction than those working a regular shift. But this top-line result masked something deeper: The company surveyed only the employees who didn't quit—but the overtime employees were the ones quitting earlier and more often. This meant that the sample of employees surveyed was not random, which meant it wasn't representative. Instead, it was biased by attrition. *Attrition bias* is omnipresent in data interpretation: a *selection bias* is produced when data are chosen in a manner where adequate randomization is not achieved. This results in a sample that is not representative of the entire population.

For example, suppose I surveyed everyone at the company and asked them if they think bullying is a problem. In that case, I would miss all the employees who quit because they were bullied so often that they couldn't take it anymore. It would be like asking only Kelly and Beyoncé if Mathew Knowles was a good manager. Neglecting to survey LaTavia or LeToya—who disliked Mathew so much they attempted to get him fired—would skew the results. On the flip side, if I interviewed everyone who quit or was fired from the company, then I would miss all the employees who still work at the company and don't think anything is wrong with the work culture.

So if you are considering working for a company and a current employee tells you how great it is, take that with a grain of salt. Similarly, if a former employee tells you how awful it was, take that with a grain of salt, too. Both perspectives may be truthful, but they are also both biased. And this rule applies to all games, not just the game of choosing where to work. The kinds of people who avoid conflict will seek cooperative games, and those who seek conflict will be inclined to play competitive games.

To correct the selection bias in the satisfaction surveys, I compared overtime employees to regular shift employees who had been at the company for the same amount of time. In this comparison, the finding was the opposite of the earlier finding: overtime workers had much lower satisfaction scores than the regular shift workers. I shared my findings with my manager, who shared it with our team's director, who shared it with the scheduling team's director. Shortly after that, I received a request for a meeting with two of the managers on the scheduling team, Jake and Jarred.

Jake greeted me in the conference room with a smile and a handshake, so it seemed like I was entering into a cooperative conversation. He pressed me about how it could be possible that the overtime workers had higher satisfaction scores but *I* was saying they were less satisfied with their jobs. I told Jake and Jarred that we didn't have the satisfaction scores of the overtime workers who were so dissatisfied they quit. Instead, we only saw the overtime workers who are usually just a few months into their job and haven't started to hate it yet.

I stepped to the whiteboard and explained. I drew a chart with the employee-satisfaction scores broken down by months in the job on the horizontal axis and employee-satisfaction scores on the vertical axis. I color coded the findings with different markers. I explained each variable and its rationale.

Jake and Jarred nodded, but they still looked confused. I waited for a question or comment about what I had just explained. Instead, Jake asked me about the source of my data. I told them I got the data from their analyst in Delhi. Jake responded: "Just Delhi? Oh, you need to include data for Mumbai and Jaipur too."

I agreed. So later that day, I received a file with the additional overtime data. I repeated the analysis to my colleague's specifications. The results were much the same. But my two colleagues were still incredulous and wanted to meet again.

GENDER STEREOTYPES IN THE WORKPLACE

In the meantime, I had my monthly one-to-one meeting with my director. She asked me how things were going and about my research project. I recounted my meeting with Jake and Jarred. "I'm not sure why they want to meet again." I told her. "The results didn't change with the new data, so I don't know what else there is to discuss. It feels like they're looking for something wrong with my analysis."

My director told me plainly that the two didn't believe my analysis because they didn't respect me. She said they probably couldn't imagine that a woman would know more than them. She reminded me that I'm the one with a PhD in economics, not them, so I should stand my ground.

That PhD could signal my abilities to my coworkers and help combat their preconceived notions, but it wouldn't make us equals—in their eyes or in the labor market. Although women earn more when they have more education, the gap between men and women is wider among the highly educated: Women without a bachelor's degree earn 78 cents for every dollar men without a bachelor's degree make; meanwhile, women with a bachelor's degree earn 74 cents for every dollar men with that degree make.[2]

A study from Harvard, NYU, and the University of Denver found that "women are underrepresented in careers where brilliance is valued." Furthermore, the study found that men were more often associated with brilliance than women.[3] Participants were shown pictures and words and asked to sort them into categories such as "male," "female," "brilliant," and "funny." The study found that people associate men with brilliance as much as they associate women with family, another pervasive gender stereotype.[4] The result held among children and adults as well as women and men, and carried across the United States and the world.

So no matter where I went in the world, chances were people assumed I wasn't brilliant. It wouldn't matter if I waved my three economics degrees in people's faces—in fact, doing so would likely make things worse, as it would make me come off as braggadocious and insecure. And there was no guarantee my credentials would change anyone's perceptions anyway, because sexist perceptions are untethered from reality.

Regardless, I was moved by how matter-of-fact my director was about her conclusions on gender bias. I usually hesitate to call out sexism when I perceive it, even when I know my senses are supported by research. Hearing it from her felt affirming, because on my own, I couldn't tell definitively why Jake and Jarred were giving me a hard time. It's not like they were walking around with red heads for the world to see. And I wanted to give them the benefit of the doubt, not because they had earned it, but because it's impossible to get any work done if

I believe everyone is out to get me. However, I wasn't doing myself any favors by ignoring red flags. My director was likely speaking from experience. She was the youngest woman to be promoted to the director position at the company. I'm sure she had encountered her fair share of Jakes and Jarreds along the way. Still, she wasn't offering to intervene on my behalf. She told me to handle it myself.

And handling it would be challenging: women who express anger in the workplace are penalized, while men usually get off scot-free or are even rewarded. Researchers at Yale and Northwestern conducted a study on how anger is viewed in the workplace. The researchers found that study participants attributed women's emotional reactions to internal personal characteristics. In contrast, men's emotional reactions were attributed to outside forces.[5] If a man has an emotional outburst, he can get away with it because people will think he was provoked—that it wasn't his fault. I, however, had to keep my cool and not let my emotions get the best of me because, as a woman, my personal reputation was at stake. To make matters worse, hits to a woman's reputation are more damaging than hits to a man's. Researchers at Harvard, Northwestern, and Stanford looked at how penalties for misconduct differed by gender in the financial advisory industry. Compared to male advisers guilty of wrongdoing, female advisers had a 20% higher chance of losing their job and a 30% lower chance of finding a new job. This result held even after accounting for differences in occupation, worker productivity, and the nature and frequency of the misconduct.[6]

EVADE OR CONFRONT?

I wished I could hide from Jake and Jarred. In another competitive game, the pursuit–evasion game, also known as a cat-and-mouse game, it's easier for the mouse to evade when there are lots of hiding spots. The nice thing about working for a big company was that I could usually hide behind my never-ending list of research requests. I always had a long list of projects to work on, so if a difficult colleague made a request, I could drop them down in the queue if I felt like it. But not this time. Since this was a direct request from the senior vice president, I couldn't deprioritize it. And unfortunately, Jake and Jarred's team had provided the dataset, so they had a seemingly legitimate reason to involve themselves.

In the hawk–dove game, there is a binary choice: be passive like a dove, or be aggressive like a hawk. There is no in-between. When confronting a hawk, a player's aggression must match or exceed that of their opponent to win.

As I walked into the conference room to meet with Jake and Jarred, they sat, arms crossed, opposite me. Again, they went into the same line of questioning. However, this time it felt more like a cross-examination than a research discussion. Jake prodded: "The satisfaction scores are higher for the overtime workers. That's what the senior vice president asked you to look at. So why are you doing this extra analysis?"

"The overtime workers are more likely to quit. I have to take that into account when interpreting the satisfaction scores," I replied.

"Do you have any idea how disruptive it will be to change all of the schedules? You have to be absolutely sure," Jake declared.

"I am 99% sure. According to my analysis, there is only a one percent chance the result is a statistical fluke." I was talking about the p-value—the statistical measure that gives the probability of the null hypothesis. In this case, the p-value was actually *less* than 1%.

"What data did you use again?" Jarred asked.

"The data you sent me."

"What data is that?"

I rolled my eyes. These dudes doubted my research abilities, and they didn't even know what data they sent me. "The employee IDs from the three India offices. I have employee IDs for all of the workers from last quarter."

"Oh, that's not enough. You need data for the whole year."

"Why?" I snapped.

"What do you mean, why?"

"Why do I need more data? Like I said, there is only a one percent chance the result is a fluke. So more data isn't going to change anything." I could sense my message wasn't getting across. "It's like I'm looking at a picture of a dog, and you're telling me my photo isn't good enough—I need to get an HD picture. But I don't need high definition to know I'm looking at a dog. The dog isn't going to disappear just because I increase the number of pixels. I can see the dog's floppy ears, I can see its droopy tongue, I can see its square nose. I don't need to zoom in to see the drool dripping off the dog's tongue to know I'm looking at a dog."

This response must have pissed off Jarred, because he exploded on me.

"*You don't know that!*" he yelled, banging his fist on the conference table. "It doesn't make sense. There's more data!" he shouted through tight lips. "This isn't over."

Jake looked horrified. Jarred had taken it too far. Jarred must have sensed Jake's eyes on him because he hung his head and looked down at the table like he was ashamed. I sat silently, waiting for an apology, but Jarred kept looking down. He wasn't apologizing, because he wasn't sorry for how he spoke to me. He was embarrassed that he got emotional and blew their cover. Jake and Jarred didn't like my research results, regardless of what data I used. They feared the senior vice president would tell them to eliminate mandatory overtime, creating more work for them. So instead of doing their jobs, they would rather bully me out of doing mine.

But the nature of this opposition made me even more resolute. I had seen over and over again instances of company employees making decisions that were convenient for them without thinking twice about how it would affect the employees on the ground who make the company function. If I let Jake and Jarred get away with this, I would be allowing them to bully not just me, but also the thousands of workers in my dataset. So I announced: "This is a waste of time. I will analyze the full year's data even though I know it won't change anything. Then I'm going to send it to the senior vice president. You can talk to him about it if you still have doubts."

As I predicted, the results came back the same. Jake and Jarred stood down. Based on the research results, the senior vice president directed the staffing team to eliminate mandatory overtime.

IDENTIFYING ENEMIES AND ALLIES

In games, players either play with or against each other. Sometimes it's clear whether or not the other players will help or hurt you, and sometimes that information is hidden, causing an information asymmetry. To complicate matters further, sometimes the players themselves don't know whether they want to cooperate or compete as individuals.

Foraging birds often work together to find food, but they all put in different levels of effort. The foraging behavior of birds such as geese, great tits,[7] and spice finches[8] has been modeled by ecologists in the producer–scrounger game. In the game, some birds in the flock will choose the producer strategy: they fly around searching for food for the benefit of the flock. Other birds will choose the strategy of scrounger: they wait on the sidelines, enjoying the sun or taking a birdbath, and wait for one of the sucker producer birds to find some food. Then they sidle up next to them and enjoy the food the producer bird worked so hard to find. Some birds always choose to produce no matter what. It's part of their personality.[9] Conversely, some birds always choose to scrounge. But a set of birds switch up their strategy depending on the amount of food available. When food is scarce, they take matters into their own hands (or beaks, rather): they take the initiative to search for food themselves. But when food is bountiful, they lay about, choosing the scrounging strategy.

Based on only one interaction, it's impossible to know whether a player's strategy is determined by their environment, their personality, or both. It's unfortunate that when women act aggressively, that choice is usually attributed to their character, but men's anger is attributed to their environment. Even so, I still want to give Jarred the benefit of the doubt. Maybe he was just having a bad day. The truth is, both personal characteristics and environment can determine player actions, whether the player is a man or a woman, human or animal.

SIGNALING STRENGTH

The red-headed finch wears its aggression on its face. But humans are capable of concealing their aggression—or their cowardice. For example, your opponent might act macho but be quick to back down in an actual confrontation. Or they may act friendly but be aggressive when pressed. So you must figure out who your opponent really is. And you also want to lead your opponent to believe you are not the one to mess with. Economists call this *signaling*: credibly and intentionally conveying information about yourself to another person.

Beyoncé has taken this tactic to protect her privacy. She rarely appears in celebrity magazines unless she has final approval over the photographer and concept.[10] When Beyoncé decides to make a personal announcement to the world, she does it on her terms—like when she created events out of her pregnancy announcements, revealing her baby bump during an MTV Video Music Awards performance in 2011 and a high-art photography project in 2017.[11]

Ironically, Beyoncé's attempts at privacy make paparazzi shots of her all the more valuable because when supply goes down, the price goes up; scarcity increases value. As a result, photographers can earn thousands of dollars from selling her image. For that much money, it makes financial sense to spend all day tracking down Beyoncé instead of spending the day at a D-list celebrity event.

This puts Beyoncé in a dilemma. The more she avoids the paparazzi, the more valuable her photos are, and the more the paparazzi hound her. To get around this problem, Beyoncé undercuts the paparazzi, making their photos worthless.

In 2019, Beyoncé staged a photo shoot of herself in a red sequined ball gown beside her husband, Jay-Z, posed in a white tuxedo. She posted the photos to her Instagram account, and the images spread to celebrity magazines and blogs. Why did she do this? The paparazzo Miles Diggs who goes by Diggzy commented on Instagram, "The sole reason these photos have been posted is because I was patient, and worked hard to get the shot. She can't let the little people [the paparazzi] succeed."[12]

The paparazzo went on to say in another post, "Beyoncé can post whatever TF [the fuck] she wants, whenever TF she wants. . . . What I am saying is she only post [sp] her photos if someone gets a shot of her walking the streets, so that the media can use them for free. Y'all would be mad too if you worked your ass off for thousands of dollars and then someone put it in a shredder."[13]

Apparently, this photographer learned that Beyoncé would be attending her niece's *Great Gatsby*–themed party and waited patiently to snap a photo of her outside the event. He was upset that Beyoncé posted a posed and glamorous picture of her and her husband in the same outfits pictured in his shot. Now magazines wouldn't buy Diggzy's photograph, because Beyoncé gave away a better one.

In a final clarifying comment, Diggzy stated, "She takes a photo that took about 8 hours of work, and is worth thousands of dollars, and then gives it out for free out of spite. She can post whatever she wants whenever she wants, but just know the reason behind it."[14]

But Beyoncé likely wasn't acting out of spite. She was letting the paparazzi know that if they ever caught a photo of her, she would make it worthless. She was signaling that she would punish anyone trying to make money from her image without her consent. Beyoncé understands that she can't stop the paparazzi from harassing her, but she *can* change their incentives. She can devalue the payoff the paparazzi receive from harassing her. The celebrities the paparazzi choose to hunt for photographs are based on payoffs and costs. Once a photographer learns that Beyoncé will always sabotage their payoff in their repeated game, their best option is to target a different star.

When Jake and Jarred tried to bully me, I stood my ground not only because I needed to win the battle—I also wanted to win the war. This wasn't a one-shot interaction, but a repeated game. Unlike *one-shot games*, where players make decisions without considering the future repercussions, *repeated games* are played multiple times, allowing players to observe and respond to each other's actions over time. In repeated games, players can build a reputation that can influence other player's beliefs and choices.

I wanted to signal that in the future, I was going to be a hawk. I wanted to signal that if they tried to undermine my research again, they would hit a brick wall. I wanted them to go tell their colleagues about what happened, so all the bullies in the office would receive my signal. Then I could succeed at my job without interference. I had to choose the hawk strategy to win.

GAME RECAP

The next time you're confronted by a bully or potential bully at work, follow these steps:

When evaluating a new place of work's culture, ask former and current employees for their opinion. Because of attrition bias, former employees may be overly pessimistic about the company. Current employees may be overly positive. Get both perspectives.

Identify your coworker's objectives. If you and your colleagues share the same goals, your work relationships will be like a cooperative game. However, if a coworker's goals interfere with your objectives, then you are playing a competitive game. If your opponent is clever, they may conceal their true objectives to avoid confrontation. In that case, put yourself in your opponent's shoes and think about what they likely desire and fear to take an educated guess at their hidden goals.

Determine whether your opponent will back down. If your opponent is trying to conceal their objectives, it may be because they don't want to be outed as the competitive type or, worse, a bully. Bullies hurt productivity in the workplace, and in functional workplaces, bullies are reprimanded. If your workplace frowns on bullying, publicly calling your opponent out on their behavior may induce them to back down. Shine a flashlight on their behavior. Include your manager and the bully's manager on emails. Don't take one-to-one meetings with the bully. Have at least one witness who can validate your experience.

Determine whether you want to evade your opponent. You have the choice of whether or not to face your opponent. If you want to avoid fighting them, you may be able to evade them, but evading can be time-consuming and limiting.

Determine whether backing down will make you a future target for bullying. Losing or winning against your opponent can damage your reputation and affect future games. If you are seen as a pushover type, you may be targeted by more bullies in the future.

Use this opportunity to learn who your genuine allies are. If your manager doesn't have your back, it's time to change teams. If you can't change teams, it's time to apply for a new job. You will get ahead at work only if your manager has your back.

If you want to face your bully, push them to the point of backing down. When you confront your bully, act like a hawk. Make them understand that fighting you will be more costly than backing down.

7
GETTING PROMOTED

Earning a promotion empowers an employee to take on more responsibility within their organization, receive a higher income, and gain a title that may come with more respect. It's a powerful reward that can motivate employees to work harder. Unfortunately, it's not always the hardest workers who earn promotions. That's because true meritocracy—a system in which power is determined by ability and effort—is impossible.

THE MERITOCRACY MYTH

Meritocracy in a workplace is impossible because no matter how the criteria for promotion are designed, there is no way to guarantee that the promotion will go to the employee who worked the hardest. That's because employers don't actually *know* which employees are the hardest workers.

Is it the employee who worked the most hours? Or is it the employee who produced the most output? If neither can be measured, perhaps it is the employee with the best customer feedback, or the best reviews from coworkers? None of these measures is perfect, and hinging a promotion on any one of these factors can cause employees to ignore the rest.

To make matters worse, bosses can have subjective and biased views on what "hard work" looks like. A study from MIT Sloan School of Business found that women received substantially lower ratings for potential than men, despite outperforming them and being less likely to quit. The researchers estimated this type of gender bias is responsible for up to 50% of the gap between promotions received by men versus women.[1]

Because there isn't a perfect way for employers to identify the most-worthy employees, promotions are never perfectly meritocratic. That is especially true when promotion opportunities are scarce and political games play a role in decision processes. "Working hard" won't guarantee that hard work is recognized.

So, if an employee wants to earn a promotion, they can't just keep their head down and work hard. They need to be strategic. They must understand the promotion game's rules and then use backward induction to identify the moves that will guarantee a promotion.

THE CHALLENGES OF PERFORMANCE EVALUATIONS

I fixated on winning a promotion as soon as I started working at the tech company. I knew that being a top performer was a necessary but not sufficient condition for my promotion. Like how a bird requires wings to fly, but not all winged birds are capable of flight, there were performance criteria for me to meet, but meeting those criteria would not guarantee my promotion.

Employers use promotions and other rewards to incentivize workers to be productive. But, typically, the criteria used don't fully or accurately measure worker performance. As a result, a worker may fail to win the promotion game if they focus too much on being a good employee without meeting the requirements set.

Economists call this the *principal–agent problem*. Anytime a principal (boss) hires an agent (employee), a problem arises. This is because the boss's and the employee's goals are not aligned: the boss wants the employee to work as hard as possible; the employee wants to work only hard enough to earn a good wage.

The boss may attempt to get the employee to work harder by observing the employee and making threats to withhold wages if the employee is seen slacking off. However, the boss can't micromanage perfectly because the boss can't monitor everything the employee does. The boss often only sees the employee's output: the finished work. The boss can't tell if the result was a fluke or the product of hard work by the employee. A boss could investigate how much effort the employee puts in. However, the employee might be pretending to put in effort when actually slacking off.

For example, suppose a boss tells their employee to enter data into a computer spreadsheet. In that case, the boss can only partially observe whether the employee is using all their work time on the project. The boss could put a motion detector on the employee's mouse and software on the employee's computer to track what applications and web pages are open. Still, the boss won't know if the employee is working or just tapping out the syncopated beat of a Beyoncé song on the keyboard.

Presumably, the boss wants the employee to enter data quickly and accurately. However, if the boss rewards speed, the employee will be incentivized to ignore quality. If the boss rewards only quality, the employee will slow down to ensure they make no errors. Maybe the boss cares mostly about quality, but when there is a tight deadline, the boss cares more about expedience. However, workers won't change their behavior if that prioritization isn't reflected in performance metrics.

To make matters more complicated, the boss won't know how much luck was involved. For example, the data may have contained typos and errors that the employee had to spend extra time cleaning up. Or the data might have included pages and pages of repeated information, so the employee could just use the copy-paste function to input most of it. Ideally, the boss wants their employee to put in maximum effort daily. Unfortunately for the boss, it is often impossible to distinguish who is trying from who is faking it.

This back-and-forth is ultimately a fight about economic surplus. The employer's economic surplus is the worker's output minus the cost of employing the worker. The worker's economic surplus is their wage minus the personal cost of their effort at work. The tension comes from the fact that effort (working hard) decreases the worker's economic surplus but increases their employer's.

The boss wants the worker to act in good faith and put in maximum effort. However, effort is costly to the employee. The employee would be happier taking breaks and working under less pressure. But the boss's inside option is degraded whenever the worker slacks off. As a result, the boss is getting slightly less out of the employment relationship.

Similarly, whenever the boss stands over the worker's shoulder, monitoring their work, demanding maximum effort, the worker's inside option is degraded. The employment relationship will go on as long as the boss and employee are better off continuing it versus terminating. And the passive-aggressive fight over economic surplus goes on.

The principal–agent problem can also appear in relationships other than boss-employee, like the one between a musical artist and their record label. According to press accounts and interviews, Beyoncé and her record label were not aligned while working on her debut solo album, *Dangerously in Love.* She felt pressure from her record label to include more commercial-sounding songs. After hearing the album, the executives told Beyoncé she didn't have a single hit song on the album.[2] The record label executives (who were the principals) had different goals and incentives than Beyoncé, the agent. The executives were mainly concerned with maximizing profits and minimizing risks. But Beyoncé was more interested in creating an album that reflected her artistic vision. Beyoncé's risk-taking paid off in the end: five songs from the album made it to the top five on the music charts.

Another example of the principal–agent problem is seen in the relationship between a homebuyer and the homebuyer's real estate agent. Homebuyers expect their real estate agents to show the homes that best meet their preferences. But traditionally, a buyer's agent is paid a percentage of whatever price the buyer ultimately pays for their new home. This misalignment in incentives can lead to an unscrupulous real estate agent pushing expensive homes on a buyer who would prefer a more affordable home. In response, some real estate brokerages and agents have tried to better align incentives by basing their compensation on a flat fee or customer reviews instead of a percent of the home's sale price.

In any principal–agent problem, incentives can be somewhat aligned by designing reward systems. Rewards include cash bonuses, raises, and promotions. By winning a prize like a promotion, the employee gets something of value in exchange for more effort. For example, effort might be measured by the number of hours an employee works. In contrast, the output might be measured by the number of projects the employee completes. The boss could also pit employees against one another and reward only top-performing employees. Economists call this a *tournament* because there are winners and losers, just like in a sports tournament.

In one study, the economist Edward Lazear used performance data about auto-glass installers at Safelite Glass Corporation. Lazear looked at how changing the way employees were paid affected their work. Initially, workers were paid an hourly wage. However, in the experiment, some workers were paid a piece-rate pay. Under piece-rate compensation, a worker was paid more for each additional glass windshield installed. Lazear found that workers increased their output by 44% on average when the company changed from paying employees an hourly wage to a piece-rate pay.[3] When pay was based on output, unproductive workers were more likely to resign or not seek employment with the auto-glass company in the first place. On the other hand, top performers worked harder and produced more when they were paid based on output. Since top performers earned more under piece-rate pay, the company could hire more effective workers and retain its top performers more successfully.[4]

But economic theory suggests that making promotions too competitive can demotivate workers. Research published in the *Journal of Political Economy* introduced a game-theory model that shows how the more competitive a workplace contest (like a promotion) is, the more discouraged employees become.[5] This happens because increased competition can motivate people to try harder. However, it can also discourage people because winning is less likely. The economists found that increasing the size of the competition, the inequality of the prizes, or the number of people competing can all decrease the effort put forth by players. The research also suggests that larger competitions may be less effective at motivating effort than small ones.

Workplace competitions can motivate teams but can also cause players to try to game the system. Researchers conducted an experiment at a fruit farm in the UK to see how different ways of rewarding employees who work in teams impacted the farm's productivity. At the fruit farm, the workers were divided into teams of five, and their main job was to pick fruit from different fields. When they first arrived at the farm, they were randomly assigned to a team by the general manager for their first week. After that, they could choose their team members at a weekly meeting as long as all members agreed to be on the same team. [6]

Teams were overall more productive when rewards were given to the teams based on rank (first place, second place, and so on.) But over time, workers gamed the system by avoiding the unproductive workers. The most productive workers banded together to maximize their odds of being a part of the team with the best chance of getting the biggest reward. With all the top performers on one team and no bottom performers weighing them down, each winning team member didn't have to work so hard to earn first place.[7]

Clearly, reward systems have the power to change employee behavior. However, for any reward system to work, employees must trust that the boss can discern who deserves the reward. There are objective output measures for auto-glass installers and fruit pickers. Even though the boss can't observe how much effort workers put in, it's easy to tell which workers have fixed the most windshields or collected the most strawberries. But for white-collar workers like myself, even output is subjective. There is no objective way to compare the productivity of one economist to another, let alone compare an economist to a product manager, a graphic designer, or a software engineer.

However, at my Big Tech job, my performance was undeniable. My team had never worked with an economist before, so they were blown away by my abilities. Whatever question they had, I

128   SEVEN

could find the answer. And if I couldn't find the answer to their specific question, I could uncover the answer to a better question they didn't think to ask. Productivity was down last month for our Spanish-language employees—what happened? "It looks like the less-productive employees all have the same supervisor. Maybe that has something to do with it." Why are employees in Shanghai quitting more frequently than the employees in Nanjing? "It looks like the employees who quit reported higher dissatisfaction with their pay. The cost of living is higher in Shanghai than in Nanjing. Maybe we should reevaluate compensation." Why did the Phoenix employees take so many breaks last month? "The site manager says the air conditioning was malfunctioning in one of the buildings, and the data shows it was mostly the employees in that building taking extra breaks." At the time, I believed that promotions were meritocratic, so I was happy to perform.

Economists at Northwestern University and the Barcelona School of Economics conducted an experiment on the effects of meritocratic promotions at the Ministry of Health in Sierra Leone. Before the experiment, the workers at the Ministry of Health thought that promotions were being given out unfairly, based on who had the most connections with senior leaders. So the researchers created a new promotion process that was based only on performance metrics, introducing it to half of the workers. When the promotion process became more meritocratic, worker productivity increased compared to when promotions were given out unfairly. In fact, productivity was even higher when the pay increase that came with promotion was large. However, large pay increases *demotivated* employees when promotions were unmeritocratic.[8]

I had checked off the necessary requirement to be perceived as a top performer. Still, there was more to securing a promotion. I also had to play a political game that would require backward induction.

BACKWARD INDUCTION:
THE SECRET PATH TO VICTORY

The best way to identify a winning strategy for any game, whether in a board game or a real-life getting-promoted game, is to begin at the end. Imagine what success looks like at the end, then work your way backward to identify all the moves needed to guarantee that success is the outcome. Game theorists call this technique *backward induction*. Under this strategy, you think about your end game during your early game to make the best opening moves.

I hate playing the board game Catan because I know how the game will end, and it's always with me losing. Catan, previously known as Settlers of Catan, was developed in Germany and first released in 1995. However, it wasn't until a decade later that the game took off in popularity and indoctrinated a new generation into the fun and competitive world of strategic board games.

In Catan, three to four players create settlements, trade resources, and race to collect ten victory points. The game is simple enough to learn that a new player can beat an experienced player. This makes it an excellent first taste for anyone new to strategic board games. But the fact that a new player can win with little experience means the winner is not determined primarily by skill in a traditional sense. The winner isn't necessarily the person who manages their resources the best or has the luckiest dice rolls or card draws. Ultimately, the winner is determined by who manages their likeability the best.

In a three-player game, the player with the most and second most points race to get to ten points, while the person in

130 SEVEN

third place is usually too far behind to catch up. However, the last-place player can still impact the game's outcome by making trades. Whoever the player in last place makes favorable trades with will have an advantage that is often large enough to guarantee that the selected favorite player wins. The least-skilled player becomes the kingmaker, with the power to crown the winner.

Great Catan players perform backward induction to see this outcome coming. One friend I used to play with would go out of his way to help the last-place player throughout the game to earn their favor. Unfortunately, I can't pull off that level of social manipulation while also trying to manage the cards in front of me, which is why I almost always lose at Catan.

It's hard enough to focus on the tasks in front of you, but great players can focus on the future and the present at the same time. They can see the end game and work backward to figure out the path to victory. They can identify the kingmakers, and they focus their efforts on those key players.

In the film *Get Out*, the Black protagonist Chris uses backward induction to outsmart the family of white liberals who kidnap him and try to use his brain for their own purposes. In the film, Chris and Rose, a white woman, visit Rose's parents at their secluded estate. Chris notices strange behavior from the people he encounters at the estate and suspects something is amiss and his safety is in danger.

To escape the estate, Chris works backward from the end of the situation. He collects clues and pieces together the full extent of the family's plan to take over his Black body by harvesting his brain. Chris then uses this knowledge to anticipate the actions of the white family and outmaneuver them. For instance, he realizes the family would need to hypnotize him to harvest his brain. So, he essentially plays dead and pretends to be sedated under hypnosis while still conscious. Like how a mallard will fall to the ground and play dead as a final defense against predators, backward induction allows Chris to solve the problem of how to protect himself and get out.

Backward induction can be used to identify a winning strategy in any game that involves multiple steps or choices. It can be implemented in trivial board games and the life-and-death games of horror films. In the real world, backward induction can be used to identify a winning strategy for advancing your career.

Since my performance alone wouldn't guarantee my promotion, I needed a strategy. I needed to work backward from my goal of getting promoted to identify the steps and ways my promotion might either pass or fail each step.

Promotions were scarce at my company, so many top performers got passed over each year. On top of that, there was no guarantee my manager would want to put me up for promotion. It was entirely up to her discretion whether to put in the time and effort to write my promotion document, gather references, and advocate for me. On top of that, other people on my team had been there longer and still hadn't been promoted. Those employees might quit if passed over again. According to a 2019 ADP Research Institute report, one team member's promotion is correlated with higher turnover among the other team members: teams with a promoted employee had an 8% greater turnover rate than teams with no promotions.[9]

My manager was clever, though. She had strategic reasons for promoting me. As a manager, her performance was judged based on her team's success. And my promotion would increase the chances of us reaching our team goals. So in a way, my manager's success hinged on my success. And as an extension, my manager's *manager's* success depended on my success. The executives at the top of the corporate hierarchy weren't producers, so

132   SEVEN

their success and salaries depended on the performance of all the employees under their umbrella.

CORPORATE HIERARCHIES

According to the *management-hierarchy theory*, firms divide employees into layers determined by employee characteristics such as knowledge or tasks performed. In an ideal firm, the most knowledgeable workers belong to the top layer. That way, the knowledgeable lead those still learning about the business.[10]

The problem with this structure is that the more layers added to a firm, the less equal pay becomes. Economists at Yale, Johns Hopkins, and Princeton studied the organizational structures of manufacturing firms in France. They found that firms that add employees tend to add layers of hierarchy at the top and reduce pay at the bottom. However, firms that stayed small tend to keep their organizational structure. As a result, these small firms paid their average worker more than they would have made at a sizable hierarchical firm.[11]

The Big Tech company I worked for followed this pattern. Its hundreds of thousands of employees were divided into hierarchical layers, with employees at the top making far more than those at the bottom. I started out as a level 5, which meant only level 6s and above could weigh in on my performance assessment and impact my chances of promotion. Anyone above me knew my opinion as a level 5 would never impact *their* promotion decisions, so they could safely ignore me without career repercussions. That's why my manager wanted to promote me to level 6—I would have more influence over more of my coworkers. That way, our team would have more influence within the company.

INFLUENCING THE KINGMAKERS

But my manager was not a kingmaker. My manager, level 7, and all the other managers in my department would submit their promotion recommendations to the directors within our department, the level 8s. They would narrow down the list to fit within the budget. That list would go to our vice president, level 10, for final approval.

The bargaining between directors was a black box. Each director had their own agenda, and their multilateral negotiations could go in unpredictable directions. But the end game was foreseeable.

At large organizations, it is especially tough for executives to discern productive leaders from unproductive ones. Of course, the senior executives at my company tried their best. But employee satisfaction scores, performance metrics, the reports of directors and managers, and observations during office visits were unreliable. The satisfaction scores didn't explain why employees were happy or unhappy. The metrics didn't tell executives if the problems were with the employees, the management, or the job itself. Managers' reports might be biased. And observations at offices and warehouses might be more theatrics than an accurate representation of daily life for employees. This meant managers had to have precise and accurate bullshit detectors to successfully lead a department with multiple layers of management.

So I knew when the vice president would go to look at the list of promotions from the directors, he would be looking for bullshit. And if he suspected bullshit, there would be hell to pay. That was the endgame in my backward induction. If the vice president recognized my worthiness for promotion and did so publicly, the directors would fall in line and support my promotion, if not genuinely then, out of fear.

Most of my colleagues avoided being on the vice president's radar altogether. He was a scary guy. He was usually friendly, but when he suspected one of his employees was bullshitting him, he transformed into a raging bull. He would drill in on his target, asking a barrage of questions, until the employee cracked and either admitted that what they initially said was incorrect, uninformed, or incomplete.

Each week, my team would deliver a readout of our progress toward goals to the vice president and his team of directors. No one on my team wanted to give this readout, but I volunteered. In graduate school at the University of Chicago, my research was scrutinized by economists with legendary bullshit detectors. I knew how to eradicate any last trace of it from my research. I wanted the vice president to see that I was the real deal. Not only that, I wanted all his directors to see me publicly pass his bullshit tests with flying colors. That way, the directors would fear the vice president asking them: "Why isn't Daryl being promoted?" It didn't matter if the question was unlikely. The fear would keep my promotion safe.

Usually, the vice president took what I said at face value, but he tried to make me break once. We were rolling out new software to our employees—software that had taken years to develop. It was supposed to improve productivity, yet productivity was declining. The software team claimed nothing was wrong, but my analysis showed that employees found the software unreliable. The vice president was tense about these results because so much had been invested in the software. He grilled me: "What about the Nanjing employees? We didn't translate the software for them until April. When did their scores start going down?" I was prepared for all these questions and calmly referred to my table of results broken out by geography and date. I was not afraid because the facts were on my side. It was clear the software was to blame. He began nodding with me, and his anger turned to warmth.

That warmth continued in all our interactions, and the directors noticed. Now the directors would come to me with their research requests; that way, when the vice president pressed them on how they knew something, they could simply say, "Daryl researched it," and the vice president would accept that as a viable answer. By getting the kingmaker's approval, I had just about everyone's approval, and my promotion was in the bag—or so I thought.

THE IMPORTANCE OF ALLIES

It turned out there was another kingmaker. Two weeks before my promotion materials were due, my manager asked me if I knew a level-7 economist who would cosign my promotion. She apologized for not telling me about this requirement earlier. I was the first economist on her team, and she didn't know about this rule.

No one came to mind for me to ask. There were no level-7 economists working on employee satisfaction. I had only discussed my research with level-6 and level-5 economists. I could see this promotion slipping away from me. My manager was in the process of moving to Europe for a new assignment. She would be my manager for this promotion cycle but not the next one. Earlier that week, I found out I was five weeks pregnant, which meant I would be on maternity leave during the start of the next promotion cycle. It was now or never.

It was going to be hard to convince the other economists at the company that I deserved to be promoted when plenty of economists at my level with more job experience had been waiting longer.

Job tenure is an easy and objective measure for giving out promotions. However, it doesn't have much to do with ability. When hiring, this company stuck to the "50% rule": every new hire needed to be stronger than 50% of current employees in similar roles. So to get hired in the first place, I had to demonstrate to my interviewers that I would perform better than at least half of the economists at my level. This criterion introduced *selection bias*—new employees should always exceed the median performance of those who had been there longer. So, it would be nonsensical to give employees who were hired before me preferential treatment because, by design, the newer employees should be stronger performers.

Still, I was worried that the desire for the perception of fairness would trump actual meritocracy. I needed to convince at least one level-7 economist that I deserved to be promoted, despite being in my role for less than a year.

Luckily, I did know one level-7 economist. Her research was different from mine—it focused on markets, not employee productivity. But I had gotten to know Colleen at our monthly lunches with the other women economists at the company. We would get together to talk about the challenges we faced as women in the economics profession: colleagues not taking us seriously, men taking credit for our work, coworkers overstepping professional boundaries, and so on. Colleen had heard me discuss my work at these lunches, even if it was mostly venting. I sent her a message about the promotion asking if she would be willing to send my manager a paragraph-long endorsement. She immediately came to my rescue. I was so grateful to have her on my side.

Having more women in leadership positions leads to higher earnings for top-performing women. But bottom-performing women earn less. That's according to research published in the *Economic Journal.* The researchers posited that women leaders are better at discerning top-performing women from bottom-performing women than men, which leads to a more meritocratic allocation of wages.[12]

For someone like me, who was a hair away from being promoted, having just one woman in leadership to vouch for me made all the difference. Colleen was the only top economist at the company I could ask because she was the only one who had heard me talk about my work. I didn't have many interactions with the top men economists. But I had socialized with Colleen, and in those informal interactions, she could discern my worthiness for promotion. The top men economists wouldn't have had a clue about my abilities.

Several weeks later, I received news that the directors and vice president had officially approved my promotion. That same day, I heard the rumor that our vice president was begrudgingly leaving the company. The kingmaker was being dethroned. It felt like I had won first place at a sandcastle-building contest right before the tide came crashing in. The castle I built was a reflection of my skills, but the timing of the wave was complete luck.

I was ecstatic and demoralized at the same time. For months, my primary focus was getting promoted, and all the work I put into ensuring my promotion had nothing to do with my actual job. If promotions were doled out meritocratically, I shouldn't have had to waste all that time. And since I barely pulled off the promotion by the skin of my teeth, it made me not want to play the promotion game ever again.

The highly competitive environment at my workplace was discouraging. I didn't know what to do with those feelings when I was supposed to be celebrating my promotion.

GAME RECAP

When trying to get promoted, follow these steps:

Understand how performance is measured and whether your performance makes you eligible for promotion. For example, your performance may be measured by inputs, like the hours you spend at your desk; outputs, like your finished work product; or a combination of criteria. Find out from your manager exactly what criteria qualifies you for promotion.

Understand the promotion process and all the people who can push your promotion forward or hold it back. My manager would initiate my promotion after I met her promotion criteria. Next, the directors could cut me from the promotion list. If I didn't have a level-7 economist endorsing me, my promotion would be automatically rejected. The promotion list would ultimately go to the vice president for final approval.

Identify the people whose opinions truly matter—the kingmakers. Only three people truly had power over my promotion: my manager, my vice president, and one level-7 cconomist of my choosing. The directors seemingly had the power to push back my promotion. However, their fear of the vice president meant they had little power.

Identify the objectives of the kingmakers. For example, my manager wanted to reward my performance and make her team more influential. My vice president wanted a bullshit-free promotion list. Colleen, the level-7 economist, altruistically wanted me to succeed.

Understand how much luck is involved in the process. I got lucky with my promotion. It could have died for lots of reasons outside my control. For example, if my manager had switched roles earlier, my vice president had left the company earlier, or there were no women level-7 economists to bond with, I would never have been promoted.

Approximate how long it might take to get promoted. Although luck was on my side for this promotion, I knew I couldn't expect to be so lucky again. The bar for my next promotion would be even higher. It might take me four, five, or six years to get promoted again.

Reevaluate whether you want to fight for a promotion or would be better off switching to a new role or company where a promotion is more achievable. For example, my promotion experience made me reluctant to stay at the tech company and keep working toward another promotion. Instead, I would have to figure out a different way to advance my career.

8
BALANCING FAMILY AND CAREER

In life, you play multiple games simultaneously, each with different objectives: the career game, the housing market game, the family game, and so on. The decisions you make in one game often impact your ability to attain your objectives in other games. For example, buying a home in an area with few job prospects may interfere with your career objectives. Spending too much time playing the career game can interfere with family objectives. You may also find your personal goals in direct conflict with your family's, friends', and acquaintances' expectations.

SOCIAL PRESSURES AND GENDER NORMS

I know I have an unusual marriage. It is uncommon that I, the wife, am the breadwinner in the marriage. In over 70% of heterosexual, dual-income marriages, the man outearns the woman.[1] And, in less than 10% of marriages, the wife is the sole earner.[2] Statistics show that my marriage is not just unlikely, but also predicted to end in divorce.[3]

One reason husbands typically outearn their wives is that women are paid less than men. In 2021, the median earnings for women were 17% lower than for men.[4] There are many reasons why this gender pay gap exists, and they aren't mutually exclusive. Contributing factors include gender differences in occupation and industry, gender differences in roles and expectations in the workplace and at home, discrimination, women taking time off from work for child rearing, and women working fewer hours.

Factors related to workplace ability, like schooling and job experience, do not play a meaningful role in the gender pay gap, according to research from economists at Cornell University.[5] If these factors mattered, we would have seen a reduction in the gender pay gap in the last few decades when women became more educated and more likely to work. But that did not happen.

However, the gender pay gap doesn't fully explain why in so many couples, the husband earns more than the woman. Research from Marianne Bertrand, Emir Kamenica, and Jessica Pan found that in heterosexual marriages there are unexpectedly few marriages where the woman slightly outearns the man. The authors posit that couples prefer the husband to outearn the wife. This motivates couples to make decisions that prioritize the husband's earnings in situations where the woman could potentially earn just as much as, if not more than, her husband.[6]

This preference likely comes from social norms or pressures. For example, when I was pregnant with my first child, one of my coworkers casually asked me who would watch my child when I came back from maternity leave. I told her my husband would be a stay-at-home dad, so I didn't need to worry about childcare. I did not ask her opinion about my choice, but she gave it anyway. My colleague told me that Adam would have difficulty making parent friends because stay-at-home moms won't want to have play dates with a stay-at-home dad. Before this comment, I had only received the occasional confused look when I told people that I was the primary breadwinner and my husband did the domestic work. This was the first time someone outright said that my family, including my unborn child, would be socially punished for this decision.

Maybe she had a point. We *didn't* have any friends in the same situation as us. We fantasized about a friendly couple moving in next door with kids our same age, where the wife worked and the husband stayed at home. Surely, we would be best friends with this couple. We would share the same values, support the same politicians, and have similar attitudes about screen time, processed food, and the safety of trampolines. We would enjoy the same hobbies, sports teams, and music. We would go on vacations together and send our kids to the same schools and summer camps.

But this was a narcissistic fantasy. We weren't willing to change our goals just to fit in. Adam wanted to be a dad who was always around for his kids, because his dad was never around. His dad was a stranger to him, and his goal as a parent was to be the opposite.

Adam and I met the summer before our freshman year at MIT at a program organized by the Office of Minority Education. We began dating the summer before our junior year. By the time I applied to graduate school in my senior year, Adam was willing to rearrange his life to prioritize our relationship and my career goals. Adam initially considered joining the Navy to work as an engineer on nuclear submarines. However, he soon realized it would be difficult for us to maintain a relationship with him away at sea for most of the year. Additionally, Adam wouldn't be able to be a present father with that kind of career. He realized that being a father was the most important thing to him, so he stopped focusing on his career game and instead made sure I could concentrate on mine.

Our marriage made the most sense for our economic and family objectives. Still, I understand that our arrangement would be less than ideal for most heterosexual couples, especially ones that maintain gender norms around domestic work.

On average, couples like ours, where the woman outearns the man, are more likely to divorce. [7] One contributing factor may be that when women earn more than their husbands, they still do a disproportionate amount of housework on average. On top of that, the typical single mom spends *less* time on chores than the typical married mom.[8] If a woman is earning most of the money, doing most of the housework, and doing more housework than if she were single, it is understandable why divorce would look good compared to her inside option of staying married. But luckily, that's not an issue in my marriage, because Adam doesn't see housework and childcare as inherently feminine.

Our agreement that social norms shouldn't matter is why our marriage works for us. And that disregard for social norms has saved us money. We saved around $4,000 by forgoing a diamond engagement ring and another $30,000 by eloping at the courthouse instead of having a big wedding.[9] With the saved money, we paid off our student debt and bought a used car with cash.

Our alignment of priorities is why we have been married for ten years and have been together continuously for 16. It hasn't been easy, though. That's because marriage isn't just one game. Instead, it involves several games played simultaneously with different objectives.

MARRIAGE IS A GAME

Marriage is a *negotiation game.* As discussed earlier, a marriage involves compromises that need to be negotiated. For example, decisions about money, work, chores, children, and aging parents must be agreed upon. If the inside terms of the negotiation are worse than the outside options for either spouse, the negotiation will fall apart, along with the marriage.

Marriage is a *commitment game*. Every day we play commitment games with our future selves. For example, when I buy an elliptical machine for my home, I commit to using it. If I don't follow through on that commitment, the purchase becomes a costly mistake. However, it is much easier to sell an elliptical machine than to get a divorce. If you or your partner cannot predict what you each want one, five, or ten years into the marriage, you may wake up one morning and ask for a divorce.

In economics, *time inconsistency* refers to a situation in which a person's preferences shift over time to the point where they cannot make optimal choices if the consequences come in the future.[10] When I purchase an elliptical machine today, I do so with the intention that my future self will want to exercise on it. Similarly, when people get married today, they do so with the intention that their future selves will also want to be married. However, sometimes our intentions differ from reality. When it comes time to use the elliptical machine, I may not feel motivated to exercise. When intentions don't align with actions, it's easy to make regrettable choices. That applies to the choices of whether to buy the elliptical machine and whether to say "I do."

It's hard to anticipate what your future self will be like because it is common for a person's objectives to change over time. Believing that your future preferences will be the same as your current preferences is a form of projection bias.[11] *Projection bias* is the tendency for individuals to overestimate the extent to which their current preferences, attitudes, or beliefs will remain consistent over time. People underappreciate how their choices, experiences, and environment can change themselves. For example, projection bias can cause a hungry shopper to buy too many groceries.[12] When someone is hungry, they tend to underappreciate how their taste might change after going home and having a meal. Likewise, an engaged couple may similarly underappreciate how their relationship objectives might change after the honeymoon phase.

To combat projection bias when deciding to get married, make an educated guess about your future self and try to imagine multiple scenarios. This is the same exercise I recommended for deciding to buy a home. But when it comes to marriage—which comes with even more emotions than purchasing a home—it's essential to take a step back and view the relationship objectively. (It may help to pretend your relationship isn't your own but that of a close friend.) Think through the best-case scenarios and the worst-case scenarios for the relationship. Weigh each scenario by its likelihood, and make a decision that makes you the best off in the most likely scenarios while still making plans for less likely scenarios. If the default divorce laws in your state or country don't adequately protect you against the worst-case scenarios, then a prenuptial agreement may be in order. (Note: This is a topic so nuanced that it would require another book.)

THE BENEFITS OF COMMITMENT

To make matters more complicated, the negotiation and commitment games within a marriage can affect each other. For example, when a couple constantly engages in brinkmanship to win every marital negotiation, that is a sign the couple is not committed to the relationship. The movie *Two Can Play That Game* warns of the dangers of brinkmanship. In the end, Vivica A. Fox's character learns that her constant threats to leave her boyfriend have weakened her chances of having a healthy, committed relationship.

In game theory, *brinkmanship* is when players engage in a high-stakes game of chicken. Players attempt to gain the upper hand by taking increasingly risky actions to force the opposition to retreat. This strategy is often used when players are locked in a dispute and neither side is willing to compromise. For example, during a cold war, a country may threaten to use nuclear weapons to force the other side to agree to their demands. In a relationship, a partner may threaten to go nuclear: threatening a breakup to force the other partner to give in. However, for this tactic to be effective, the threats must be credible. No cheap talk.

But who would want to be in a relationship when they are constantly treated like the enemy? Winning a short-term game of brinkmanship can degrade a partner's expectations about the value of the relationship moving forward and increase the likelihood that, eventually, the relationship will end.

Making a binding and externally forced commitment, like getting legally married, can help end relationship brinkmanship. That's according to research published in the *Journal of Law, Economics, and Organization*. In the researchers' economic model, commitments with consequences end any brinkmanship. Brinkmanship is an irrational strategy when both sides know they would be worse off breaking the commitment.[13]

So getting married can make a relationship more stable, but it doesn't make life easy. It's easier to worry only about personal goals. Being married is like participating in an endless group project. When things are going well, it's easy to recognize your partner's hard work, but when things are going badly, it's tempting to assign blame to your spouse. At 3 a.m., when the baby is crying, there's poop on the crib sheets, and the laundry is sitting wet in the washing machine, it's hard to stay rational. It's hard to remember you're both on the same team. You can't get mad at the baby, so you get mad at each other; you blame each other or yourselves.

I've learned that the only way to win a fight like that is to take a deep breath and repeat the mantra "You're doing the best you can; we both are." Because that kind of a fight isn't about negotiating terms, it's about accepting adversity as a fact of life.

Two Can Play That Game has a happy ending: both Fox and Chestnut verbally commit to stop playing games and instead work on creating the type of relationship they want to commit to, in good times and bad. It would be interesting to see a sequel that addresses whether that verbal agreement was a strong enough commitment to keep them together.

Half of first marriages end in divorce, and the share is even higher for second and third marriages.[14] Therefore, it is safe to assume that most couples consider divorce at some point.

Getting married is like locking yourself in a gated garden and throwing away the key; divorce is like picking the lock. Divorce is costly, but when the outside option of ending the marriage is more valuable than remaining married, the cost can be worth the gain.

Some people will never choose to pick the lock. They value the idea of marriage too much; it's too important, for personal, religious, or social reasons. Others see divorce as a viable outside option, especially when the garden is dead, dying, or unhealthy.

Even without divorce, all marriages end at some point. If a marriage doesn't end in divorce, it will end in death, so either way, one person is going to have to go on independently for a short or long rest of their life—a reminder to not take options for granted, because options can go away.

MARRIAGE AS A FINANCIAL STRATEGY

Marriage isn't just about negotiation and commitment games. Marriage can be gratifying. A marriage can produce happiness, love, and intimacy. On the other hand, marriage can simultaneously be an economic investment. And couples may have to make tradeoffs between those two objectives.

Research published in the *Journal of Political Economy* found evidence that couples make tradeoffs between picking a partner they love versus selecting a partner that is a good economic match. The study defined a good economic match as one where spousal income is uncorrelated or, even better, negatively correlated.[15]

When marital income is correlated, each partner's income is somehow connected. For example, a software engineer's and a data scientist's incomes would be *positively correlated* because they both earn more money when the tech industry is booming and less when tech companies are in dire straits. When spousal income is *negatively correlated*, incomes are connected but in opposite directions. For example, a real estate agent specializing in luxury housing and a real estate agent specializing in foreclosure would have negatively correlated incomes—the luxury real estate agent earns more when the housing market is up, but the foreclosure specialist has more business when the housing market is down. According to the research, when incomes are negatively correlated, the marriage lasts longer than one where spouses' incomes are positively correlated.[16]

Income stability is just one way that the economic whole of a marriage is greater than the sum of two single individuals. A married couple will typically have a higher after-tax income than what they would have had as two singles, thanks to the United States tax code's subsidization of marriage. On average, married men earn more than unmarried men. However, research from sociologists at Harvard and Princeton suggests that this relationship is just a coincidence and that the isolated act of getting married doesn't impact earnings for men.[17]

And then, on top of the objectives of love and money, marriage can also be about household production. *Household production* refers to the various goods and services produced or provided within the household for the consumption and well-being of its members, such as home maintenance, home organization, cooking, child rearing, and emotional support.

The Nobel laureate Gary Becker was the first economist to model a family as a firm that produces children, among other products and services. Becker considered children to be both consumption and investment goods. Children can bring happiness to parents in the present and contribute to a household's income and a married couple's financial security in the future. A couple who sees their children as a source of joy may prioritize providing a fun childhood. Meanwhile, a couple who sees their children as an investment may prioritize education or other activities that increase financial success in adulthood. The economist Emily Oster expanded on Becker's ideas in her book *The Family Firm*, which instructs parents to make decisions about family as if it were a business.[18]

Love, money, and children are a lot of priorities to juggle. In my marriage, we handle this by dividing our areas of focus. I focus on my comparative advantage of making money, and Adam focuses on his comparative advantages in household production. That way, we can each play to our strengths and be maximally productive as a couple. Ignoring gender, this kind of marital arrangement is traditional. In 1967, 49% of mothers were stay-at-home moms. However, by the end of the century, that share dropped to 23% and then increased to 26% in 2021[19] Meanwhile, the share of stay-at-home dads increased from 5% in 2000 to just 7% in 2021.[20]

When I became pregnant with my first child, I thought my marital arrangement meant my career was safe. I assumed I wouldn't face a career penalty for motherhood. However, I still had to physically give birth and recover from that birth. I still needed to take maternity leave.

WORKING WHILE PREGNANT

In 2017, Allyson Felix reached the height of her running career after taking home three gold medals in the 2012 Olympics in London and another two gold medals at the 2016 Olympics in Rio de Janeiro.[21] With this athletic success came endorsement offers. Brands wanted access to the shine Felix had worked hard to achieve; that way, their shoes, and clothing would give customers the illusion of possessing Felix's essence. However, in 2018, Felix, at 32 weeks of pregnancy, developed the life-threatening condition preeclampsia, and had to give birth to her daughter prematurely via C-section to save both their lives. This event not only put her life at risk but also put her career and means of supporting her family in peril because her endorsement deal at Nike gave no protections or accommodations for pregnancy.[22]

Up until that point, the games Felix played supported one another. Following her passion for pushing herself to her athletic limits helped her achieve both success on the track and success concerning endorsement deals. But once she began pursuing her other passion of motherhood, she had a significant disadvantage when winning an endorsement.

After recovering from her pregnancy and surgery, Felix negotiated a new contract with Nike. She asked for maternity leave to be included in her contract, to which Nike said no. Even though Felix was willing to accept lower compensation, Nike wouldn't negotiate on maternity leave.

What was Nike thinking? Felix was willing to sacrifice money in exchange for maternity leave, so it would seem that Nike and Felix could come to mutually beneficial terms in their endorsement relationship. However, like LaTavia and LeToya had, Felix misunderstood Nike's perspective. Nike wanted their logo on the backs of victorious athletes. Nike seemed to believe that pregnant women, and women who had recently given birth, were unlikely to win races. From this perspective, it becomes clearer why Nike didn't want to endorse athletes who were pregnant or would become pregnant soon.

Felix was a winning athlete, and she was confident she would continue to win even while pregnant or breastfeeding. But Nike seemingly had preconceived notions and stereotypes about what mothers are capable of. Nike still wanted to endorse women to maintain their brand value among women consumers, but apparently not pregnant women. At the time, Nike had an ad campaign called "Dream Crazier" that made it seem like they supported women athletes unequivocally. Felix went to the press to call out Nike's hypocrisy and bias against mothers.

This tactic worsened Nike's outside option. When the public became aware of Nike's lack of support for pregnant athletes, their brand value went down among women who similarly struggle with pregnancy discrimination. And in response, Nike began offering maternity leave to its sponsored athletes in 2019. But by this time, Felix had started her own footwear brand, Saysh.

Felix continued winning medals. In 2020 she became the most decorated US athlete in Olympic history. Clearly, Nike underestimated Felix's ability to perform postpartum.

※ ※ ※

A study from Cornell sociologists had participants evaluate job application materials that indicated the parental status and gender of the candidate. Mothers received lower scores for perceived competence and were offered lower wages than childless women, childless men, or fathers. However, men were not penalized at all for being fathers.[23]

It can become a self-fulfilling prophecy if employers assume mothers and expecting mothers underperform at work. This is because if employers expect mothers to underperform, they won't bother to accommodate the needs of mothers. Employers may rather see a mother quit so they can employ an outside worker who is not a mother. And without accommodation, many mothers will underperform and leave the workforce altogether.

Research from the US Census Bureau found that women were 18% more likely to leave the workforce in the months following childbirth. A woman's likelihood of reentering the workforce declined with each additional child she has. For the mothers who continued to work, their earnings fall by about $2,000 for the first three months after giving birth. In the long run, they ended up earning less than they would have, had they never had children.[24]

The wage penalty is larger for women with more education in higher-earning fields. That's according to research from economists at the Norwegian School of Economics. They found that women in fields such as business and law faced a substantially larger wage penalty than women in areas where the hours are more flexible.[25]

In a study published in the *American Economic Review*, economists compared the earnings of women who successfully gave birth via IVF (in vitro fertilization) to women whose IVF did not result in a birth. The two groups of women should have been similar in earnings, background, and desire to have children, so these results identify the direct effect of having a child on future earnings. The study found that having a child had negative, large, and long-lasting impacts on women's earnings. The average differences between mothers' wages compared to childless women's wages underestimated the career consequences for women on the cusp of deciding whether or not to have children.[26]

But I wasn't thinking about any of these statistics when I decided to become a mother. I knew most of the studies included moms who didn't have a supportive husband like I had. Still, I was probably overoptimistic about how demanding and time-consuming motherhood would be. According to researchers at the National Bureau of Economic Research, women underestimate the impact of having children on their earnings. Women like me, who have a college degree and grew up with a working mother, underestimate the effects the most. This is a new phenomenon. Earlier cohorts of mothers underestimated their ability to work after having a baby. However, more recent cohorts of mothers *overestimated* the likelihood they would continue working. The researchers posited that this is because the cost of raising children has been going up since the 1980s; meanwhile, expectations have been slow to catch up to reality.[27]

I was focused primarily on the issue of maternity leave. I knew that the more time I had to spend with my newborn, the better off my baby would be. According to a review of maternity leave health impacts published in the *Harvard Review of Psychiatry*, paid maternity leave positively affects mothers' and children's health.[28] Mothers who have paid maternity leave are less likely to experience postpartum depression, and their babies are more likely to thrive.[29] And yet, paid maternity leave is not guaranteed or the norm in the United States. The Family and Medical Leave Act of 1993 grants eligible employees 12 weeks of unpaid leave following a birth. But, when it comes to paid family leave, as of 2022, only a quarter of employed Americans in the private sector are given that benefit by their employer.[30]

The Big Tech company I worked for provided 20 weeks of paid maternity leave: four weeks preceding the due date and another 16 weeks postbirth. So I thought I was set. This would give me the time I needed to prepare for the birth, recover, and bond with my child. That generous amount of leave may have benefited my health and my child's health, but unfortunately, it may have hurt my career.

Research published in *Labour Economics* found evidence that employer-paid maternity leave causes employers to pay women of reproductive age less money. The economists studied a policy change in Germany that altered rules so that firms there no longer had to pay directly for maternity leave. Instead, costs were pooled across all firms. Firms responded by paying their female employees more. Before the rule change, firms could predict that a female hire of reproductive age would cost them more than a male or an older female hire. After the rule change, each hire would cost a firm an equal amount in maternity leave expenses, regardless of their reproductive potential. When firms paid out of pocket for maternity leave expenses, they effectively punished women of reproductive age for the increased cost by paying them less. It is unclear if this was deliberate or the result of unconscious bias.[31]

UNCONSCIOUS BIAS

In economic models, people make choices "on the margin." When a boss decides whom to give a raise to, the boss doesn't need to think about every raise they have ever given. They think only about the marginal benefits and marginal costs of awarding a raise to one worker over the other. If two workers have performed equally well, tiny differences matter a lot. Minor differences can have large economic consequences. An unconscious preference for a worker who is childless can amount to large differences in pay if there aren't set policies in place to prevent bias.

Unconscious bias is often subtle. It can be difficult to see unless it's happening right in front of you. When I was pregnant,

I witnessed what appeared to be the kind of unconscious bias that leads to decreased earnings for pregnant women and new mothers. In September, my manager arranged for me to sit in on my department's third-quarter performance evaluation discussion. My manager planned to make *me* a manager once my promotion was officially approved. That way, I could take on more projects and contribute even more to the team. By attending the evaluation discussion, I could learn about my future management responsibilities.

The six managers who reported to our director gathered around the conference table with our designated human resources representative. The HR rep gave an introduction to the process:

"I hope you all came prepared with your performance designations for each employee you manage. We would love to label each of our high-performing employees 'top tier.' But remember, we only give that designation to one in five employees. We don't want to assign all 'top tier' evaluations to senior employees. The same goes for the 'least effective' designation. We want to aim for about five percent of employees in the bottom-tier designation, and it shouldn't only go to junior employees. We will discuss the evaluations and try to get a nice distribution of performance designations. If the distribution doesn't look right to leadership, we will have to do this all over again, so let's avoid that. Once the leaders approve, the evaluations will go to HR. We will do a final inspection to ensure there isn't any gender bias or anything like that. Any questions?"

The managers went around the room discussing each employee's evaluation. Travis, a middle-age manager who had been at the company for about five years, went last, and that's where the discussion stalled. Travis wanted two of his employees to be labeled "top tier." However, he was getting a lot of pushback from the other managers about having more than one "top tier" performer on his team of three. Travis went back and forth for a long time. "Brittany has gone above and beyond in the last year, but Conor pulled off a really tough project . . . Brittany had excellent feedback from her own team, but Conor had stellar feedback from other teams . . ."

It seemed like an impossible decision, but finally, Travis settled on Conor: "Conor's performance has gotten better and better in the last several weeks."

I felt offended on Brittany's behalf. It seemed like Conor was benefiting from *recency bias*. Recency bias is the tendency people have to give more weight or consideration to recent events or information when making decisions. The last two months seemed to matter more than what occurred during the rest of the year. However, this was supposed to be an evaluation for the entire year. It seemed unfair because Brittany didn't have the opportunity to further improve her performance over the last two months. Brittany was out on maternity leave.

At that moment, Brittany's expected earnings dropped. Brittany's manager said she was just as worthy of receiving the "top tier" designation as her male colleague, but she lost the tiebreaker. And that tiebreaker seemed to come down to Conor being present in the office while Brittany was on maternity leave taking care of her firstborn child. Without a "top tier" designation, Brittany would not receive a raise. That raise would have included stock-based compensation that would have vested over the next four years, so this hit to her earnings would likely last at least that long.

The discussion moved on to which employees would get the "least effective" designation. No manager wanted to call anyone on their team a low performer. But the meeting could end only once the managers identified at least one more employee to receive the lowest rating. The HR rep went down the names on the list until she homed in on a woman on Travis's team. "I don't want to call Marcia a low performer," Travis said. "I don't think it's fair, because she's on medical leave." I had noticed Marcia hadn't been in the office recently, but I didn't know she was out on leave or for what reason.

"Medical leave shouldn't matter one way or the other," the HR rep said. "Base your evaluation objectively on her performance before she went on leave."

"Well, her performance was slipping in the weeks before she went on leave. She missed deadlines."

All the managers looked at one another to see if anyone would defend Marcia. But no manager could stick up for her without risking their own employees' performance designation. "It sounds like Marcia's performance was below average," the HR rep said. As a result, Marcia was labeled "least effective," which meant she would not receive a pay increase. On top of that, she would be placed on a performance improvement plan as soon as she returned.

Researchers at MIT and Indiana University found a consistent result across three experiments on how the presumption of meritocracy disadvantages women in the workplace. In an experiment, the researchers asked study participants who had managerial experience to evaluate hypothetical workers while varying the gender of the employees and the stated core values of the hypothetical business. The researchers found that when a business presented itself as meritocratic, professional managers favored male employees over female ones. As a result, the managers assigned the men higher financial compensation.[32]

I can't say that there was any explicit gender discrimination going on at the Big Tech company. And I don't know whether these designations went through. An executive or HR employee may have changed these performance assessments before they became official. But it didn't feel like a coincidence that both women employees had their performance scores demoted while they were out on leave. Taking just a few months off work for legitimate reasons probably wouldn't hurt their performance when they returned. Still, it was enough to impact their earnings for years into the future because compensation decisions, like all decisions, happen on the margin.

My promotion was officially approved just before Halloween, five weeks into my second trimester. I could have let everyone know about my pregnancy then. But I continued to conceal it for another month. I didn't want it to bias people's beliefs about my performance any longer than necessary.

DISCRIMINATION AND THE PERSISTENCE OF STEREOTYPES

No one, myself included, knew whether becoming a mother would make me a less productive employee, but that's what happens statistically. In economics, *statistical discrimination* in the workplace occurs when an employment decision is based on statistical information about an employee's group identity. Some common stereotypes about pregnant women's ability to work include the idea that pregnant women are less capable or less committed to their jobs, that they are more likely to take time off or miss work, and that they are less able to handle the physical and mental demands of the workplace. These stereotypes can lead to discrimination and adverse treatment of pregnant women at work.

These stereotypes can result in all mothers and expecting mothers being penalized in the workplace regardless of their actual performance or propensity to quit. This kind of bias can reinforce historical discrimination. Historically, mothers have performed worse at their jobs because they faced obstacles, such as overt harassment or a lack of accommodations. However, the stereotype that women are inferior workers may persist even after obstacles are removed. It's challenging to eradicate this complex bias, even after a workplace has genuinely tried to even the playing field for mothers. I managed to get promoted before giving birth to my first child. But as a mother, I was now playing a game with different rules.

GAME RECAP

When you're making plans related to your relationship, marriage, or decisions about having children, follow these steps:

Identify your and your partner's goals within the relationship. For example, discuss goals around career, children, where to live, and anything else you find important in life.

Identify where your goals are aligned and where your goals conflict. For example, if your partner wants a stay-at-home spouse, five kids, and to live on the East Coast, but you want a career outside the home, no kids, and to live on the West Coast, your goals are in conflict.

Align your goals now and in the future. Commit to a relationship only once you and your partner align your goals. Be cautious about obligating yourself to a goal you may regret later on. And don't pressure your partner into making commitments they may want to break in the future. In the honeymoon stage of your relationship, you may be willing to sacrifice your goals for your partner's. However, your future self may be reluctant to fulfill that commitment. Don't engage in brinkmanship with your partner as a way to prioritize your personal goals over relationship goals. Instead, fully commit to the relationship goals.

If your goals involve children, understand how this might impact your career. If you are thinking of becoming a mother or primary caregiver, plan for career setbacks. Most women underestimate the impact of having children on earnings. This can vary depending on how supportive your workplace is of mothers. Workplaces that provide generous maternity leave, mothers' rooms, and flexible work schedules are typically better for mothers. Also, note how often colleagues who are mothers earn promotions or raises.

9
KNOWING YOUR WORTH

A change in the way others perceive you can happen at multiple moments in life. How you are perceived by others can change after graduating from school, getting married, or having children. It can also vary based on your environment or how you present yourself. When people discover you are part of any stereotyped group, your perceived value might change. In these instances, it's a good idea to reassess your self-worth instead of relying on other people's evaluations. Reassess your inside and outside options to find the best path forward.

REASSESSING INSIDE OPTIONS

It's hard to know precisely how pregnancy affected my career prospects. Still, when I returned to work from maternity leave, I had the palpable feeling that I was returning to a worse job than the one I had left just five months before.

Research published in the *Journal of Business and Psychology* has found that women often experience a decline in job satisfaction after giving birth. The psychologists found that women's job satisfaction was substantially higher before their pregnancies than during or after. In addition, better workplace maternity-leave policies were associated with better job satisfaction.[1]

My employer's maternity leave policies were better than most. I received 20 weeks of paid leave, and when I returned, I had access to mothers' rooms for pumping breast milk. The reason I felt unsatisfied didn't have to do with any policy directly related to maternity. For example, before having a baby, it was a job perk that I got to travel the world and learn from people with entirely different cultures and perspectives than my own. But now that I had a newborn, the last thing I wanted to do was spend weeks abroad.

I didn't want to spend time at the Seattle office either. My original manager, director, and vice president, and many of my favorite colleagues were gone. They had either transferred to a different department or left the company altogether. Unfortunately, this was common. Teams at my company continuously lost and gained members like the Ship of Theseus. The turnover rate was around 3% each week. So during my 20-week maternity leave, I should have expected up to half my coworkers to be gone before I returned. I was starting from scratch with new leadership and a partially new team. Luckily, I was promoted before my leave, but the path to my next promotion would be much more difficult. Maybe impossible. And if I wasn't trying to advance to the next level, if I wasn't trying to get promoted, I didn't know what to do with myself.

It was like I was playing a simplistically designed video game where level 6 is identical to level 5, but with the difficulty turned up a notch. Winning the last level felt like a fluke, so I was not optimistic about beating the next level. Plus, without my previous manager, previous director, or favorite colleagues around me, the game stopped being fun. Climbing the promotion ladder felt meaningless. I already had enough money to afford a good life for my family. Chasing pay raises and promotions felt as purposeful as chasing a high score in a video game—a video game that was of someone else's design.

According to the 19th-century economist Alfred Marshall, the more a person has of something, the less value they get out of having even more of that thing. It's the law of diminishing marginal returns. Psychologists and economists have found that even money follows this law regarding happiness. Money matters the most for happiness when you have less of it. Although the experience of happiness is idiosyncratic, Purdue University researchers attempted to find the relationship between happiness and money by assessing life satisfaction through survey questions. According to the 2018 study, the ideal salary level for an individual was $95,000 globally and $105,000 in North America. After that point, money didn't buy increased well-being.[2]

There are two ways income might affect happiness. *Absolute income* is the dollar amount a person earns. It impacts how much a person can purchase or save for things that bring joy. However, *relative income* is how much a person earns in comparison to others. It impacts a person's class and financial status in society.

High-income countries tend to have higher ideal salaries than low-income countries because relative income affects happiness. However, relative income matters less for happiness than absolute income. That's according to a study from the National Bureau of Economic Research that examined happiness across and within countries. For example, suppose a person's earnings were to increase from $50,000 per year to $75,000. In that case, it would increase their happiness no matter what country they live in—even in developing countries where the average income is less than $5,000 per year. And if that same person's earnings were to increase by $25,000 again to $100,000, the second increase would bring less additional happiness than the first.[3]

Since I was already earning more than enough to meet my needs, getting a raise wasn't going to make me much happier. And chasing promotions couldn't make me happy either, when my employer's reputation was in decline. Two years earlier, when I told people I worked for the Big Tech company, they would tell me how much they loved shopping on our app. But now when I told someone who my employer was, they asked me how I could sleep at night working for a company that mistreats its low-wage workers. I would explain it was my job to figure out how to make employees *more* satisfied at work. But that justification felt more and more hollow as negative news reports surfaced about the company—like reports about low-wage workers having to urinate in bottles for lack of bathroom breaks.

The value of my inside options at my employer had diminished. It didn't matter that I used to like my job and my colleagues before I went out on maternity leave. If I clung to the past, I'd fall for the sunk-cost fallacy. So instead, I had to decide whether my happiness and earnings potential would be better staying versus moving on to my best outside option.

UNDERSTANDING REFERENCE POINTS

In 2005, Taraji P. Henson had recently starred in the Academy Award–nominated hip-hop drama *Hustle & Flow*. The film's success propelled Henson into the Hollywood elite. She was now being vetted for David Fincher's next film, *The Curious Case of Benjamin Button*, for the part of Queenie, Benjamin Button's Black caretaker. Brad Pitt and Cate Blanchett had already signed on to the movie with million-dollar contracts.[4]

Henson knew that although she had just won a Screen Actor's Guild Award, she could expect only a fraction of what her famous costars received. Still, she was incredibly disappointed with the deal her agent was able to negotiate. She was offered a paltry $150,000, and she would have to pay for her own accommodations on location in New Orleans. After Henson paid for her hotel, plus her manager, agent, and other work expenses, she was left with only $40,000.

Although Henson was coming off a financial and critical success, the producers of *Benjamin Button* likely assumed she wouldn't have great outside options. After all, Hollywood provided very few roles to Black actresses.

Benjamin Button ended up grossing $335 million. Henson's $150,000 was a drop in the bucket, making her even more upset that the producers extended her so little. Henson was nominated for an Academy Award for Best Supporting Actress for her performance in the film. Still, to her, that was only further proof that the producers undervalued her.

Henson was sick of being undervalued. She knew that if she kept agreeing to such low pay, producers would take it as evidence that she was indeed worth so little. In her own words: "They wanna pay what?! Honey, a ZERO is missing. If you come to Taraji P. Henson, you NEED to come with that MONEY!"[5] So for her next film, Henson worked for somebody who would pay her what she believed she was worth.

The director Tyler Perry employed Black actors all the time and looked at Henson's talent instead of her race when making an offer for his film *Acrimony*. Perry paid Henson an amount in the high six figures. After that, Henson had a reference point to use in her negotiations. Any time a producer assumed she was worth less than white actors and actresses, she could point to what Perry paid her as proof of her value. She could use it as a reference point.

For a negotiation to be successful, both players must prefer their inside option to their outside option. However, there may be many results that fit those criteria. For example, the producers of *Benjamin Button* should have been willing to pay Henson an extra $100,000 over finding another actress to play the part. But the producers had more negotiating power.

Negotiating power is loosely defined. According to the economist Abhinay Muthoo, it depends primarily on each player's outside options, propensity for taking risks, and willingness to wait.[6] Because negotiating power is inexact and hard to discern, you can assert your power simply by setting a high reference point.

In economics, a *reference point* is a benchmark against which an individual evaluates their current situation or makes decisions. It serves as a point of comparison that influences the decision-making process. Setting a reference point in a negotiation game lets other players know your expectations. It also signals that any offer below the reference point will be considered a loss. In contrast, any offer above the reference point will be regarded as a gain.[7]

In behavioral economics, *loss aversion* is the tendency to avoid losses over achieving similar gains. It works just like the endowment effect: losing something you feel belongs to you hurts more than never having had that thing in the first place. By setting a reference point, Henson signaled to movie producers that she felt entitled to a certain amount for her work as an actress. Anything less than that amount would be perceived as a loss, so don't bother offering anything lower.

Unfortunately, you can't always control the reference point that will be used by your opponent, and most of us don't have connections like Tyler Perry to help. Setting a reference point above your true outside option is called bluffing. If your opponent thinks your outside options are lower than your stated reference point, they may call your bluff. For example, the producers of *Benjamin Button* used the typical payment for a Black actress to determine Henson's offer. Henson felt she was owed the standard amount for a prestige actor, regardless of race or gender. She could reset the reference point for her offers only when she gained proof of how much money she could make in her outside option of acting in Tyler Perry films.

HIGHER-ORDER BELIEFS

To excel at negotiating, you must be able to put yourself in the position of your opponent. A player must have empathy. The first level of empathy is knowing your opponent's outside options and objectives. The next level of empathy is understanding your opponent's preconceived notions about you. What does your opponent think are your outside options and your goals? What would change your opponent's beliefs about you?

Game theorists call this kind of empathy *higher-order beliefs*. First-order beliefs are a player's initial beliefs or knowledge about the game. In contrast, second-order beliefs involve a player's beliefs about the first-order beliefs of other players. Similarly, third-order beliefs are a player's beliefs about the second-order beliefs of other players, and so on.

Unfortunately, operating under higher-order beliefs means you must be willing to have empathy for ignorant people. You must empathize with people who stereotype based on race, gender, sexual orientation, religion, disability, age, appearance, height, and so on. Being empathetic in a negotiation doesn't mean going easy on your opponent, though. It means you understand how your opponent thinks. You see the assumptions they will make based on the way they think, and you do your best either to defend against it or use it to your advantage if you can.

170   NINE

WHEN TO KEEP YOUR MOUTH SHUT

As an American, I rarely get the opportunity to haggle over price. However, outside the United States, bartering is more common. On one work trip, I traveled to Beijing with a few colleagues from Seattle headquarters. On our day off, we shopped for souvenirs at an indoor mall to get a break from the smoke-filled air outside.

Unfortunately, China's fast industrialization came with a negative side effect. It's what economists call an *externality*: a side effect or consequence of an economic activity that affects parties who did not choose to bring about that effect. The smoke emitted by factories caused harm to those nearby, but the factory owners did not bear the entire cost of this harm. This allowed the factory owners to make more products and profit, resulting in even more pollution. The mall offered a state-of-the-art air filtration system to counteract the industrial smoke that blanketed the city, attracting tourists and professionals like us inside.

Unlike at an American mall, where the price is nonnegotiable, bartering was the norm here. My colleagues and I split up to shop and met two hours later to eat. At lunch, I showed my middle-aged, blond-haired, blue-eyed colleague what I had bought: a set of silk pajamas for 100 yuan (about $15). My colleague's jaw dropped—he had purchased the same silk pajamas, but paid 300 yuan.

In economics, the maximum amount of money a person is willing to spend on a product or service is called their *willingness to pay*. Willingness to pay is typically higher for wealthier people simply because they have more money to spend. Willingness to pay is also higher for people who strongly prefer the good or service. When negotiating over a product like silk pajamas, the seller will try to make an educated guess about the buyer's willingness to pay. So either the shop owner thought my coworker liked the pajamas way more than I did, or the shop owner thought my coworker had way more money than I did.

While browsing the shop's selection of silk garments, the clerk asked me if I was visiting Beijing for school. I could understand why she assumed I was a college student. I was wearing my everyday work attire: jeans, sneakers, and a jaunty hat—the same clothes I would have worn in college.

I told her I was there for work. She furrowed her brow and put her hand to her chin as if she couldn't process what I said. She asked me what I was studying at school, and instead of correcting her again, I just said, "Economics."

I wondered if she was stereotyping me based on my clothes or my brown skin. Earlier, while browsing cosmetics, I noticed the wide selection of skin-whitening creams available for sale. She probably saw my brown skin as a signal of low economic class. I couldn't know why I got a deal, and I didn't care. Her misconception allowed me to score a student discount on those silk pajamas. Why should I correct her?

In chess, there are two types of positions a player can be in. In the most common type of position, a player is better off making the next move. On the other hand, in a *zugzwang* position, having to move puts a player at a disadvantage. *Zugzwang* is German for "compulsion to move"; game theorists use the term to denote any move that directly changes the expected outcome of a game from a win to a loss. In chess, that means flipping the advantage.

White always starts off with a tempo advantage. Because of their first-mover advantage, the white player can achieve checkmate faster than the black player, so at the onset, white is expected to win. However, if the black player can manage to put the white player in a zugzwang, the advantage flips to black.

Suddenly the black player is happy being on the defense. Zugzwang describes a situation where a player must make a choice, but each available option makes the decision-maker worse off.

Businesses can find themselves in zugzwangs. For example, businesses are usually better off avoiding social issues like civil rights. That's because taking a position might alienate a segment of customers and hurt their sales. But after the murder of George Floyd, American businesses were compelled to disclose their positions on racism and police brutality. They were forced into a decision because doing nothing was a much worse option. A statement from Netflix read: "To be silent is to be complicit. Black lives matter."[8]

In a negotiation, a player can force their opponent to make the first move. A player can compel their opponent to set a reference by keeping their mouth shut. But this is a good strategy only when you believe that your opponent will set a favorable reference point based on what they think of you. That's when you have your opponent in a zugzwang.

In Beijing, I had the shop clerk in a zugzwang. Usually, being stereotyped based on my brown skin puts me at a disadvantage. But sometimes, I want my opponent to underestimate me. Since I desired a lower price, I could use her misassumptions about me to my advantage. So instead of making the first move and setting a reference point for our negotiation on the price of the pajamas, I kept my mouth shut, compelling her to make the first move to her detriment: she set a price lower than what I was actually willing to pay—a lower price than what she thought my white colleague would pay. But in salary negotiations, I am usually better off moving first. It's advantageous for me to be aggressive and state my reference point to stop potential employers from undervaluing me, like the movie producers undervalued Henson.

SIGNALING OUTSIDE OPTIONS

Some birds, such as peacocks, are known for their vibrant and colorful feathers, which they use to attract mates and demonstrate their fitness to potential partners. These feathers can grow over five feet long and are used by peacocks to attract peahen mates. However, having such large and colorful feathers is energetically expensive for the birds.[9] To grow and maintain their trains, peacocks must consume large amounts of food, which can be challenging to find in their South Asian forest habitats. Additionally, the feathers are heavy and can make it difficult for the birds to move quickly or to fly. As a result, peacocks must devote a significant amount of energy and resources to their appearance, which can affect their overall health and fitness.

Similarly, individuals who engage in conspicuous consumption may use their possessions and material wealth to attract attention and show off their status to others. Just as the bright feathers of a peacock serve as a visual display of the bird's health and attractiveness, luxurious items and expensive experiences can display an individual's wealth and social standing. The term *conspicuous consumption* was first coined by the economist Thorstein Veblen in 1899. Veblen argued that wealthy members of society engage in conspicuous consumption to flaunt their wealth and distinguish themselves from the rest of the population.[10]

Conspicuous consumption is often frowned upon by economists and penny-pinchers because it may not provide objective benefits to the individual or society. Instead, these purchases act as a signal of social status. An overindulgence in conspicuous consumption may lead to financial instability at an individual and societal level.[11]

However, I completely understand the urge to signal high status. For example, the economists Kerwin Charles, Erik Hurst, and Nikolai Roussanov found that Black and Hispanic consumers were more likely to signal their status through conspicuous consumption than their white counterparts. The researchers identified purchases of items that would be visible in social interactions—things like clothing, cars, and jewelry. Black and Hispanic consumers spent $2,300 more per year on these items compared to white consumers with similar levels of wealth and education. The authors posited that Black and Hispanic people benefited more from signaling wealth than their white counterparts. That's because conspicuous consumption can challenge negative stereotypes by demonstrating success, affluence, and social standing.[12]

In some negotiation games, a player will want to signal to their opponent that they are wealthy. But in other negotiations, a player will want to signal that they are not. When negotiating salary, an employee can gain an advantage by dressing and acting like money comes effortlessly to them. This signals that the employee is confident they could get a higher salary from a different employer. When negotiating the price of an item, a shopper can gain an advantage by dressing and acting like they can't afford a high price. In all negotiations, it's advantageous to act like you are knowledgeable about the market and will get a better deal elsewhere if necessary.

When I was shopping in Beijing, the shop owner probably assumed I had less money than my white male coworker. She probably wouldn't have made that assumption if I had been wearing luxury clothing or flashy jewelry. In my zugzwang bargaining position, I was happy to let the shop owner assume I was of lower status. Her assumption allowed me to get a discount on the silk pajamas I was purchasing.

However, if I were applying for a loan or a job, or negotiating a salary, engaging in conspicuous consumption would put me at an advantage. That's because my attire would signal that I am doing well and have solid outside options.

BLUFFING

There are other ways to signal the strength of outside options besides conspicuous consumption. For example, while applying for a job, an applicant may tell the recruiter that they are happy and satisfied with their current position to signal the strength of their outside option, whether or not that's actually true. They could tell the recruiter that any new opportunity would have to be significantly better in salary or title. Or, if a job applicant is currently unemployed, they could tell the recruiter that they are applying for other roles with companies that are excited to move forward.

As I was returning from maternity leave, a recruiter from Redfin sent me a direct message on LinkedIn. The recruiter was looking for Redfin's next chief economist. I was surprised she reached out, because I wasn't currently working in housing economics. I wouldn't have thought I was qualified, but the recruiter thought so and encouraged me to apply. I was underestimating my job prospects.

After maternity leave, I was flirting with the idea of leaving my employer. But I wasn't ready to go until a significantly better opportunity came around. That gave me the upper hand with Redfin. At this point, I didn't care about making slightly more money—weirdly, that made me a better negotiator. Making an extra $10,000 didn't matter to me, which made me unafraid to ask for an additional $100,000.

Suppose a player sets their reference point too high—higher than their opponent's willingness to pay. In that case, the player runs the risk that their opponent will walk away from the negotiation. Since I was already making an excellent salary at a good job, I wasn't worried about that risk. And because I wasn't afraid, my negotiating power was strong.[13]

My job at the tech company wasn't what it used to be, but it was still a good job, a solid inside option. Having a reliable inside option made me more willing to take a risk when negotiating with Redfin. After all, if I pushed too hard with Redfin, I still had my tech job.

Before I talked to the Redfin recruiter, I knew she would ask me how much I was currently earning. All recruiters ask that question. They try to use it as a reference point. I fell for that trick before, and because I had revealed my hand, I couldn't negotiate a better offer.

Many workers falsely assume they won't earn much more than their current salary after switching jobs. One study found that employees who could have earned 10% more working for a different employer falsely assumed they could increase their income by only 1% if they switched jobs. Researchers at the National Bureau of Economics Research surveyed German workers and matched the results with data on employee incomes at different companies in similar roles. The workers underestimated their outside options by mistakenly using their current salaries as a reference point instead of investigating how much more they could have actually earned from other employers.[14]

I wasn't going to let my current salary be my reference point this time. The recruiter was trying to figure out the lowest possible amount I would accept when it came time to negotiate. And she would base that on my outside option, which was my current compensation.

Researchers at MIT and University of Minnesota business schools found that job applicants can negotiate higher pay when the employer lacks information about their income history. The researchers came to this conclusion based on an experiment. In the study, they provided employers with job applicant profiles for which income histories were assigned at random. The researchers found that job offers came with lower wages when the employer could see how much the applicants made at their previous jobs. Employers also considered more applicants when they couldn't use income history to filter applications. Instead, they asked more questions during interviews to discern how much the employee was worth. As a result, the applicants with hidden income history received offers 9% higher than their counterparts who had their income history revealed to the employer.[15]

I wanted the highest offer possible. So I needed to make the recruiter believe it would take a higher number than my current salary to get me to accept an offer. The number had to be believable and be below the recruiter's budget for the role. So I needed to estimate the recruiter's budget. Unfortunately, there wasn't much data for chief economist salaries online. However, I discovered directors could earn $250,000 to $400,000 per year. So I estimated a chief economist could make as much as a director. So, I settled on the high end, $400,000 as my opener, to avoid overthinking.

I reassured myself that my reference point was perfectly reasonable and that I shouldn't be ashamed to ask for it. My skills and job experiences were rare. Plus, the economy and the housing market were doing well. Redfin was worth more than a billion dollars. So I rationalized that they could afford to pay whatever salary I asked for.

When the recruiter asked me how much I currently make, I replied: "I won't apply for this job unless the compensation is at least $400,000." After my promotion, my target compensation increased from under $200,000 to $230,000. However, I expected to earn more than that if I stayed because the stock price had doubled since I started, bringing my expected annual compensation to around $300,000. For all I knew, the stock price would keep increasing, so I didn't know how much I would earn in the next year or two. All that information was none of the recruiter's business anyway. She just needed a number to enter in her spreadsheet that she could reference during a negotiation.

I wasn't worried about the recruiter rejecting me over asking for $400,000. I liked my job enough that I wasn't going to risk going somewhere new for less than $350,000. If Redfin was willing to pay me at least $350,000, they wouldn't stop the interview process because I asked for $400,000. The difference would just be wiggle room for final negotiation.

I mustered the audacity to ask for such a high number because I wasn't attached to the Redfin opportunity yet. At this point in the interview process, I knew nothing about the Redfin team, so I had more fears than hopes. What if the work culture was toxic? What if I didn't like the daily tasks? What if I didn't like my colleagues? This fear of the unknown would usually keep me from taking a risk. But when it came to negotiating compensation, it kept me from accepting less than I deserved.

During my job interview, my fears faded. Everyone at Redfin was so friendly and earnest. Redfin had a good reputation as an employer. Unlike other real estate brokerages, Redfin paid their agents a salary with health benefits. The housing market research I would do in this role seemed super interesting. I would get to talk to the media, communicating the economics of the housing market, which seemed like a fun and creative exercise.

Since the Redfin job involved communication, I made sure to highlight all the public speaking and writing I did at the tech company in my interviews. I pulled stories from my first job experience at the Boston Fed and told of what it was like studying the housing market at the peak of the foreclosure crisis.

I got the job. When the recruiter returned to me with an offer of around $360,000, I was ecstatic. It was 10% less than what I had initially asked for. However, now that I was confident I would enjoy working for Redfin, it was more than enough to motivate me to make the switch. I was 30 years old and already the chief economist of a unicorn tech company. Looking back, I can't believe I managed to maintain such a fast tempo to get to that milestone so quickly.

Every now and then, I check in on how much chief economists make, so I can judge whether Redfin is still paying me fairly. Since the data isn't online, I collect my own data by taking calls with recruiters to throw outlandish numbers around to see how the recruiters react. In early 2021, I noticed that a credit card company was hiring a chief economist. I wasn't looking to leave Redfin, but I was curious about the role—specifically, how much they offered. During an introductory call with a recruiter, I said I would consider applying only if the compensation was at least $500,000. The recruiter said that was outside her budget. But six months later, she called me back, asking if I was still interested in applying. She must have received clearance to increase compensation after failing to fill the position. I still didn't want the job, though. The work seemed dull and outside my comfort zone—I would have to pitch products to clients. But I made a mental note for future negotiations to set my reference point at half a million dollars.

KNOWING YOUR WORTH

Once I had an offer in hand from Redfin, the next step was to tell my manager I was leaving. I could have acted like Vivica A.

Fox in *Two Can Play That Game*: I could have flaunted my outside option from Redfin just to get my employer to raise my pay. However, I was sure they wouldn't match Redfin's offer. Before I went out on maternity leave, I witnessed my colleague get passed over for a raise while she was out on her maternity leave. So, I wasn't surprised to learn from my manager that she downgraded me from top tier to mid-tier while I was out on maternity leave too. She had been my manager for only a few weeks before my leave started, so she didn't know much about my performance at work. Therefore, based on these higher-order beliefs, I didn't expect her to fight to increase my compensation.

When I walked into my manager's office to tell her about my offer from Redfin, I knew she couldn't offer me a better deal, given my mid-tier designation. So I hoped she would react to my news by saying something like: "That's amazing! I'm sad to see you go, but at the same time, I'm happy for you."

Instead, she replied: "I've seen lots of employees take on responsibilities that were too much for them. You're not ready to be a chief economist. Stay, and with some more experience, you'll be ready eventually."

I understood what she was trying to do. She was trying to make me think my outside option, the Redfin offer, was unsafe and uncertain. She wanted me to believe I couldn't make it on my own, like I was a LaTavia or a LeToya. Her comments pissed me off.

Higher-order thinking means knowing what your opponent thinks of you and using that to your advantage. But sometimes your opponent will have such a low opinion of your self-esteem that they will try to convince *you* that *your* beliefs are incorrect. They'll try to trick you into thinking your outside options are worse than they really are.

In the dating world, this tactic is called *negging*. Psychologists at the University of Nottingham described negging as the "purposeful lowering of a woman's self-esteem to increase perceived attractiveness of the man."[16] For example, when a man tells a beautiful woman that he doesn't mind the ugly mole on her face, that is an instance of negging. The man is trying to make the woman think she is unattractive and that other men wouldn't want her, so she will accept his romantic advances.

In game theory, negging occurs when a player attempts to lower their opponent's perceived value of their outside options to make their inside option seem better. Although negging has yet to get much attention from game theorists or economists, I learned firsthand that the negging tactic can be used by employers.

A player using a negging strategy assumes their opponent's beliefs can be manipulated. Negging would work only on someone with an incoherent sense of self. Only someone who doesn't know whether they are worthy or unworthy could be persuaded by one single comment.

In statistics, *Bayesian inference* provides a framework for interpreting events logically. It provides a framework for updating beliefs based on new information or evidence. For example, suppose I flip a coin and it comes up heads. Would you assume that the coin always lands heads up? Certainly not. You would believe the coin is like every other coin you've encountered, landing tails up half the time.

So if you receive one negative comment from a manager, or anyone else, you shouldn't assume that you are unworthy, incapable, or whatever other insults appear in your internal monologue. Consider from a logical perspective whether your critic is wrong. Consider whether your critic stands to gain from manipulating you.

After my manager said I couldn't make it without her, I logically considered every other instance in my life where I had taken on a difficult challenge and succeeded. At this point in my career, I knew I could achieve anything I set my mind to.

I was a Beyoncé. My historical evidence for success outweighed my manager's one negative comment. I got mad that my manager tried to manipulate me, and that she thought I could be manipulated. I became indignant. I gave my official two weeks' notice, feeling no remorse.

GAME RECAP

The next time you evaluate your worth in the labor market, follow these steps:

Determine how much value you're getting out of your current job. For example, is your current job providing you with enough money, enough promotion opportunities, enough fun, or enough purpose? If the answer isn't a confident yes, it is worth looking into outside options.

Identify whether there are better opportunities outside your current job. Often it's easier to obtain an upgraded title by going to another employer rather than getting promoted at your current employer. Try applying for jobs that are a step up in title.

Set a high reference point for your potential next employer. If your potential next employer assumes your outside options are better than they actually are, let them keep their false assumption. On the other hand, suppose your potential employer thinks your outside options are worse than they actually are. In that case, you will have to correct their view by setting the highest possible reference point that allows your employer to meet their hiring objectives. For example, I thought the Redfin recruiter might lowball me based on my target compensation at the tech company, so I set the reference point at $400,000. This was the highest number I felt I could reasonably ask for.

Never let one negative comment or experience shake your self-worth. The logical way to evaluate your self-worth after receiving a negative comment or going through a negative experience is to consider all your knowledge and experiences before that point. Then ask yourself if the negative comment or experience provides enough evidence to offset everything else you know about yourself.

10
OPTIMIZING YOUR LIFE

Winning a job offer, a raise, or a promotion are all examples of external prizes. External rewards are determined and awarded by entities other than yourself. However, there are many games where the prize is determined internally. Spending or saving money in a way that brings you meaning and happiness is an internal prize.

It is easy to see whether a promotion has been won or lost from an outside perspective. But with internal rewards, winning is a subjective experience. Only you can decide if you're spending, saving, or investing the right amount. Only you can determine if you're happy with the amount of time you are working versus engaging in other fulfilling activities. Only you can judge whether you enjoy your home, the community you surround yourself with, or the city you live in.

WHEN OPTIMIZING ISN'T AN OPTION

For the early parts of my career, I didn't worry much about whether I was saving the optimal amount. I was concerned only with whether I could cover my basic expenses, like rent and food. My internships and graduate school stipend didn't pay enough for me to have money left over for long-term financial goals.

In economics, a *corner solution* refers to a situation where a decision-maker faces limited options, and that causes an extreme choice. It occurs when one or more of the available options are unattainable. For example, a hawk may prefer to hunt for fish in a nearby lake over hunting for rodents in the surrounding forest. But in the winter, when the lake is frozen, diving for fish isn't an option. Rodents may not be the hawk's ideal meal, but the hawk's options are limited.

Many people would like to spend more but can't because their lack of money limits their options. People who have missed debt payments in the past may not have the option to borrow money because their credit score disqualifies them from loans.

Many people would like to save more, but the marginal benefit of spending money on current needs, like housing or food, is always greater than the marginal benefit of saving money for future needs. So, for them, any additional dollar received is logically spent in the present instead of going into a rainy-day fund or retirement savings.

Even though it can sometimes be perfectly rational to subsist without any savings, it comes with a psychological toll: a psychological disadvantage on top of a financial disadvantage. The behavioral economists Eldar Shafir and Sendhil Mullainathan wrote about this in their book *Scarcity: Why Having Too Little Means So Much.*[1] When people face scarcity, like a lack of time, money, or other resources, it consumes their thoughts and impairs cognitive abilities. This makes it difficult or impossible to make optimal decisions about saving, investing, or other significant economic considerations.

The effects of scarcity on a person's ability to make decisions make it even harder to escape poverty. When you're consumed by stress, it's easy to forget to pay a bill. And a quick fix for stress might be the dopamine from making a purchase even if you know you can't afford it.

There are no easy fixes for scarcity at the individual level. Government assistance in the United States is also scarce. The only way out is to find peace despite your financial situation and to focus on increasing your earnings. Instead of worrying about whether your lack of savings is a moral failing, focus as best you can on advancing your career until you finally have some breathing room.[2] And if you aren't living in scarcity, it's time to clarify your saving and investment goals and start thinking strategically about how to reach them.

SAVING

Some bird species, such as chickadees, nuthatches, jays, and crows, save food by storing it away. Many bird species recall where they hid their food and what kind of morsel they hid in each location. Storing seeds helps a bird get through the winter and allows seeds to disperse and forests to stay strong.[3]

In the forests of Yellowstone, for example, a single Clark's nutcracker has been observed storing 100,000 seeds in one year. When a cached seed is left abandoned, it has the potential to germinate and grow into a tree. Whitebark pines rely on nutcrackers to disseminate their seeds. This interdependence has grown in importance as disease threatens whitebark pine forests and the birds that live in the woods.[4]

Birds save seeds to protect themselves against starvation when food is difficult to find. A bird that saves a seed in the fall to eat in the winter is making a bet: the bird bets it will survive till winter, when seeds will be more scarce and, therefore, more valuable than in the fall. The bird makes educated guesses about the future to decide how much food to save. If the bird expects a consistent, reliable food source in the coming months, it may be more likely to eat now or forage less and not bother saving. On the other hand, if the bird expects a worse future, it will proceed cautiously and build more reserves to reduce the risk of starvation.

People may save for the same reasons. Having enough cash savings to cover your expenses for several months can help protect you if you lose your job or have an emergency expense. The saved money will be more valuable during trying times.

The permanent-income hypothesis, first proposed by the University of Chicago economist and Nobel laureate Milton Friedman, suggests that people, and evidently some birds, make decisions about their spending based on long-term expectations about their earnings. According to this hypothesis, people have a certain level of income that they expect to have over the long term called their *permanent income*. However, this "permanent income" cannot be objectively calculated, because it is based on a person's subjective feelings about the future.[5]

Since future income is unknowable, expectations about the future play a role in people's decisions about spending and saving. For example, if someone expects to have a lot of expenses soon, they might save more money to be prepared. On the other hand, if they expect to have a lot of income coming in, they might be more likely to spend money on things they want.

People's spending and saving decisions are influenced by their *tolerance for risk*, which is their willingness to place a bet to potentially gain a reward. For example, someone with a high tolerance for risk will be more likely to take on high-risk investments. In contrast, someone with a lower tolerance for risk might be more cautious and save more in cash or low-risk investments.

Finally, how much a person cares about future events can influence their spending and saving decisions. For example, someone more concerned about the future might be more likely to save money for retirement or emergencies. In contrast, someone more focused on the present might be more likely to spend money in ways that bring them happiness today.

INVESTING

When I got my first big Redfin stock vest, I had to decide what to do with the money. I wanted to sell the stock as soon as possible. If bad luck caused a severe housing market crash, I might be out of a job and left owning devalued stock. I wanted to diversify and spread my money across investments with less volatility. I was too tied to the swings of the housing market, given that I owned a home, owned Redfin stock, and was employed by Redfin.

But after I sold the stock, I had to decide what to do with the cash. With every second that went by, the cash became less valuable simply due to inflation.

Inflation occurs any time the amount of money floating around in the economy increases without an increase in stuff to spend that money on. When that happens, money becomes less valuable because it isn't as scarce; a dollar can no longer buy as much as it used to.

The amount of money flowing around in the economy increases nearly every year. That's because the Federal Reserve adds money to the economy to keep it growing. The Fed diligently attends to this task because if the amount of money in the economy were to decrease, it could cause a *deflationary spiral*.

In a deflationary spiral, people delay spending money because that money could go further in the future—a consumer might not buy a car for $25,000 today if they can get it for $24,000 next year. If people think prices will continue decreasing, the purchasing delays will never end. The economy spirals down until a recession, or even a depression, wreaks havoc on all of us.

It's the Fed's job to prevent recessions. So, the Fed continually adds money to the economy, like a gardener watering a plant. The gardener carefully assesses how much water is needed to nurture the ecosystem. Likewise, the Fed watches the economy carefully to assess how much money needs to be added to keep it growing slowly and steadily. The Fed wants to avoid a deflationary spiral, so it adds money to the economy. However, if it adds too much (overwatering the garden,) it risks hyperinflation, where prices increase faster than consumers and businesses can keep up with.

Even under stable inflation, my money was losing value. However, if I invested, that money could grow like a seed into a plant. The way birds store seeds can resemble an investment. The more seeds that are stored, the more trees will grow in the future. More trees mean more seeds, which helps future bird generations find food in their ecosystem. But there are many types of seeds and many trees that could populate a forest. When you save your money, you contribute to the economy's future. Suppose you put your money in a cash savings account. In that case, the bank lends that money to people and businesses who will put it to use in the economy. Suppose you buy a stock with your money. In that case, you become a partial owner of a company that intends to grow. Suppose you use the money to pay for your children's college education. In that case, you are helping your children attain an education they can put to work in the economy. Every time you invest, you are betting on the future and simultaneously changing the economy's future in some form. Even if all you do with your money is buy up land and leave it undeveloped, your choice to do nothing affects the future.

Betting on the status quo is usually a safe bet. In 2023, Apple Inc. was the most valuable company in the world. And Apple is also the best bet for what company will be the most valuable ten years from now. Microsoft might overtake Apple, but Microsoft is the underdog, given that Apple is currently in the lead.

If certain types of trees grow strong and healthy in today's ecosystem, there is a good chance those types of trees will still be the strongest and healthiest decades from now. When it's impossible to know where the future is headed, the best guess is that it will be the same as the present. Investing in an index fund that tracks the stocks or bonds of the total stock market is a safe investment in the status quo.

Economists love index funds. Index funds provide diversification, allowing investors to spread their risk across many different companies and industries. This can help reduce risk and protect against losses from any single company or industry. As long as an investor holds their money for several years, an index fund should provide a strong return. Of course, the stock market experiences swings up and down, so it's unwise to put emergency savings into the stock market. But if you can hold off on selling an index fund, you should see a strong return on investment.

Economists also like index funds because they tend to have low fees and expenses. Index funds cost less because they are passively managed, which means an algorithm instead of an investment professional manages the fund. Index funds are pegged to the performance of a specific market index, such as the S&P 500, instead of just one company's stock. Since index funds mimic the current landscape of corporations, they are a bet on the status quo.

But when I look around at the economy's status quo, there are a lot of companies I would prefer dead. The downside of index funds is that because they purposefully include a large and diverse set of companies, they often contain morally questionable companies—for-profit prisons, for example. ESG (environmental, social, governance) index funds aim to offer the same diversification benefits of index funds. However, they exclude morally reprehensible companies and companies with unsustainable practices. There is a downside, however. ESG index funds come with higher fees because a person or people need to make judgments about which companies qualify for inclusion. And there is subjectivity involved—people can reasonably disagree about what qualifies as a morally responsible company.

Despite all the negatives of ESG index funds, I still prefer them over total market index funds. I am hoping and betting on a future better than the status quo.

REBALANCING WORK AND LIFE

Once I felt secure in my savings, the most scarce thing in my life became my time. As a result, I became hyperaware of how I spent my time. I scrutinized whether each moment contributed to my happiness or purpose, including my hours spent at work.

Economic models often assume that work is an exchange of time and effort for money. Work is costly to employees because it takes them away from their outside options. Those outside options include enjoyable hobbies, time with family, or time asleep. But ample research supports the notion that workers are motivated by things besides money, like purpose-driven goals or enjoyment of the work itself.[6]

In a survey, researchers at Cornell presented college students with six pairs of hypothetical job descriptions where pay, working conditions, and tasks were the same. However, the social responsibility of the employers differed. For example, in one job pairing, students had to choose between writing ads for Camel cigarettes or the American Cancer Society. When asked which job they would rather have, most students preferred jobs associated with socially responsible employers. Students said they would need to be paid 50% more to work for Camel cigarettes over the American Cancer Society.[7]

In another study, researchers at MIT and the University of Pennsylvania paid remote workers to complete a paid task labeling medical images. The workers were randomly assigned to three different groups. One group was told nothing about the task, another group was told they were labeling images of tumor cells for medical research, and another group was told their work would be discarded and never used for anything meaningful. The researchers found that having meaning increased participation and productivity. The group that believed their work was for important medical research labeled the most images.[8]

To improve my motivation at work, I focused on the aspects of my job that I found meaningful. I intrinsically enjoy economics, and I believe the communication of economics is an important public service. So, I focused on doing those aspects of my job well. Once I stopped seeing my work as just a means to an end, I became more motivated to do my best work—not because I aimed for a promotion or raise but because I liked seeing the fruits of my labor. I enjoyed producing research and writing that was good.

But even though I enjoyed my work, I detested the pointless and unnecessary aspects of my job. I hated working from the office. I loathed my commute, especially in my first months at Redfin, when I was still nursing my first child. I remember riding the bus home, getting stuck in traffic, and feeling the physical pain from engorgement and the mental anguish of missing my infant's last feeding before bedtime.

My personal cost of commuting was unsustainably high. Even though I was making more money than I ever had before, I was commuting longer than I ever had before.

The *commuting-time paradox* is the idea that, even as people earn more money and transit options improve, people's commute times stay the same. In one study published in the *Journal of Urban Economics*, economists posited an explanation premised on negotiating power. When an employer offers an employee a higher wage, the employee becomes more willing to commute to get that wage. In the economist's model, an employee ends up commuting the same length of time no matter how much money they earn.[9]

And then, the pandemic hit in 2020. I was sent home from the office indefinitely. Working from home relieved constraints on my happiness across time and space. Without my commute, I had extra hours in my day. I was able to nurse my second child, born in April 2020, from the comfort of home instead of lugging leak-prone bags of breast milk back from the office. I felt guilty that my life had improved amidst a pandemic and a recession wreaking havoc on less fortunate people's lives.

Redfin changed its policy to permit employees to work from anywhere after it became evident that the pandemic would last longer than one year. My options for where to live suddenly expanded from the Seattle metro area to anywhere in the country. Economic theory predicts that an increase in choices should lead to an increase (or at least not a decrease) in utility or happiness.

But psychologists and behavioral economists have found evidence that this may not always be true, which results in a paradox of choice.[10] Having more choices can make it harder to decide and lead to regret if a choice doesn't turn out how you expected. Also, when there are many options, it can cause "analysis paralysis," where you can't decide at all because there are too many choices—and even if you do pick one, you might feel like you missed out on other options that might have been better.

As I spent more time in my Seattle home, isolated from friends and family, I had plenty of time to think about my choice of location. I originally came to Seattle for the growing job opportunities in its tech scene. But now, tech jobs like mine could be done anywhere. So I reflected on whether my family and I would be better off living elsewhere, and where that place would be.

It was a strange time to ponder making a permanent move because no one knew what aspects of the pandemic were temporary and what would be permanent. According to a Redfin research survey, 75% of homebuyers reported that the pandemic changed their preferences. The most common preference change was an increased desire for more indoor or outdoor space. Private space increased in value, with public areas deemed unsafe due to the contagious coronavirus. This change in preferences led to a surge in demand for homes with more bedrooms and larger yards. With city amenities like restaurants and bars shut down, many homebuyers left for suburban and rural areas where large homes were more affordable. This boom in housing demand was further fueled by record-low mortgage rates, which made borrowing to buy a house much more affordable.[11]

But only certain kinds of people could take advantage of these affordable mortgages. Anyone living in scarcity, like those out of work or worried about losing employment, were unable to buy a home. It was mostly the wealthy who could afford to purchase not only one house but also second homes and investment properties. Purchases of second homes doubled during the pandemic.[12] The share of homes purchased by investors increased from around 15% in 2019 to 20% in late 2021.[13] Even though it was primarily wealthy people buying homes, the changes in their behavior rippled throughout the country. For example, in 2018, only about 18% of people looking to buy a home searched outside their metro area. However, by 2022, 24% of homebuyers were looking to move out of town.[14]

I debated the pros and cons of leaving Seattle. The cons were mainly in the present. Doing anything during a pandemic felt risky, and that included moving. Plus, I had a newborn baby and didn't want to deal with the added stress. I was lucky enough to be employed and financially secure during the pandemic, so I could move if I wanted to. However, I remained on the fence about whether to move.

According to research by Steven Levitt, people who are on the fence about making a big life change are usually better off making the change. Levitt asked people to flip a coin to help them decide about a major life change they were unsure of, like quitting a job or ending a relationship. The people who were told by the coin to make a change were more likely to actually make that change. They were also happier with their decision and felt better about it six months later than those told by the coin to keep things the same. This finding suggests that people are generally too cautious when making big decisions that can change their lives and might need an outside push to help them overcome their status quo bias.[15]

❊ ❊ ❊

And then the smoke came rolling in; I got my outside push. I had moved to Seattle in August 2016. In the summers of 2017, 2018, and 2020, the area experienced severe wildfire smoke events that made the air unsafe to breathe for over a week. These smoke events used to be uncommon, but hotter summers and overgrown forests along the West Coast contributed to worse and more frequent fires.

Halfway around the world, climate change has led to increased drought in the Australasian habitat of the grey teal. With its slender build, long, thin legs, and long, pointed beak, the bird is well suited for foraging for food in shallow waters, which may dry up or become flooded with the weather. So, to find water, the grey teal travels great distances. Fortunately, the bird has adapted physically to this need with long, narrow wings that allow it to fly long distances with minimal effort. Because the grey teal is willing to fly a thousand kilometers to find a suitable habitat, the species can better adapt to climate change.[16]

Like the grey teal, people pay attention to changes in the climate when deciding where to live. For example, research I authored with economists at USC and MIT found that homebuyers are less likely to purchase a home with a high flood risk when presented with flood projections alongside real estate listings on Redfin's website and app. In a randomized experiment, we found that Redfin users who viewed homes with a high flood-risk score went on to bid on those with moderate risk. In contrast, users not shown flood-risk data did not change their buying behavior. This research provided the first definitive evidence that the risks posed by climate change have the power to change where people choose to live.[17]

When I told my husband about the reports of smoke rolling in, he packed our bags. I initially argued that we should stay and tough it out with our air filters. But then Adam argued back that we would be miserable, trapped inside. I could tell from the look in his eyes that his claustrophobia had put him into fight-or-flight mode. Adam would rather drive a thousand miles to his hometown in Wisconsin than stay confined in a house surrounded by toxic air. I was working remotely, so nothing was keeping us in Seattle. I chose to put Adam's feelings first, even though I didn't feel the same urgency. Besides, after spending six months sheltering in place from the pandemic, I could use a change in scenery. Plus, the pandemic had isolated us from friends and family, and we had both in Wisconsin.

We packed our van in a matter of hours and started driving over the Cascade mountains to escape the smoke chasing us east. Finally, after three days on the road, we arrived at our short-term rental in Lake Geneva, Wisconsin. With the summer season still lingering, we relished our time outdoors, swimming in the spring-fed lake and exploring the oak and maple forests blooming with wildflowers.

Once we were in Wisconsin, the decision of where to live was no longer about whether to leave Seattle. Instead, the decision was about whether to return. Without status quo bias, I began to see the city in a new light.

※ ※ ※

There is a lot to love about Seattle—the snowcapped mountains, the evergreen forests, the summer sunsets that last until 9 p.m. But the city felt like it was on the decline. The cost of living was on the rise while livability was degrading, and the root of these issues can be traced back to housing policy.

Seattle, like many other cities, has seen a decline in affordable housing over the years. As high-paying jobs in the tech sector attracted well-paid workers (like myself) to the area, the demand for housing increased. However, the city did not prioritize the need for housing. As a result, many homeowners, seeking to increase the value of their homes, opposed the development of new housing. These homeowners could easily block the construction of apartment buildings and multifamily housing by fighting changes to zoning rules.

With the supply constricted, more people competed for homes, which drove up prices. As a result, housing costs grew dramatically. In addition, the overall cost of living swelled. As a result, consumer prices in the Seattle metro increased by 60% from the end of 2010 to the end of 2020.[18] In 2019, Seattle became the most expensive city for renters outside California.[19]

The increase in housing costs slowly caused more and more problems for the city. As rents go up, so does the number of housing-insecure or unhoused people. Since higher housing costs disproportionately affect lower-income people already struggling financially, economic inequality tends to rise with rents. Residents who can no longer afford to live in the city often move to the more affordable suburbs and surrounding cities, leading to more driving, traffic, and pollution. Slowly but surely, as the cost of housing increases, the quality of life deteriorates.

Now that I had experienced a slower pace of life, without smoke, traffic, or corporate offices, I didn't want to return. Living in a big city provides more job opportunities, a diversity of cultures, and more things to do on a Friday night than living in a small town. These were all important to me in my 20s, but now that I was in my 30s with two kids and a well-established career, I preferred peace to excitement.

After moving to Wisconsin, my quality of life improved. I'm closer to family. There is no traffic. I live within walking distance of the beach. There is a thriving tabletop-game scene (Lake Geneva is the birthplace of Dungeons & Dragons). My kids have access to high-quality public schools. Now that we live in a small town, we have a greater sense of community. Having a community in a big city is possible, but it seems to take more effort. In the city, if I met a mom at the playground and didn't get her number, I would probably never see her again. But living in a small town, there are more opportunities for recurring spontaneous interactions that turn acquaintances into friends. We see the same cast of recurring characters around town. They know who we are, where we live, and our kids. Growing up in a city, I became accustomed to being anonymous, but our kids are recognized at the playground, the grocery store, and the library. When they are teenagers, they won't be able to get away with anything because I'll hear about it through the local grapevine.

Having a sense of community inspired Adam to become civically engaged. He volunteers and serves part time for the local government as a village trustee. This is great for me, because now I have someone to complain to about our village's lack of affordable housing.

I had to take a slight pay cut for my employer, Redfin, to approve my move. Still, the benefits outweighed the cost, and I knew I could initiate a renegotiation at the right time.

GAME RECAP

The next time you're deciding whether to spend, save, or invest your money, follow these steps:

If you live in scarcity, worry less about saving and focus instead on increasing your earnings. Trying to pinch pennies even more will add more stress to an already stressful situation. It's OK to delay decisions about saving until you feel you are meeting your present needs. Focus on advancing your career for the time being. But once your current needs are met, it's time to optimize your savings.

Evaluate your current spending habits. Are you spending money in ways that bring you happiness and purpose, or are you spending money on conspicuous consumption? If you're spending your money on conspicuous consumption, evaluate if you're getting benefits beyond the perception of higher social status. If not, consider cutting back on luxury purchases.

Set aside money for emergencies. An emergency savings fund can help you cover your bills and expenses during a job loss or other personal financial crisis. Your money will be more valuable when you don't have as much of it. This money should be kept in a cash savings account so you can access it when needed.

Set savings goals for retirement, college funds, or buying a home. After you have set money aside for emergencies, start saving for your future. These savings can be put into diversified investments like index funds that offer high returns and low risk if you let them grow for many years.

Think about how your investments may shape the future. Think through whether your investments match up with your values. Investing can help you reach your values-based goals in addition to your financial goals.

Assess how your local cost of living may be impacting your ability to save. Also, assess the quality of life in your location and whether it adds or detracts from your happiness. If you are on the fence about moving somewhere new or making another significant change, you will likely be better off taking the leap of faith.

11

SELLING A HOME

Earlier I said that buying a home is often the most significant financial decision a person will make in their lifetime. The penalty for making the wrong decision might be foreclosure and financial ruin. And the reward for making the right decision might be hundreds of thousands of dollars in wealth accrued. Of course, some of that wealth will come from the work you put into the home through maintenance and renovations. But a large part of that wealth will come simply from the fact that homes, and especially homes in desirable places, are scarce.

The housing market is like a game of musical chairs, where each round, the number of people playing keeps increasing but the number of chairs stays the same. This makes the game difficult for any player, but existing players have an advantage. Each round, anyone who already has a seat has the option to keep their seat.

Homeowners have already won the game. They have the luxury of sitting out rounds and holding on to their home as long as they can pay their mortgage, insurance, and taxes. And, when homeowners go to sell their home, they will benefit from the fact that the housing market is fixed in their favor. The housing market is a prime example of how capitalism can go astray, with winners being able to hold on to their position while others struggle to catch up.

ASSESSING HOME VALUES

As I prepared to sell my Seattle home, I wondered how much it was worth and how it compared to the value of homes in Wisconsin. The value of my Seattle home came from the land underneath it and the building on top of it. In Seattle, land values make up a significant portion of home prices, at 42%. However, land accounts for around 20% of home values in Midwest metros. Furthermore, the home structure costs more to build in Seattle than in the Midwest, contributing to the difference in home values.

It's more expensive to develop property in Seattle compared to the Midwest because it is more expensive to pay construction workers a living wage in Seattle. As of 2019, only 7% of homes in the Seattle metro area were affordable to the typical local construction worker. However, in Midwest metros like St. Louis, Cleveland, and Chicago, the majority of homes for sale were affordable to local construction workers.[1] When housing becomes unaffordable to the people who work in the area, it creates a vicious cycle: the more expensive housing is, the more expensive it becomes to hire workers to build more housing. To make matters worse, NIMBY homeowners block new housing construction by effectively outlawing the development of apartment buildings and multifamily homes.

Up and down the West and East Coasts, cities have become entrenched in this vicious cycle. Nationally, the demand for housing had been outpacing the supply for some time. As a result, home prices grew 52% between 2012 and 2019.[2] During this period, 8.4 million new households were formed in the US. However, only 6.8 million new housing units were constructed.

PREPARING TO SELL

As a housing economist, I was well aware of the economic forces in the background pushing up my home's value. I anticipated that my house would be worth more than when I bought it. While living in the home, I spent $75,000 on new plumbing, electrical, and heating and cooling systems. After my real estate agent told me that renovating the kitchen, bathroom, and other features could increase the home's value by an additional $150,000, I invested another $75,000 in renovations.

I liked my house the way it was. I liked the 1950s pink tile in the kitchen. I didn't mind that the dishwasher was decades old. But buyers tend to like homes that look new and photograph well. So, I could either sell my house as is to a flipper or someone looking for a fixer-upper, or I could invest in the improvements myself to expand my pool of potential buyers.

Since I wasn't in a rush to sell and had the funds to pay for the renovations, I chose to upgrade the home. It's not every day you can get a 50% return on investment, after all. And since I was the owner-occupant, I wouldn't have to pay capital gains tax on the profit. With the United States tax code on my side, it was an easy way to turn money into more money.

The US tax code is full of rules that benefit homeowners. A common tax break for homeowners is the mortgage interest deduction. With the mortgage interest deduction, homeowners may subtract interest paid on mortgages from their income so they can pay less in taxes. This includes second homes, which gives wealthy Americans extra incentive to collect properties. Although there is a cap on the deduction, the tax break overwhelmingly benefits wealthy Americans. It is a *regressive tax*, meaning it takes from the poor and gives to the rich. A *progressive tax*, on the other hand, takes from the wealthy and gives to the poor.

While my family and I stayed in Wisconsin and searched for a new home to buy, I had the Redfin Concierge Service renovate our Seattle property. With mortgage rates at a record low and home prices in Wisconsin being about a third of what they were in Seattle, I could afford to carry both mortgages simultaneously. (My mortgage in Wisconsin would cost me a quarter of what my mortgage in Seattle cost.) As a result, I didn't have to worry about selling our Seattle home to have enough money to buy a new one in Wisconsin. Most home sellers can't pull this off, which is why mostly well-off people with the means to juggle two mortgages moved during the pandemic.

During the pandemic, the wealthy benefited from cheap interest rates set by the Federal Reserve. In 2020, as middle- and low-income Americans struggled with unemployment and missed rent or mortgage payments, second-home purchases doubled and luxury home sales growth quadrupled.[3] By 2022, the monthly mortgage payment on a midprice home increased by 50%, pricing out anyone on the verge of being able to afford a house a year earlier.[4] I was one of the wealthy, lucky ones who bought a home at the most opportune time.

We purchased our Wisconsin home in November and set our sights on selling our Seattle home in February at the start of the 2021 homebuying season. However, by January, the housing market was more competitive than my agent or I had anticipated.

SETTING THE PRICE

Homes similar to mine were selling for $1.25 million—$100,000 more than we expected and over $400,000 more than I initially paid. The Fed's low-interest policies during the pandemic supercharged the demand for homes. And many tech employees working from home were leaving San Francisco and Silicon Valley for Seattle. Comparatively, Seattle provided a lower cost of living and zero state income tax.

The state of Washington's tax structure is regressive. Without any income tax, the state relies primarily on sales taxes. Since low earners tend to spend most of their money and high earners tend to save most of their money, sales taxes disproportionately burden the poor. Seattle also has famously high alcohol taxes.[5] An alcohol tax is a type of sin tax. Sin taxes raise revenue while discouraging undesirable or harmful behaviors like drinking, gambling, or smoking. Discouraging alcohol consumption through taxes can improve public health by reducing alcohol-related deaths and diseases. But sin taxes are usually regressive. This is because poor people spend a disproportionate amount of income on alcohol and other vices.

Seattle also collects property taxes on homeowners, but Washington homeowners contribute less to their state's tax revenue than homeowners in the rest of the country.[6] Overall, a high-earning homeowner can expect to pay less in state taxes in Washington than in most states, which has made Seattle an attractive alternative to homebuyers from California.

I priced my home less than what similar homes were selling for, at just under $1.2 million. It's generally better to err on the side of pricing too low rather than too high. If I priced too low, I would likely receive multiple offers, sparking a bidding war. On the other hand, pricing too high could result in zero offers.

Because of a February snowstorm, we pushed back our home sale by a week. It seems silly, but the timing does matter in real estate. Homes tend to have the most success drawing in buyers when they are first listed, much like how a movie attracts its largest audience on opening weekend. If a home gets 100 views on its Redfin listing page on the first day, it will typically receive only 51 views by the second day and 25 views by the seventh day.[7] Had I listed my home for sale during a week when everyone was focused on a freak snowstorm, I would have doomed its premiere.

SELECTING A BUYER

I listed my home for sale on a Thursday and set an offer review date for the following Tuesday. By Tuesday, I had received four offers, each of which included a letter from the potential buyer. However, I made a conscious decision not to read the letters, as I didn't want the personal stories to bias my decision-making. It is illegal for a seller to consider factors such as race, marital status, gender, sexual orientation, or age when deciding whom to sell a home to. However, homebuyers sometimes include this information in their letters to appeal to the seller's emotions. For example, the letters might consist of family photos and stories about how much their children will love the backyard or how much grandma will appreciate the guest bedroom. I didn't want to see any of that.

When people make decisions based on who they like rather than who is the best fit for an opportunity, it can create a pattern where certain groups are always favored over others. This can lead to a lack of diversity and representation in the housing market, just like in the job market.

For example, suppose home sellers consistently choose to sell their house to the person they like instead of the person who offers the most money. In that case, they may contribute to a system where certain groups of people are consistently left out of the housing market. Similarly, suppose a boss always hires their friends instead of the most qualified job candidates. In that case, they may be perpetuating a system where certain groups of people have limited opportunities for work. In both cases, this lack of diversity and representation can negatively affect those consistently unfavored.

In 1957, the economist Gary Becker proposed a theory of racial prejudice that predicted discrimination against Black people would eventually fade due to economic competition. Becker differentiated between discrimination that was the result of racial prejudice and discrimination that was the result of stereotyping. According to his theory, taste-based discrimination, which is rooted in people's dislike or hatred of a group, cannot survive in the free market. This is because companies that are prejudiced against hiring Black workers would not be as successful as those that employ a diverse workforce. If Black workers are just as productive as white workers but cost less to employ, firms that hire only white workers will be at a disadvantage. This is because they aren't making efficient use of the available workforce.[8]

Similarly, home sellers who are prejudiced against Black homebuyers would be at a disadvantage because they aren't receiving every possible offer. For example, suppose a racist white homeowner refuses to sell their home to a Black homebuyer willing to pay $550,000 but would sell to anyone else for $500,000. In that case, an enterprising white investor could flip the house by buying from the racist seller and reselling to the Black buyer, earning $50,000. Racism solved.

However, in 1982, the economist Matthew S. Goldberg updated this flawed theory. Goldberg considered that racial hiring discrimination may be driven by nepotism or favoritism. Under Goldberg's model, past policies and attitudes can lead to persistent inequality in employment and wages for those who aren't receiving preferential treatment, even with economic competition.[9]

Goldberg's model of discrimination would similarly predict that favoritism toward certain groups would perpetuate housing discrimination of the past. For example, suppose a home seller isn't exactly prejudiced against Black homebuyers—the seller just prefers buyers who grew up in the neighborhood. And the neighborhood happens to be historically white. Instead of selling to an investor who might flip the property to a Black buyer, the home seller prefers to sell to a local white family who intends to live in the home indefinitely. In this scenario, the Black homebuyer never gets the opportunity to buy the house at the market rate.

Before the Fair Housing Act of 1968, it was legal for real estate agents to steer Black buyers away from white neighborhoods.[10] It was legal for a deed to include language that forbade the home from ever being sold to a person of color.[11] It was legal for an entire municipality to declare itself a sundown town. In sundown towns, Black people were permitted to work during the day. However, they were prohibited from living in town or even staying past sundown.[12] And because of that history, just 45% of Black families own a home today, compared to 74% of white families.[13] If home sellers, who are majority white, give preferential treatment to buyers who remind them of themselves, that perpetuates inequality in housing.

And even though I'm not white, I'm not immune to unconscious bias. No one is. Nepotism is often driven by an altruistic urge. Helping someone out who is a friend, family member, or someone you just like can make you feel good. But charity doesn't always make the world fairer. On the contrary, when bias plays a role in who does and doesn't receive a helping hand, it makes the world more unfair. The flaws of individual players accumulate into a flawed game, a flawed system.

It was easy to eschew my biases and simply take the highest offer, no matter who it came from. My top bid was $1.27 million, while the next best offer was $1.25 million. If I had chosen the second bidder simply because I liked their letter, I might as well have given them $20,000 out of my own pocket.

GAME RECAP

When you prepare to sell your home, follow these steps:

Assess your home's value. Your home's value depends on its historical value (how much you bought it for), how much the land value has increased, and how much the property has improved or deteriorated since you purchased it. Talk to your real estate agent and research the prices of similar homes in your area to assess the home value. The Redfin estimate or algorithmic prices are a good starting point, but these often don't consider property improvements or other unique aspects of the home.

Make last-minute improvements. You can make improvements big and small to improve the value of your home. Significant issues like outdated plumbing can scare away buyers, and minor modifications like landscaping or fresh paint can attract buyers. However, not every improvement will yield a higher price, so research trends in your local market and consult with your agent.

Set your price a little low instead of too high. You have only one debut for your home, and you want *any* buyer who might make an offer to take a look. You are better off having too many offers versus none at all, so price your home on the low side.

Pick a buyer objectively. Don't give preferential treatment to buyers you like for personal reasons. To avoid bias, select the strongest offer.

12
A CODE FOR WINNERS

The rules of the economy are flawed. They are so flawed that one woman made it her life's goal to reveal its perverse rule system to the American public. And her mission gave us the classic game *Monopoly*.

Monopoly, originally titled the Landlord's Game, was poorly designed on purpose.[1] Lizzie Magie, the game's inventor, designed the rules so that the player who happens to land on and buy valuable spaces like Boardwalk gains such a significant advantage they become uncatchable. No matter what choices and moves the other players make, the player who purchases the most valuable spaces first is fated to win.

Lizzie Magie, a turn-of-the-20th-century polymath and follower of the economist Henry George, designed the flaw in the board game Monopoly to reflect what she saw as the main flaw in the American economic system. This flaw was that landowners may extract value from the economy without contributing anything in return. In Monopoly, a player gains the ability to collect rent from opponents as soon as they purchase an empty property. Players who do not own any property cannot earn rent in the game. This gives the player fortunate enough to land on Boardwalk in the first round a significant advantage, which only grows as the game progresses until all other players go bankrupt.

And no one player alone can make Monopoly more fair. Passing over the opportunity to buy Boardwalk doesn't fix the game flaw. It only opens the door for another player to buy it. One person's moves are inconsequential to the fairness of the system. The rules are what matter and need to be changed.

The game, with its original rules, is not much fun. It's a common trope for the player in last place to flip the board rather than watch their opponent win in such an inglorious manner. So over time, groups of players have modified the rules of Monopoly to give those falling behind a chance to catch up. In one common rule modification, the taxes, fines, or other penalties paid throughout the game are placed under the Free Parking space. When a player lands on Free Parking, they receive the Monopoly dollars underneath. This redistribution of money makes the game more competitive because the player in first place must play to win or risk being surpassed by players who receive a free boost.

Under this rule modification, the Free Parking space serves as a *public good* in the game. Taxes collected in the game are used to fund a project with the potential to benefit everyone. Real-life examples of public goods include public parks, public education, public safety departments, and public housing.

Henry George believed the value of land should be used to fund public services rather than relying on taxes on labor, consumption, and capital.[2] He argued that land value was created not by the efforts of the individual landowner but by the community as a whole through the development of infrastructure, schools, and other public goods. George advocated for taxing the land, with the proceeds used to fund public services and infrastructure, to create a more equitable distribution of wealth and encourage the efficient use of land resources.

When Monopoly was invented at the turn of the twentieth century, landowners in the United States could win the capitalism game without much effort, which is still true today. If you are lucky enough to buy land in a place gaining population and popularity, you can make a fortune without lifting a finger. And if you live in one of those places and pay rent, you will slowly see your economic position deteriorate unless you actively fight to increase your earnings.

I'm an excellent example of this. I collected hundreds of thousands of dollars in wealth not through hard work, but by owning my home. And I did this while tens of thousands of Seattle residents went homeless. I arguably deserved the money I made working, but I had nothing to do with the value of the land I owned. That came from scarcity. Even if my home's structure was bulldozed to rubble, the land underneath it would continue to increase in value because residential land is rare.

Every time a new person moved to Seattle for a fresh start, the value of my home's land went up. Every time a tourist booked an Airbnb that could have been rented out to someone needing a permanent home, the value of my home's land went up. Every time a NIMBY prevented land from being developed into new housing, the value of my home's land went up.

As a society, we vilify the homeless for seeking shelter on public land. However, we turn a blind eye to the fact that landowners are essentially squatting on public property too. Despite their title, landlords do not literally have a divine right over the land they occupy.

The public should leverage the power to tax the value of the land, ensuring that its worth benefits all members of society. We do in fact do this to a small extent. Land taxes are a part of property tax, but they don't come close to recapturing the land's full value.

The value of land in a city like Seattle is not due to any single landowner but rather the collective efforts of everyone who directly or indirectly made the city into a thriving metropolis. The fact that landowners get to collect the rewards while others go homeless is beyond unfair.

In the introduction of this book, I made the claim that anyone can achieve economic security with the right strategy, but that's a lie. There are people drowning financially who don't have the resources to identify or implement a strategy. And just because some people can seemingly, magically pull themselves up by their bootstraps doesn't mean everyone can.

Capitalism is broken, but it has an easy fix—or, at least, the fix is easy from an economic standpoint. Tax the land, and redistribute the wealth to the players in the economy who have fallen behind. That way, we can all have a better chance at winning.

That's the kind of game I want to play.

I titled this book *Hate the Game* because I don't want you to hate yourself for playing the game of capitalism in its current unfair form. Despite the numerous issues with the rules, playing to win does not make you complicit in the system's flaws. The reality is that there are severe economic consequences for losing. However, once you are in a position of power and can shape the rules of the game, let your hate of the game fuel your desire for change.

EPILOGUE

Once I settled into Wisconsin, I discovered I possessed the agency to create the life I value most. Before, my life had been designed around my career aspirations. The city I lived in, the commute I endured, and even the clothes I wore were all designed around my desire for achievement. But moving to Wisconsin was the reset I needed to begin seeing my life from a more holistic perspective.

And then, out of the blue, I got a call from an executive recruiter asking me to apply to be the next president of the Federal Reserve Bank of Boston. The previous president had stepped down abruptly amidst a scandal surrounding questionable stock trades. So the Boston Fed announced they would search far and wide for a new president, and in that search, they discovered me.

I immediately began imagining myself in the role. I would be the first woman of color and youngest Fed president if selected. It was as if someone had tapped me on the shoulder and offered me the opportunity to participate in the Miss America pageant, and already I was envisioning myself standing on stage in a gown and sash, wearing my crown.

I thought back to my internship at the Boston Fed. My first job as an economist—wait, were they going to subject me to another drug test? They wouldn't ask the president to do that, right? Wait, wouldn't that be worse, if they required their workers to take drug tests but didn't require the same of the executives?

I looked at the CBD balm on my bathroom counter and wondered if it would set off a test. I had been applying the balm to my hip to help ease the pain that never faded after my second pregnancy. The product was federally legal thanks to the 2018 Farm Bill. Still, a drug test doesn't know the difference between hemp-derived THC and cannabis-derived THC. I thought about my upcoming visit to California. Would I have to abstain from cannabis even though it was legal there?

I felt myself spiraling into an endless internal debate over whether I could work for an organization whose rules don't align with my values. So I resolved to protest when the issue arose. I'm done urinating in cups. If they wanted me to be the Boston Fed president, they would have to eliminate drug testing for all employees, not just me.

And then it occurred to me that I would have to move my entire family to Boston, even though we were happy in Wisconsin. Adam was excited for me and unconditionally supportive as always, but I knew he was happy in his hometown. He felt a connection with his community for the first time in over a decade.

Was I really going to reorganize all my priorities that I set for myself? I moved to Wisconsin for good reasons—reasons that made sense, given my values. Were my values so weak that I would switch them up as soon as a shiny new trophy was dangled in front of me?

I still went through with the interview. The recruiter said it would be a good networking opportunity, which was a valid point. But instead of trying to make myself as appealing as possible to the Boston Fed Board of Directors, I presented an authentic version of myself. No illusions and no compromises. I told them about my background studying behavioral economics, my work studying employee satisfaction at the tech company, and my role studying the housing market for Redfin. I didn't exaggerate my knowledge of monetary policy or my experience as an executive. If they wanted me, they would have to accept the real me.

After the interview, the recruiter called to tell me that I was not selected. The job and honor of becoming the first Black woman to preside over a Federal Reserve Bank rightfully went to a much more qualified and experienced economist, Dr. Susan Collins. However, the recruiter told me the board was impressed by my interview and that I could still become a Fed president one day. I just needed to acquire more experience in senior management. I explained that I liked my job and wasn't interested in taking on more management duties. I was done playing games I didn't enjoy just to win a prize.

With this newfound clarity about my values, I negotiated with Redfin for reduced hours and increased flexibility to have more time to spend on the activities I value, like writing this book.

I have the career I want. I have the life I want. All I wanted from the beginning was to go to the beach, dance to my favorite music, and play the games I enjoy. And you can catch me doing just that. I'll be at the beach, dancing with my kids, playing the Hokey Pokey.

That's what it's all about.

ACKNOWLEDGMENTS

I would like to thank everyone who supported me in the creation of this book.

Thank you to my editor, Chad Zimmerman, for his invaluable guidance throughout the entire writing process. Your expertise and insightful feedback have played a significant role in shaping this book into its final form.

I am also deeply indebted to my reviewers and test readers. Your thoughtful suggestions have greatly enriched the content of this book.

To my husband, Adam, I cannot thank you enough for your love and support. Thank you for being the best dad to our kids and making us laugh every day. Thank you to our extended family who provided encouragement and childcare.

With gratitude,

Daryl

GLOSSARY

ambiguity aversion. The tendency to prefer known risks over unknown risks when making decisions under uncertainty. Also known as *uncertainty aversion*.

anchoring effect. A tendency to overfocus on an initial piece of information while making decisions.

asymmetric information. A situation in which one party involved in a transaction or negotiation has more or better information than the other party.

attrition bias. A type of selection bias where participants quit or drop-out of a study, program, or job at different rates across comparison groups, leading to systematic differences between the groups.

backward induction. A method of reasoning where one starts from the end of a game and works backward to determine the optimal strategy or decision at each step leading up to that point.

bait-and-switch. A deceptive tactic where a seller advertises an item or service at a low price to attract customers, but then, on gaining the customer's interest, substitutes the advertised item with a different product that is more expensive or less desirable to customers.

Bayesian inference. A framework for interpreting events logically, whereby beliefs are updated based on new information or evidence.

behavioral game theory. The branch of game theory that incorporates insights from psychology to model and analyze how an individual actually behaves in strategic interactions, rather than assuming perfectly rational decision-making.

brinkmanship. When a player or party deliberately creates a situation with potentially severe consequences if an agreement is not reached. The strategy is intended to force the other party to back down or make concessions.

commitment game. A game where one or more individuals commit themselves to a particular course of action that affects the outcomes for all involved parties.

commuting-time paradox. The idea that, even as people earn more money and transit options improve, people's commute times stay the same.

comparative advantage. The ability of an individual or group to produce a good or service at a lower opportunity cost than others.

competitive game. A game where players act in their self-interest, and the outcome for one player is often at the expense of others. See also *cooperative game.*

conspicuous consumption. The practice by an individual or household of spending money on goods and services primarily for the purpose of displaying their wealth or social status to others.

cooperative game. A game where players can form coalitions and work together to achieve goals or outcomes that may be shared. See also *competitive game.*

corner solution. Occurs when the ideal choice for a decision-maker is the most extreme choice within a set of limited options.

data cleaning. Fixing or removing incorrect, corrupted, or mis-formatted data within a dataset to avoid bad or misleading results.

decision fatigue. The feeling that leads to the declining quality of decisions made by an individual after a prolonged period of decision-making or when faced with a large number of choices.

deflationary spiral. The phenomenon in which people delay spending money because of a belief that their money could go further in the future due to declining prices.

demand. The willingness of consumers to purchase a product or service at a particular price.

diversification. The strategy of spreading investments or resources across a variety of assets, industries, sectors, or other categories.

economic surplus. The net gain that a person or group reaps from a business transaction. It represents the difference between the total value or benefit received and the total cost or sacrifice incurred.

endogenous preference formation. A model for how internal values and preferences develop over time. In the model, preferences are not fixed but are shaped within the eco-nomic system itself. Preferences are formed as a result of an individual's experiences and the environment, and individu-als adopt worldviews that shape their judgments about their experiences.

endowment effect. Refers to the phenomenon where people tend to assign a higher value to the things they own or feel attached to.

ESG (environmental, social, governance) index funds. An index fund that includes investments only in companies that meet criteria based on environmental, social, or governance factors.

evolutionary game theory. The branch of game theory applies the concepts of game theory to the survival of animals and the natural selection of animal behaviors.

expected utility theory. A fundamental concept in economics, which posits that individuals weigh uncertain outcomes according to their likelihood and the net benefit when making decisions.

external reward. A form of compensation or incentive that comes from an external source rather than being inherently satisfying or enjoyable.

externality. A side effect or consequence of an economic activity that affects parties who did not choose to incur that effect.

Federal Reserve. The central banking system of the United States, which sets interest rates and monetary policy to control inflation and unemployment; a.k.a. *the Fed*. The Fed includes 12 member banks, including Boston, and a Board of Governors in Washington, DC, a.k.a. *Federal Reserve Board*.

first-order beliefs. A player's initial beliefs or knowledge about the game.

game theory. The branch of mathematics and economics that studies how people make strategic decisions when the results depend on the decisions of others. It examines how people or groups interact, taking into account their preferences, strategies, and likely outcomes.

gender pay gap. The difference in average or median earnings between men and women in the workforce. Contributing factors include gender differences in occupation and industry, gender differences in roles and expectations in the workplace and at home, discrimination, women taking time off from work for child rearing, and women working fewer hours.

halo effect. A cognitive bias where a person's overall impression of a product, brand, corporation, or individual is influenced by specific attributes or qualities, such as physical appearance or social status.

hawk–dove game. A game in which two players square off to gain a reward and have the choice to act like either bully hawks or pushover doves.

herding. The tendency of individuals to follow the actions of a larger group, without independently evaluating the information or options.

higher-order beliefs. Beliefs that go beyond initial beliefs or knowledge of a game. See also *first-order beliefs*, *second-order beliefs*, and *third-order beliefs*.

household production. The various goods and services produced or provided within a household for the consumption and well-being of its members, such as home maintenance, home organization, cooking, child rearing, and emotional support.

human capital. The skills, knowledge, education, training, and other attributes embodied in individuals that contribute to their ability to perform labor and create economic value.

hypothesis testing. The process of comparing the probability of living in a world where a fact is true to the probability that a fact is false. It is a statistical analysis to determine whether the observed data provides enough evidence to reject or fail to reject a hypothesis.

index fund. A type of investment fund. These funds track the performance of stocks or bonds of the total stock market or a subset of the market to achieve diversification.

inflation. The phenomenon in which money becomes less valuable due to an increase in the supply of money, causing an increase in the demand for goods and services which increases prices.

inside option. In the context of a negotiation, the payoff a party obtains from reaching an agreement.

internal reward. the inherent satisfaction, enjoyment, or fulfillment that an individual derives from engaging in a particular activity. Also known as an *intrinsic reward*.

land value (tax). The potential value of a parcel of land, not including property or other improvements to the land. A land value tax is distinct from property taxes, which tax a portion of the value of land and property combined.

law of diminishing marginal returns. *In the production of goods and services:* As the quantity of one input is increased while keeping other inputs constant, the incremental output or return derived from each additional unit of the input will eventually diminish. *In individual utility*: The more a person has of something, the less that person will value getting more of that thing.

law of large numbers. As the number of observations in a sample grows larger, the average of the sample will tend to get closer to the true probability for the population.

leisure time. The time that individuals engage in activities other than work.

loss aversion. The tendency to avoid losses over achieving similar gains.

management-hierarchy theory. A workplace leadership structure where employees are divided into layers determined by employee characteristics such as knowledge or tasks performed.

marginal benefit. The additional benefit or usefulness gained from making a choice or taking an action.

marginal cost. The extra cost that comes with making a choice or taking an action.

meritocracy. A system or society in which individuals' success and advancement are primarily determined by their abilities, talents, and achievements, rather than by factors such as social class, wealth, or family background.

mortgage interest deduction. A tax break that allows a homeowner to subtract interest paid on home mortgage from their taxable income.

Nash equilibrium. A stable state within a game where no player has an incentive to deviate from their selected strategy, given the strategies chosen by the other players.

negative reciprocity. The act of responding to a negative action with another negative action, often as a form of retaliation with the intention to harm an opponent.

negatively correlated. When the values of two variables tend to move in opposite directions.

negativity bias. A psychological phenomenon describing the tendency of individuals to give more weight or attention to negative information, experiences, or stimuli compared to positive ones.

negging. *In game theory:* When a player attempts to lower an opponent's perceived value of their outside options to make their inside option seem better. *In the psychology of dating:* when a person intentionally lowers the self-esteem of a potential dating partner to increase their own perceived attractiveness.

negotiating power. The ability and leverage that a party possesses in influencing the terms, conditions, and outcomes of a negotiation. Depends on each player's outside options, propensity for taking risks, and willingness to wait.

negotiation game. A situation in which two or more parties engage in discussions, interactions, or strategic decision-making with the aim of reaching a mutually acceptable agreement.

NIMBY. The acronym for "Not in my backyard"; refers to home-owners who oppose new housing construction or other development.

null hypothesis. Represents the world, conditions, and assumptions that would be consistent with a hypothesis being false.

one-shot games. An isolated game where players make decisions without considering the future repercussions.

opportunity cost. The value of an individual's or group's outside option to an agreement or decision.

optimal foraging theory. A conceptual framework in ecology that explores the strategies and decision-making processes used by organisms when obtaining and consuming food in order to maximize their energy gain or likelihood of survival.

optimism bias. The tendency to overestimate the likelihood of favorable outcomes and underestimate the likelihood of unfavorable outcomes.

outside option. In the context of a negotiation, the payoff a party obtains when no agreement is reached. It is the best alternative to a negotiation agreement.

***p*-value.** A statistical measure giving the probability that no effect would be detected if the data was drawn again under the same circumstances. Used to statistical evidence against a *null hypothesis*.

paradox of choice. When an increase in choices leads to a decrease in utility or happiness.

GLOSSARY 231

permanent-income hypothesis. Suggests that individuals make decisions about their spending based on long-term expectations about their earnings.

piece-rate compensation. An incentive system in economics where individuals are paid based on the quantity of output or work they produce rather than receiving a fixed salary or hourly wage. This type of compensation is one of many methods used by employers to align the interests of workers with the goals of the employer.

positively correlated. When the values of two variables tend to move in the same direction.

present bias. The tendency of individuals to place a higher value on immediate payoffs compared to future payoffs.

principal–agent problem. The misalignment in goals and incentives between a principal who assigns tasks and an agent who performs tasks.

producer–scrounger game. A game that models the tradeoff between two primary foraging strategies—being a "producer" and being a "scrounger." Producers actively search for food and scroungers wait and watch to take advantage of food found by scroungers.

progressive tax. A tax that is more burdensome on the rich than the poor.

projection bias. A cognitive bias where individuals assume that their current preferences, attitudes, or beliefs will remain relatively stable over time.

public good. A project, product, or service with the potential to benefit everyone. Examples include public parks, public education, public safety departments, and public housing.

recency bias. The tendency to give more weight or consideration to recent events or information when making decisions.

reference point. A benchmark against which an individual evaluates their current situation or make decisions. Serves as a point of comparison that influences the decision-making process.

regressive tax. A tax that is more burdensome on the poor than the rich.

relative income. How much a person earns in comparison to others.

repeated game. A game that unfolds over multiple periods, allowing players to observe and respond to each other's actions. In repeated games, players can build a reputation that can influence other player's beliefs and choices.

scarcity. The inherent imbalance between the limited availability of resources and the insatiable desire for those resources.

second-order beliefs. A player's beliefs about the first-order beliefs of other players.

selection bias. A situation where the sample used for analysis is unrepresentative of the broader population, leading to skewed or inaccurate results.

signaling. The credible and intentional conveyance of information about yourself to another person or player.

sin tax. A tax that discourages an undesirable or harmful behavior like drinking, gambling, or smoking.

starting conditions. The initial set of rules, circumstances, skills, resources, and difficulties that players face in a game.

statistical discrimination. A form of stereotyping where a decision about a person is based on statistical information about that person's group identity. Distinct from *taste-based discrimination*.

status quo bias. The tendency of individuals to prefer the current state of affairs and exhibit resistance to change.

GLOSSARY   233

strategic voting. In game theory, a situation where voters do not cast their ballots according to their true preferences but instead vote strategically to achieve a specific outcome. Voters may vote strategically when they anticipate that their preferred candidate or outcome is unlikely to win or when they want to prevent a less desirable outcome.

sunk-cost fallacy. The cognitive bias where individuals continue with a project after devoting time, money, or effort to it, despite the costs outweighing the benefits moving forward.

supply. The willingness of sellers or producers to provide a good or service at a particular price.

survivorship bias. The tendency to focus on successful outcomes or "winners" in a particular field while ignoring or dismissing those that did not make it through a selection process. This bias can cause a skewed perception of what factors lead to success.

taste-based discrimination. Discrimination or prejudice rooted in an individual's preferences or tastes. Distinct from *statistical discrimination*.

tempo. The speed at which a player can execute a strategy within a game.

third-order beliefs. A player's beliefs about the second-order beliefs of other players.

time inconsistency. When an individual's preferences change over time, leading to inconsistencies or conflicts in their choices at different points in time.

tolerance for risk. The willingness to place a bet to potentially gain a reward; a.k.a. *risk tolerance*.

tournament. A competitive structure or incentive system where individuals or groups compete against each other to achieve a certain goal or outcome. The concept is often used to describe situations where participants engage in a contest or competition, and the rewards or incentives are based on relative performance rather than absolute achievements.

traditional game theory. The branch of game theory that assumes rationality and selfishness drive people's strategic choices.

ultimatum game. A type of negotiation game in which the first moving player makes a take-it-or-leave-it offer and the second moving player either accepts or rejects the offer.

undifferentiated product. A product or service that is identical or very similar to those offered by competitors in the market.

utility. The value a person gets from doing something. This concept is used to quantify the subjective well-being or happiness that individuals derive from their choices.

willingness to pay. The maximum amount of money a person is willing to spend on a product or service.

winner's curse. A phenomenon in auctions where the winning bidder ends up paying more for an item than it is actually worth. It occurs when bidders in an auction have incomplete information about the true value of the item being auctioned, and the winning bidder is the one who overestimates the item's value the most.

zugzwang. German, "compulsion to move." Used by game theorists to denote any move that directly changes the expected outcome of a game from a win to a loss.

NOTES

INTRODUCTION

1. Melissa Koller, "Income Inequality Down Due to Drops in Real Incomes at the Middle and Top, but Post-Tax Income Estimates Tell a Different Story," Census.gov, September 12, 2023, accessed January 22, 2024, https://www.census.gov/library/stories/2023/09/income-inequality.html.

2. Doug Irving, "What Would It Take to Close America's Black-White Wealth Gap?," RAND, May 9, 2023, https://www.rand.org/pubs/articles/2023/what-would-it-take-to-close-americas-black-white-wealth-gap.html.

3. Jill E. Yavorsky, Lisa A. Keister, Yue Qian, and Michael Nau, "Women in the One Percent: Gender Dynamics in Top Income Positions," *American Sociological Review* 84, no. 1 (February 2019): 54–81, https://doi.org/10.1177/0003122418820702.

4. Raj Chetty, David Grusky, Maximilian Hell, Nathaniel Hendren, Robert Manduca, and Jimmy Narang, "The Fading American Dream: Trends in Absolute Income Mobility since 1940," *Science* 356, no. 6336 (2017): 398–406.

CHAPTER 1

1. See Milton Friedman, *Capitalism and Freedom* (University of Chicago Press, 1962).

2. Lily Katz, "January Was the Most Competitive Month on Record for Homebuyers," Redfin Real Estate News, February 23, 2022, https://www.redfin.com/news/real-estate-bidding-wars-january-2022/.

236 NOTES TO PAGES 15-26

3. Katz, "January Was the Most Competitive Month."
4. Anne C. Gielen and Jan C. van Ours, "Layoffs, Quits and Wage Negotiations," *Economics Letters* 109, no. 2 (2010): 108–11.
5. Marta Lachowska, Alexandre Mas, Raffaele Saggio, and Stephen A. Woodbury, "Wage Posting or Wage Bargaining? A Test Using Dual Jobholders," *Journal of Labor Economics* 40, no. S1 (2022): S469–93.
6. Shushanik Margaryan, Nils Saniter, Mathias Schumann, and Thomas Siedler, "Do Internships Pay Off? The Effects of Student Internships on Earnings," *Journal of Human Resources* 57, no. 4 (2022): 1242–75.
7. Philip Oreopoulos, Till von Wachter, and Andrew Heisz, "The Short- and Long-Term Career Effects of Graduating in a Recession," *American Economic Journal: Applied Economics* 4, no. 1 (2012): 1–29.
8. P. C. de Looff, L. J. M. Cornet, P. J. C. M. Embregts, H. L. I. Nijman, and H. C. M. Didden, "Associations of Sympathetic and Parasympathetic Activity in Job Stress and Burnout: A Systematic Review," *PLoS ONE* 13, no. 10 (2018): e0205741; Jennifer E. Ho, Martin G. Larson, Anahita Ghorbani, Susan Cheng, Erin E. Coglianese, Ramachandran S. Vasan, and Thomas J. Wang, "Long-Term Cardiovascular Risks Associated with an Elevated Heart Rate: The Framingham Heart Study," *Journal of the American Heart Association* 3, no. 3 (2014): e000668; Julian F. Thayer and Richard D. Lane, "Claude Bernard and the Heart–Brain Connection: Further Elaboration of a Model of Neurovisceral Integration," *Neuroscience & Biobehavioral Reviews* 33, no. 2 (2009): 81–88.
9. Sophie Béjean and Hélène Sultan-Taïeb, "Modeling the Economic Burden of Diseases Imputable to Stress at Work," *European Journal of Health Economics* 6, no. 1 (2005): 16–23.
10. Lisa B. Kahn, "The Long-Term Labor Market Consequences of Graduating from College in a Bad Economy," *Labour Economics* 17, no. 2 (2010): 303–16.

CHAPTER 2

1. Claire Liu, "Female Economics Professors Talk Gender Dynamics in the Field," *Brown Daily Herald*, April 1, 2021, accessed January 20, 2023, https://www.browndailyherald.com/article/2021/04/female -economics-professors-talk-gender-dynamics-in-the-field; Gary A. Hoover and Ebonya Washington, "Report: Committee on the Status of Minority Groups in the Economics Profession (CSMGEP)," *AEA Papers and Proceedings* 111 (2021):764–79.
2. Anthony Saidy, Norman Lessing, and Norman Snyder, *The World of Chess* (London: Collins, 1974). The following discussion draws from this book unless otherwise cited.

NOTES TO PAGES 27-36   237

3. "In elite tournament games": Julio González-Díaz and Ignacio Palacios-Huerta, "Cognitive Performance in Competitive Environments: Evidence from a Natural Experiment," *Journal of Public Economics* 139 (2016): 47.

4. Andreas Fagereng, Magne Mogstad, and Marte Rønning, "Why Do Wealthy Parents Have Wealthy Children?," *Journal of Political Economy* 129, no. 3 (2021): 703–56.

5. Kerwin Kofi Charles and Erik Hurst, "The Correlation of Wealth across Generations," *Journal of Political Economy* 111, no. 6 (2003): 1155–82.

6. Daniel Barth, Nicholas W. Papageorge, and Kevin Thom, "Genetic Endowments and Wealth Inequality," *Journal of Political Economy* 128, no. 4 (2020): 1474–522.

7. Michael Hughes and Bradley R. Hertel, "The Significance of Color Remains: A Study of Life Chances, Mate Selection, and Ethnic Consciousness among Black Americans," *Social Forces* 68, no. 4 (1990): 1105–20; Arthur H. Goldsmith, Darrick Hamilton, and William Darity Jr., "From Dark to Light: Skin Color and Wages among African-Americans," *Journal of Human Resources* 42, no. 4 (2007): 701–38.

8. Sum from 62 to 100 (100 choose k) * $(.5 \wedge k)$ * $(.5 \wedge (100 - k))$ = .01

9. Sum from 6 to 10 (10 choose k) * $(.5 \wedge (k))$ * $(.5 \wedge (10 - k))$ = .38

10. $.89 \wedge 22$ = .08

11. $(6/16) * (5/15) * (4/14) * (3/13) * (2/12) * (1/11)$ = 0.0001

12. Valerie K. Bostwick and Bruce A. Weinberg, "Nevertheless She Persisted? Gender Peer Effects in Doctoral STEM Programs," *Journal of Labor Economics* 40, no. 2 (2022): 397–436.

13. Claire Liu, "Female Economics Professors Talk Gender Dynamics in the Field," *Brown Daily Herald*, April 1, 2021, accessed January 20, 2023, https://www.browndailyherald.com/article/2021/04/female-eco nomics-professors-talk-gender-dynamics-in-the-field.

14. *Report of the Committee on the Status of Minority Groups in the Economics Profession (CSMGEP)* (American Economic Association, December 2022), 3, 6.

15. (9 choose 4) / (38 choose 4) = 0.002

16. Brittany Bloodhart, Meena M. Balgopal, Anne Marie A. Casper, Laura B. Sample McMeeking, and Emily V. Fischer, "Outperforming yet Undervalued: Undergraduate Women in STEM," *PLoS ONE* 15, no. 6 (2020): e0234685.

17. Hessel Oosterbeek and Reyn van Ewijk, "Gender Peer Effects in University: Evidence from a Randomized Experiment," *Economics of Education Review* 38 (2014): 51–63.

18. Vanessa K. Bohns and Lauren A. DeVincent, "Rejecting Unwanted Romantic Advances Is More Difficult Than Suitors Realize," *Social Psychological and Personality Science* 10, no. 8 (2019): 1102–10.

19. P (x successes in n tried) = (n choose x) * p ^ x * (1 − p) ^ (n − x)
    (1/3)^8 + (8 choose 1) * (2/3) * (1/3)^7 + (8 choose 2) * (2/3)^2 *
    (1/3)^6 = .02
20. Patricia A. Hutton, "Understanding Student Cheating and What Educators Can Do about It," *College Teaching* 54, no. 1 (2006): 171–76.
21. David Card, Stefano DellaVigna, Patricia Funk, and Nagore Iriberri, "Gender Differences in Peer Recognition by Economists," *Econometrica* 90, no. 5 (2022): 1937–71.
22. Eleonora Broccardo, Oliver Hart, and Luigi Zingales, "Exit versus Voice," *Journal of Political Economy* 130, no. 12 (2022): 3101–45.
23. B. Douglas Bernheim, Luca Braghieri, Alejandro Martínez-Marquina, and David Zuckerman, "A Theory of Chosen Preferences," *American Economic Review* 111, no. 2 (2021): 720–54.
24. Thomas S. Ferguson, "Who Solved the Secretary Problem?," *Statistical Science* 4, no. 3 (1989): 282–89, http://www.jstor.org/stable/2245639.
25. Daniel Kahneman, Jack L. Knetsch, and Richard H. Thaler, "Anomalies: The Endowment Effect, Loss Aversion, and Status Quo Bias," Journal of Economic Perspectives 5, no. 1 (Winter 1991): 193–206.

CHAPTER 3

1. Ernst Fehr and Ian Krajbich. "Social Preferences and the Brain," in *Neuroeconomics* (Academic Press, 2014), 193–218.
2. Gary Charness and Matthew Rabin, "Expressed Preferences and Behavior in Experimental Games," *Games and Economic Behavior* 53, no. 2 (2005): 151–69.
3. Alan B. Krueger, *Rockonomics: A Backstage Tour of What the Music Industry Can Teach Us about Economics and Life* (Currency, 2019), 84.
4. Elizabeth A. Harris, Alexandra Alter, and Adam Bednar, "A Trial Put Publishing's Inner Workings on Display. What Did We Learn?," *New York Times*, August 19, 2022, https://www.nytimes.com/2022/08/19/books/prh-penguin-random-house-trial.html.
5. Edward N. Wolff, *Household Wealth Trends in the United States, 1962 to 2016: Has Middle Class Wealth Recovered?* (working paper 24085, National Bureau of Economic Research, 2017), www.nber.org/papers/w24085.
6. George A. Akerlof, "The Market for 'Lemons': Quality Uncertainty and the Market Mechanism," *Quarterly Journal of Economics* 84, no. 3 (1970): 488–500.
7. Pam Erickson Otto, "Good Natured: Blue Jay Calls," Hickory Knolls Discovery Center, September 7, 2018, accessed January 20, 2023, https://www.stcnature.org/blue-jay-calls/; Natural Selections, "Natural

NOTES TO PAGES 58–74   239

Deceptions: Tricks Animals Play on Competitors," North Country Public Radio, March 7, 2019, accessed January 20, 2023, https://www.northcountrypublicradio.org/news/story/25373/20190307/natural-deceptions-tricks-animals-play-on-competitors.

8. Antonio J. Golubski, Nathaniel S. O'Connell, Jesse A. Schwartz, and Sean F. Ellermeyer, "A 'Crying Wolf' Game of Interspecific Kleptoparasitic Mutualism," *Biology Letters* 10, no. 3 (2014): 20140073.

9. D. Ellsberg, "Risk, Ambiguity, and the Savage Axioms," *Quarterly Journal of Economics* 75, no. 4 (1961): 643–69.

10. Daniel Ellsberg, "Risk, Ambiguity, and the Savage Axioms," *Quarterly Journal of Economics* 75, no. 4 (1961): 643–69.

11. Rosemarie Nagel, "Unraveling in Guessing Games: An Experimental Study," *American Economic Review* 85, no. 5 (1995): 1313–26, http://www.jstor.org/stable/2950991.

12. WGBH Educational Foundation and Clear Blue Sky Productions, "Jacanas and Polyandry," *NOVA: Evolution*, 2001, accessed January 20, 2023, http://www.pbs.org/wgbh/evolution/library/01/6/l_016_04.html.

CHAPTER 4

1. Alan Benson, "A Theory of Dual Job Search and Sex-Based Occupational Clustering," *Industrial Relations: A Journal of Economy and Society* 54, no. 3 (2015): 367–400.

2. Mo Costandi, "Bowerbird Builds a House of Illusions to Improve His Chances of Mating," *Guardian*, January 19, 2012, sec. Science, https://www.theguardian.com/science/neurophilosophy/2012/jan/19/1.

3. Costandi, "Bowerbird Builds House of Illusions."

4. John A. Endler, Lorna C. Endler, and Natalie R. Doerr, "Great Bowerbirds Create Theaters with Forced Perspective When Seen by Their Audience," *Current Biology* 20, no. 18 (2010): 1679–84.

5. Laura A. Kelley and John A. Endler, "Illusions Promote Mating Success in Great Bowerbirds," *Science* 335, no. 6066 (2012): 335–38.

6. Philippe Sterkens, Ralf Caers, Marijke De Couck, Michael Geamanu, Victor Van Driessche, and Stijn Baert, "Costly Mistakes: Why and When Spelling Errors in Resumes Jeopardise Interview Chances," *PLoS ONE* 18, no. 4 (2023): e0283280; Ronald D. David, Robert H. Willoughby, and Harold M. Maurer, "Dysgraphia and Superior Intelligence: A Processing Syndrome?," *Pediatric Research* 11, no. 4 (1977): 376–376.

7. Amrisha Vaish, Tobias Grossmann, and Amanda Woodward, "Not All Emotions Are Created Equal: The Negativity Bias in Social-Emotional Development," *Psychological Bulletin* 134, no. 3 (May 2008): 383–403, https://doi.org/10.1037/0033-2909.134.3.383.

240 NOTES TO PAGES 74–87

8. "Daryl—Baby Girl Name Meaning, Origin, and Popularity," BabyCenter, n.d., accessed June 30, 2023, https://www.babycenter.com/baby-names/details/daryl-63005.

9. Marianne Bertrand and Sendhil Mullainathan, "Are Emily and Greg More Employable Than Lakisha and Jamal? A Field Experiment on Labor Market Discrimination," *American Economic Review* 94, no. 4 (2004): 991–1013.

10. Richard E. Nisbett and Timothy D. Wilson. "The Halo Effect: Evidence for Unconscious Alteration of Judgments," *Journal of Personality and Social Psychology* 35, no. 4 (1977): 250.

11. Christopher G. Wetzel, Timothy D. Wilson, and James Kort. "The Halo Effect Revisited: Forewarned Is Not Forearmed," *Journal of Experimental Social Psychology* 17, no. 4 (1981): 427–439.

12. Daniel S. Hamermesh, "Beauty Pays," in *Beauty Pays* (Princeton University Press, 2011), esp. 43.

13. Timothy Feddersen and Wolfgang Pesendorfer, "Convicting the Innocent: The Inferiority of Unanimous Jury Verdicts under Strategic Voting," *American Political Science Review* 92, no. 1 (1998): 23–35.

14. Stijn Baert, "Hiring Discrimination: An Overview of (Almost) All Correspondence Experiments since 2005," *Audit Studies: Behind the Scenes with Theory, Method, and Nuance* (2018): 63–77.

CHAPTER 5

1. Taylor Marr, "Stock Market vs. Real Estate: Which Has Rebounded Better since the Recession?," Redfin Real Estate News, November 14, 2016, accessed July 2, 2023, https://www.redfin.com/news/stock-market-vs-real-estate-which-has-rebounded-better-since-the-recession/.

2. Dana Anderson, "Homebuyers Need $107,000 Annually to Afford the Typical U.S. Home—Up 46% from a Year Ago," Redfin Real Estate News, November 15, 2022, https://www.redfin.com/news/homebuyer-income-increase-october-2022/.

3. Economic and Housing Research Group, "Housing Supply: A Growing Deficit," Freddie Mac, May 7, 2021, accessed January 20, 2023, https://www.freddiemac.com/research/insight/20210507-housing-supply.

4. Robert Dietz, "A Decade of Home Building: The Long Recovery of the 2010s," Eye On Housing, National Association of Home Builders, January 6, 2020, https://eyeonhousing.org/2020/01/a-decade-of-home-building-the-long-recovery-of-the-2010s/.

5. Emily Badger, "California's Housing Crisis Is Fueled by Nimbyism," *New York Times*, June 5, 2022, accessed December 29, 2022, https://www.nytimes.com/2022/06/05/business/economy/california-housing-crisis-nimby.html.

6. See Catalyst for Change, "Litigation Resources," n.d., accessed December 29, 2022, https://catalystsca.org/litigation-resources/.

7. Dana Anderson, "Black Americans Face Bigger Financial Barriers to Homeownership Than White Americans: Redfin Survey," June 29, 2021, accessed July 2, 2023, https://www.redfin.com/news/redfin-sur vey-black-homeownership-financial-barriers/.

8. Dana Anderson, "Just 45% of Black Families Own Their Home, Compared with 74% of White Families—and the Gap Has Hardly Narrowed over the Last Decade," Redfin Real Estate News, May 17, 2022, https://www.redfin.com/news/?p=74321.

9. Katherine Schaeffer, "Key Facts about Housing Affordability in the U.S.," Pew Research Center, March 23, 2022, accessed July 2, 2023, https://www.pewresearch.org/short-reads/2022/03/23/key-facts-about -housing-affordability-in-the-u-s/.

10. Whitney Airgood-Obrycki and Alexander Hermann ,"Affordability Gaps Widened for Renters in the First Year of the Pandemic," Joint Center for Housing Studies," July 20, 2022, accessed January 20, 2023, https://www.jchs.harvard.edu/blog/affordability-gaps-widened-renters -first-year-pandemic.

11. Gene Balk, "114,000 More People: Seattle Now Decade's Fastest-Growing Big City in All of U.S." *Seattle Times*, May 24, 2018, www .seattletimes.com/seattle-news/data/114000-more-people-seattle-now -this-decades-fastest-growing-big-city-in-all-of-united-states/.

12. José Mustre-del-Río and Emily Pollard, "What Explains Lifetime Earnings Differences across Individuals?," *Economic Review QI* (2019): 35–56, esp. 46.

13. Dana Anderson, "Millennials Still Want Single-Family Homes, Even If It Means a Long Commute," Redfin Real Estate News, November 21, 2019, https://www.redfin.com/news/millennial-homebuyers-prefer -single-family-homes/.

14. Jack L. Knetsch and John A. Sinden, "Willingness to Pay and Compensation Demanded: Experimental Evidence of an Unexpected Disparity in Measures of Value," *Quarterly Journal of Economics* 99, no. 3 (1984): 507–21.

15. Meghan R. Busse, Devin G. Pope, Jaren C. Pope, and Jorge Silva-Risso, *Projection Bias in the Car and Housing Markets* (no. w18212, National Bureau of Economic Research, 2012); Dana Anderson, "The Typical U.S. Home Changes Hands Every 13.2 Years," Redfin Real Estate News, March 2, 2022, https://www.redfin.com/news/?p=73951.

16. Edward P. Lazear, "Bait and Switch," *Journal of Political Economy* 103, no. 4 (1995): 813–30.

17. Amos Tversky and Daniel Kahneman, "Judgment under Uncertainty: Heuristics and Biases: Biases in Judgments Reveal Some Heuristics of Thinking under Uncertainty," *Science* 185, no. 4157 (1974): 1124–31.

NOTES TO PAGES 96-114

18. Emil Persson, Kinga Barrafrem, Andreas Meunier, and Gustav Tinghög, "The Effect of Decision Fatigue on Surgeons' Clinical Decision Making," *Health Economics* 28, no. 10 (2019): 1194–203.

19. M. Humayun Kabir, "Did Investors Herd during the Financial Crisis? Evidence from the U.S. Financial Industry," *International Review of Finance* 18, no. 1 (2018): 59–90.

CHAPTER 6

1. "Gouldian Finch," Australian Museum, updated October 12, 2020, accessed May 14, 2024, www.australian.museum/learn/animals/birds /gouldian-finch/; Hanna Kokko, Simon C. Griffith, and Sarah R. Pryke, "The Hawk–Dove Game in a Sexually Reproducing Species Explains a Colourful Polymorphism of an Endangered Bird," *Proceedings of the Royal Society B: Biological Sciences* 281, no. 1793 (2014): 20141794.

2. Jennifer Cheeseman Day, "Among the Educated, Women Earn 74 Cents for Every Dollar Men Make," US Census Bureau, May 29, 2019, accessed January 20, 2023, https://www.census.gov/library /stories/2019/05/college-degree-widens-gender-earnings-gap.html.

3. Daniel Storage, Tessa E. S. Charlesworth, Mahzarin R. Banaji, and Andrei Cimpian, "Adults and Children Implicitly Associate Brilliance with Men More than Women," *Journal of Experimental Social Psychology* 90 (September 1, 2020): 104020, https://doi.org/10.1016 /j.jesp.2020.104020.

4. NYU Web Communications, "Men More Likely Than Women to Be Seen as Brilliant," July 2, 2020, accessed January 20, 2023, http:// www.nyu.edu/content/nyu/en/about/news-publications/news/2020 /july/men-more-likely-than-women-to-be-seen-as-brilliant-.

5. Victoria L. Brescoll and Eric Luis Uhlmann, "Can an Angry Woman Get Ahead? Status Conferral, Gender, and Expression of Emotion in the Workplace," *Psychological Science* 19, no. 3 (March 2008): 268–75, https://doi.org/10.1111/j.1467-9280.2008.02079.x.

6. Mark Egan, Gregor Matvos, and Amit Seru, "When Harry Fired Sally: The Double Standard in Punishing Misconduct," *Journal of Political Economy* 130, no. 5 (2022): 1184–248.

7. Lucy M. Aplin and J. Morand-Ferron, "Stable Producer–Scrounger Dynamics in Wild Birds: Sociability and Learning Speed Covary with Scrounging Behaviour," *Proceedings of the Royal Society B: Biological Sciences* 284, no. 1852 (2017): 20162872.

8. Luc-Alain Giraldeau, Catherine Soos, and Guy Beauchamp, "A Test of the Producer–Scrounger Foraging Game in Captive Flocks of Spice Finches, *Loncbura punctulate*," *Behavioral Ecology and Sociobiology* 34 (1994): 251–56.

NOTES TO PAGES 115–131   243

9. Ralf H. J. M. Kurvers,, Herbert H. T. Prins, Sipke E. van Wieren, Kees van Oers, Bart A. Nolet, and Ronald C. Ydenberg, "The Effect of Personality on Social Foraging: Shy Barnacle Geese Scrounge More," *Proceedings of the Royal Society B: Biological Sciences* 277, no. 1681 (February 22, 2010): 601–8, https://doi.org/10.1098/rspb.2009.1474.

10. Rozina Sabur, "Beyonce Given 'Unprecedented' Control over *Vogue* Cover Shoot," *Telegraph*, July 31, 2018, https://www.telegraph.co.uk /news/2018/07/31/beyonce-given-unprecedented-control-vogue -cover-shoot/.

11. Daniel Kreps, "Beyoncé Announces She Is Pregnant with Twins," *Rolling Stone*, February 1, 2017, https://www.rollingstone.com/music /music-news/beyonce-announces-she-is-pregnant-with-twins-122303/.

12. Janelle Okwodu, "How Diggzy Became Fashion's Favorite Paparazzi," *Vogue*, June 4, 2021, https://www.vogue.com/article/diggzy-miles-diggs -fashions-favorite-paparazzi; Honest, "How Beyoncé Finesses the Paparazzi," YouTube video, 5:22, quotation at 2:51, accessed January 20, 2023, https://www.youtube.com/watch?v=gx8M9gYmYSY.

13. Honest, "How Beyoncé Finesses the Paparazzi," at 3:15.

14. Honest, at 3:58.

CHAPTER 7

1. Alan M. Benson, Danielle Li, and Kelly Shue, "Potential and the Gender Promotion Gap," *Academy of Management Proceedings* 2023, no. 1.

2. Devin, "Concert Review: Beyoncé Reigns at Roseland Ballroom," Rap-Up, August 15, 2011, accessed January 20, 2023, https://www.rap-up .com/2011/08/15/concert-review-beyonce-reigns-at-roseland-ballroom/.

3. Edward P. Lazear, "Performance Pay and Productivity," *American Economic Review* 90, no. 5 (2000): 1346–61.

4. Lazear, "Performance Pay and Productivity."

5. Dawei Fang, Thomas Noe, and Philipp Strack, "Turning Up the Heat: The Discouraging Effect of Competition in Contests," *Journal of Political Economy* 128, no. 5 (2020): 1940–75.

6. Oriana Bandiera, Iwan Barankay, and Imran Rasul, "Team Incentives: Evidence from a Firm Level Experiment," *Journal of the European Economic Association* 11, no. 5 (2013): 1079–114.

7. Bandiera, Barankay, and Rasul, "Team Incentives."

8. Erika Deserranno, Philipp Kastrau, and Gianmarco León-Ciliotta, *Promotions and Productivity: The Role of Meritocracy and Pay Progression in the Public Sector*," Working Paper Series, no. 180 (Center for Effective Global Action, University of Caliornia: 2021.

9. The State of the Workforce: Full Research Report 2019 (Association for Development and Research of Sustainable Infrastructure), accessed

January 20, 2023, http://adpri.org/wp-content/uploads/2020/07/The-State-of-the-Workforce-Full-Research-Report-2019.pdf.

10. Luis Garicano, "Hierarchies and the Organization of Knowledge in Production," *Journal of Political Eeconomy* 108, no. 5 (2000): 874–904.

11. Lorenzo Caliendo, Ferdinando Monte, and Esteban Rossi-Hansberg, "The Anatomy of French Production Hierarchies," *Journal of Political Economy* 123, no. 4 (2015): 809–52.

12. Luca Flabbi, Mario Macis, Andrea Moro, and Fabiano Schivardi, "Do Female Executives Make a Difference? The Impact of Female Leadership on Gender Gaps and Firm Performance," *Economic Journal* 129, no. 622 (2019): 2390–423.

CHAPTER 8

1. Sasha-Ann Simons, "More Couples Are Embracing Female Bread-winners, Despite Decades-Old Stigma," NPR, February 18, 2020, accessed January 20, 2023, https://www.npr.org/local/305/2020/02/18/807050015/more-couples-are-embracing-female-breadwinners-despite-decades-old-stigma.

2. US Bureau of Labor Statistics, "Working Wives in Married-Couple Families, 1967–2011," *TED: The Economics Daily* (blog), June 2, 2014, accessed January 20, 2023, https://www.bls.gov/opub/ted/2014/ted_20140602.htm.

3. Marianne Bertrand, Emir Kamenica, and Jessica Pan, "Gender Identity and Relative Income within Households," *Quarterly Journal of Economics* 130, no. 2 (2015): 571–614.

4. "Median Earnings for Women in 2021 Were 83.1 Percent of the Median for Men," *TED: The Economics Daily*, U.S. Bureau of Labor Statistics, January 24, 2022, accessed January 20, 2023, https://www.bls.gov/opub/ted/2022/median-earnings-for-women-in-2021-were-83-1-percent-of-the-median-for-men.htm#:~:text=FONT%20SIZE%3A%20PRINT%3A-,Median%20earnings%20for%20women%20in%202021%20were,of%20the%20median%20for%20men&text=In%202021%2C%20median%20weekly%20earnings,83.1%20percent%20of%20men's%20earnings.

5. Francine D. Blau and Lawrence M. Kahn, "The Gender Wage Gap: Extent, Trends, and Explanations," *Journal of Economic Literature* 55, no. 3 (2017): 789–865.

6. Bertrand, Kamenica, and Pan, "Gender Identity and Relative Income."

7. Bertrand, Kamenica, and Pan.

8. Joanna R. Pepin, Liana C. Sayer, and Lynne M. Casper, "Marital Status and Mothers' Time Use: Childcare, Housework, Leisure, and Sleep," *Demography* 55, no. 1 (2018): 107–33.

NOTES TO PAGES 144–150   **245**

9. Megan DeMatteo, "What's an Appropriate Amount to Spend on an Engagement Ring?," CNBC, last updated September 23, 2022, accessed January 20, 2023, https://www.cnbc.com/select/how-much-to-spend -on-engagement-ring/; Lauren Schwahn, "How Much Does the Average Wedding Cost?," NerdWallet, May 6, 2024, accessed May 15, 2024, https://www.nerdwallet.com/article/finance/how-much-does-average -wedding-cost.

10. Allan Drazen, "Time Inconsistency," University of Maryland, November 2016, https://econweb.umd.edu/~seulakim/601/601Files/dra zen2019/lecture_note/TIC_2016.pdf. For the formalization of time inconsistency in economics models, see George Loewenstein and Drazen Prelec, "Anomalies in Intertemporal Choice: Evidence and an Interpretation," *Quarterly Journal of Economics* 107, no. 2 (1992): 573–97.

11. George Loewenstein, Ted O'Donoghue, and Matthew Rabin, "Projection Bias in Predicting Future Utility," *Quarterly Journal of Economics* 118, no. 4 (2003): 1209–48.

12. David K. Dodd, Richard B. Stalling, and J. Bedell, "Grocery Purchases as a Function of Obesity and Assumed Food Deprivation," *International Journal of Obesity* 1, no. 1 (1977): 43–47.

13. Michael Schwarz and Konstantin Sonin, "A Theory of Brinkmanship, Conflicts, and Commitments," *Journal of Law, Economics, & Organization* 24, no. 1 (2008): 163–83.

14. Mark Banschick, "The High Failure Rate of Second and Third Marriages," *Psychology Today*, February 6, 2012, accessed February 22, 2024, https://www.psychologytoday.com/us/blog/the-intelligent -divorce/201202/the-high-failure-rate-of-second-and-third-marriages.

15. Gregory D. Hess, "Marriage and Consumption Insurance: What's Love Got to Do with It?," *Journal of Political Economy* 112, no. 2 (2004): 290–318.

16. Hess, "Marriage and Consumption Insurance."

17. Alexandra Killewald and Ian Lundberg, "New Evidence against a Causal Marriage Wage Premium," *Demography* 54, no. 3 (2017): 1007–28.

18. Gary Stanley Becker, *An Economic Analysis of the Family* (Economic and Social Research Institute, 1986); Emily Oster, *The Family Firm: A Data-Driven Guide to Better Decision Making in the Early School Years*, vol. 3 (Penguin, 2022).

19. Jacob Galley, "Stay-at-Home Mothers through the Years," U.S. Bureau of Labor Statistics, *Monthly Labor Review: Beyond BLS*, September 2014, accessed January 20, 2023, https://www.bls.gov/opub/mlr /2014/beyond-bls/stay-at-home-mothers-through-the-years.htm #:~:text=In%201967%2C%2049%20percent%20of,to%2029%20per cent%20in%202012.

20. Richard Fry, "Almost 1 in 5 Stay-at-Home Parents in the U.S. Are Dads," Pew Research Center, August 3, 2023, https://www.pewre search.org/short-reads/2023/08/03/almost-1-in-5-stay-at-home-parents -in-the-us-are-dads/.

21. Emma Hruby, "Allyson Felix Retirement: Top Moments from Her Record-Breaking Career," Just Women's Sports, July 15, 2022, accessed July 5, 2023, https://justwomenssports.com/article/allyson-felix-world -athletics-championships-final-race-retirement/.

22. Allyson Felix, Lindsay Crouse, Taige Jensen, and Max Cantor, "Opin-ion: Allyson Felix: My Own Nike Pregnancy Story," *New York Times*, May 22, 2019, sec. Opinion, https://www.nytimes.com/2019/05/22 /opinion/allyson-felix-pregnancy-nike.html.

23. Shelley J. Correll, Stephen Benard, and In Paik, "Getting a Job: Is There a Motherhood Penalty?," *American Journal of Sociology* 112, no. 5 (2007): 1297–338.

24. Danielle Sandler and Nichole Szembrot, *Maternal Labor Dynamics: Participation, Earnings, and Employer Changes* (Center for Economic Studies Working Paper Series, CES 19–33, US Census Bureau, 2019.

25. Aline Bütikofer, Sissel Jensen, and Kjell G. Salvanes, "The Role of Par-enthood on the Gender Gap among Top Earners," *European Economic Review* 109 (2018): 103–23.

26. Petter Lundborg, Erik Plug, and Astrid Würtz Rasmussen, "Can Women Have Children and a Career? IV Evidence from IVF Treat-ments," *American Economic Review* 107, no. 6 (2017): 1611–37.

27. Ilyana Kuziemko, Jessica Pan, Jenny Shen, and Ebonya Washington, *The Mommy Effect: Do Women Anticipate the Employment Effects of Mother-hood?* (National Bureau of Economic Research, no. w24740, 2018).

28. Maureen Sayres Van Niel, Richa Bhatia, Nicholas S. Riano, Ludmila de Faria, Lisa Catapano-Friedman, Simha Ravven, Barbara Weissman, et al., "The Impact of Paid Maternity Leave on the Mental and Physi-cal Health of Mothers and Children: A Review of the Literature and Policy Implications," *Harvard Review of Psychiatry* 28, no. 2 (2020): 113–26.

29. Maureen Sayres Van Niel, Richa Bhatia, Nicholas S. Riano, Ludmila de Faria, Lisa Catapano-Friedman, Simha Ravven, Barbara Weissman et al., "The Impact of Paid Maternity Leave on the Mental and Physical Health of Mothers and Children: A Review of the Literature and Policy Implications," *Harvard Review of Psychiatry* 28, no. 2 (2020): 113–26.

30. Women's Bureau, "Paid Family and Medical Leave Fact Sheet," US Department of Labor, n.d., accessed March 4, 2024, https://www.dol .gov/sites/dolgov/files/WB/paid-leave/PaidLeavefactsheet.pdf.

31. Jonas Jessen, Robin Jessen, and Jochen Kluve, "Punishing Potential Mothers? Evidence for Statistical Employer Discrimination from a Natural Experiment," *Labour Economics* 59 (2019): 164–72.

NOTES TO PAGES 158–173   **247**

32. Emilio J. Castilla and Stephen Benard, "The Paradox of Meritocracy in Organizations," *Administrative Science Quarterly* 55, no. 4 (2010): 543–676.

CHAPTER 9

1. Theresa J. Brown, Kristie Ferrara, and Nicole Schley, "The Relationship of Pregnancy Status to Job Satisfaction: An Exploratory Analysis," *Journal of Business and Psychology* 17, no. 1 (2002): 63–72.

2. Kepa M. Ormazabal, "The Law of Diminishing Marginal Utility in Alfred Marshall's Principles of Economics," *European Journal of the History of Economic Thought* 2, no. 1 (1995): 91–126, doi:10.1080/1042771950000 0096; Andrew T. Jebb, Louis Tay, Ed Diener, and Shigehiro Oishi. "Happiness, Income Satiation and Turning Points around the World," *Nature Human Behaviour* 2, no. 1 (2018): 33–38.

3. Betsey Stevenson and Justin Wolfers, *Economic Growth and Subjective Well-Being: Reassessing the Easterlin Paradox* (working paper w14282, National Bureau of Economic Research, 2008).

4. Taraji P. Henson and Denene Millner, *Around the Way Girl: A Memoir*. (New York: 37 Ink/Atria, 2016). The following discussion draws from this book unless otherwise cited.

5. Britt Stephens, "Taraji P. Henson Isn't Taking a Penny Less Than She Deserves: 'Honey, a Zero Is Missing,'" PopSugar, January 18, 2019, https://www.popsugar.com/celebrity/taraji-p-henson-quotes-negotiat ing-her-salary-jan-2019-45692539.

6. Abhinay Muthoo, "A Non-technical Introduction to Bargaining Theory," *World Economics (Henley-on-Thames)* 1, no. 2 (2000): 145–66, definition on 148–54.

7. Daniel Kahneman, "Reference Points, Anchors, Norms, and Mixed Feelings," *Organizational Behavior and Human Decision Processes* 51, no. 2 (1992): 296–312.

8. Jena McGregor, "With Protests, Silence Is 'Not an Option' for Corporate America," *Washington Post*, June 1, 2020, accessed July 5, 2023, https://www.washingtonpost.com/business/2020/06/01/with -protests-silence-is-not-an-option-corporate-america/; Netflix, "To be silent is to be complicit. Black lives matter . . . ," Twitter, May 30, 2020, 2:30 p.m., accessed July 5, 2023, https://twitter.com/netflix/sta tus/1266829242353893376.

9. Andrea Alfano, "Do Peacocks Pay a Price for Beauty?," Audubon, October 9, 2014, https://www.audubon.org/news/do-peacocks-pay -price-beauty.

10. Thorstein Veblen, *The Theory of the Leisure Class* (Routledge, 2017), chap. 4.

248 NOTES TO PAGES 173–194

11. Veblen and Mills, *Theory of the Leisure Class*, chap. 4.

12. Kerwin Kofi Charles, Erik Hurst, and Nikolai Roussanov, "Conspicuous Consumption and Race," *Quarterly Journal of Economics* 124, no. 2 (2009): 425–67.

13. See Muthoo, "Non-technical Introduction to Bargaining Theory."

14. Simon Jäger, Christopher Roth, Nina Roussille, and Benjamin Schoefer, *Worker Beliefs about Outside Options* (no. w29623, National Bureau of Economic Research, 2022.)

15. Moshe A. Barach and John J. Horton, "How Do Employers Use Compensation History? Evidence from a Field Experiment," *Journal of Labor Economics* 39, no. 1 (2021): 193–218.

16. Kathleen Green, Zoe Kukan, and Ruth J. Tully, "Public Perceptions of 'Negging': Lowering Women's Self-Esteem to Increase the Male's Attractiveness and Achieve Sexual Conquest," *Journal of Aggression, Conflict and Peace Research* 9, no. 2 (2017): 95.

CHAPTER 10

1. See Sendhil Mullainathan and Eldar Shafir, *Scarcity: Why Having Too Little Means So Much* (Macmillan, 2013).

2. See, for example, Rutger Bregman, "Poverty Isn't a Lack of Character, It Is a Lack of Cash," filmed April 2017, Vancouver, BC, TED video, 14:48, https://www.ted.com/talks/rutger_bregman_poverty_isn_t_a _lack_of_character_it_s_a_lack_of_cash?language=en.

3. "Do Birds Store Food for the Winter?," All About Birds, Cornell Lab, April 1, 2009, https://www.allaboutbirds.org/news/do-birds-store -food-for-the-winter/#.

4. Gustav Axelson, "Soul Mates: Nutcrackers, Whitebark Pine, and a Bond That Holds an Ecosystem Together," All About Birds, Cornell Lab, October 7, 2015, https://www.allaboutbirds.org/news/soul-mates-nut crackers-whitebark-pine-and-a-bond-that-holds-an-ecosystem-together/.

5. Milton Friedman, "The Permanent Income Hypothesis," in *A Theory of the Consumption Function*, 20–37 (Princeton University Press, 1957).

6. See, for example, Lea Cassar and Stephan Meier, "Nonmonetary Incentives and the Implications of Work as a Source of Meaning," *Journal of Economic Perspectives* 32, no. 3 (2018): 215–38.

7. Robert H. Frank, "What Price the Moral High Ground?," *Southern Economic Journal* 63, no. 1 (1996): 1–17.

8. Dana Chandler and Adam Kapelner, "Breaking Monotony with Meaning: Motivation in Crowdsourcing Markets," *Journal of Economic Behavior & Organization* 90 (2013): 123–33.

9. Jos Van Ommeren and Piet Rietveld, "The Commuting Time Paradox," *Journal of Urban Economics* 58, no. 3 (2005): 437–54.

NOTES TO PAGES 194–199 **249**

10. George Loewenstein, "Is More Choice Always Better," *Social Security Brief* 7, no. 1 (1999): 7.

11. Katie Raynolds and Lorraine Woellert, "Survey: 25% of Homebuyers Are Moving Because of the Pandemic." Redfin, August 5, 2020, updated October 7, 2020, accessed May 16, 2024. https://www.redfin.com/news/coronavirus-pandemic-drives-homebuyers-to-move/.

12. Dana Anderson, "Demand for Second Homes Is More Than Double Pre-pandemic Levels," Redfin Real Estate News, May 10, 2021, https://www.redfin.com/news/second-home-demand-doubles/.

13. Sheharyar Bokhari and Lily Katz, "Investor Home Purchases Fell 30% in Third Quarter, Largest Drop since Great Recession Aside from Pandemic Start," Redfin Real Estate News, November 22, 2022, https://www.redfin.com/news/?p=75461.

14. Dana Anderson, "Homebuyers Are Flocking to the Sun Belt, Attracted to Relatively Affordable Home Prices," Redfin Real Estate News, December 19, 2022, https://www.redfin.com/news/?p=75574.

15. Steven D. Levitt, "Heads or Tails: The Impact of a Coin Toss on Major Life Decisions and Subsequent Happiness," *Review of Economic Studies* 88, no. 1 (2021): 378–405.

16. D. A. Roshier, N. I. Klomp, and Martin Asmus, "Movements of a Nomadic Waterfowl, Grey Teal *Anas gracilis*, across Inland Australia—Results from Satellite Telemetry spanning Fifteen Months." *ARDEA-WAGENINGEN* 94, no. 3 (2006): 461; David Roshier, Martin Asmus, and Marcel Klaassen, "What Drives Long-Distance Movements in the Nomadic Grey Teal *Anas gracilis* in Australia?," *Ibis* 150, no. 3 (2008): 474–84; BirdLife International, "Grey Teal *Anas gracilis*," accessed January 20, 2023, http://datazone.birdlife.org/species/factsheet/22680271.

17. See Lily Katz, Daryl Fairweather, and Sebastian Sandoval-Olascoaga, "Homebuyers with Access to Flood-Risk Data Bid on Lower-Risk Homes," Redfin, September 12, 2022, accessed December 31, 2022, www.redfin.com/news/redfin-users-interact-with-flood-risk-data/.

18. Federal Reserve Bank of St. Louis, "Consumer Price Index for All Urban Consumers: Rent of Primary Residence in Seattle–Tacoma–Bellevue WA (CBSA)," FRED, Federal Reserve Bank of St. Louis, accessed June 3, 2024, https://fred.stlouisfed.org/series/CUURA423SEHA.

19. Gene Balk, "Seattle Now Most Expensive City for Renters Outside California, Census Data Shows," NBC Right Now, July 30, 2019, updated August 4, 2019, accessed January 20, 2023, https://www.seattletimes.com/seattle-news/data/seattle-now-most-expensive-city-for-renters-outside-california-census-data-shows/.

250 NOTES TO PAGES 204–210

CHAPTER 11

1. Dana Anderson, "St. Louis, Chicago and Cleveland Are the Most Affordable Areas for Construction Workers to Buy Homes," Redfin Real Estate News, June 3, 2019, https://www.redfin.com/news/most-affordable-cities-for-construction-workers/.

2. Sheharyar Bokhari, "Value of House vs Land," Redfin, June 24, 2019, last updated October 6, 2020, accessed December 27, 2022, www.redfin.com/news/value-of-house-vs-land/.

3. Lily Katz, "Demand for Second Homes Surges 100% Year over Year in October," Redfin Real Estate News, November 19, 2020, https://www.redfin.com/news/second-home-purchases-soar-coronavirus-pandemic/; Lily Katz, "Luxury Home Sales Surge a Record 61%, Quadrupling Pre-pandemic Growth as America's Wealthiest Homebuyers Reap Gains of Uneven Economic Recovery," Redfin Real Estate News, December 23, 2020, https://www.redfin.com/news/luxury-versus-affordable-november-2020/.

4. Tim Ellis, "Housing Market Update: Typical Homebuyer's Mortgage Payment Up 15% since Mid-August," Redfin Real Estate News, September 29, 2022, https://www.redfin.com/news/housing-market-update-mortgage-payments-hit-new-high/.

5. David Hyde, "Liquor Is Everywhere Now in Washington, so Why Aren't We Drinking More?," KUOW/NPR Network, March 22, 2018, accessed May 15, 2024, https://www.kuow.org/stories/liquor-everywhere-now-washington-so-why-arent-we-drinking-more.

6. Office of Financial Management, "State & Local Government Revenue Sources: Washington State & Local Government Revenue Sources, Fiscal Year 2020," Washington Data & Research, accessed January 20, 2023, https://ofm.wa.gov/washington-data-research/statewide-data/washington-trends/revenue-expenditures-trends/state-local-government-revenue-sources#:~:text=Washington%20is%20one%20of%20a,than%20most%20any%20other%20state.

7. Tim Ellis, "Newly Listed Homes Get 3.4 Times More Online Views Than Those with a Price Drop," Redfin Real Estate News, May 25, 2019, https://www.redfin.com/news/listing-views-new-vs-price-drop/.

8. Gary S. Becker, *The Economics of Discrimination* (University of Chicago Press, 2010), chap. 7–8.

9. Matthew S. Goldberg, "Discrimination, Nepotism, and Long-Run Wage Differentials," *Quarterly Journal of Economics* 97, no. 2 (1982): 307–19.

10. Neil C. Bruce, "Real Estate Steering and the Fair Housing Act of 1968," *Tulsa Law Journal* 12 (1976): 758.

NOTES TO PAGES 210–214   251

11. Richard Rothstein, *The Color of Law: A Forgotten History of How Our Government Segregated America* (Liveright Publishing, 2017), 8, chap. 5.
12. See James Loewen, *Sundown Towns: A Hidden Dimension of American Racism.* (New Press, 2005).
13. Dana Anderson, "Just 45% of Black Families Own Their Home, Compared With 74% of White Families—and the Gap Has Hardly Narrowed over the Last Decade," Redfin Real Estate News, May 17, 2022, https://www.redfin.com/news/?p=74321.

CHAPTER 12

1. Mary Pilon, "The Secret History of Monopoly: The Capitalist Board Game's Leftwing Origins," *Guardian*, April 11, 2015, sec. Life and Style, https://www.theguardian.com/lifeandstyle/2015/apr/11/secret-history -monopoly-capitalist-game-leftwing-origins.
2. Edgar H. Johnson, "The Economics of Henry George's 'Progress and Poverty,'" *Journal of Political Economy* 18, no. 9 (1910): 714–35.

INDEX

academia, 41, 48, 50
Acrimony (film), 167
activist investors, optimal strategy
among, 43
ADP Research Institute, 131
advantages and disadvantages, 8, 25,
29, 51, 53, 171, 186; for Black players
on *Big Brother*, 31–32; in chess,
26–27
Aesop's Fables, 48
affirmative action, 40, 47
ageism, 37
aggression, 115
Airbnb, 215
Akerlof, George, 57
alliances, 32, 35
ambiguity aversion, 59, 223
analysis paralysis, 195
anchoring effect, 95–96, 223
anger, in workplace, 111
anxiety, work-related, 78–79
Apple Inc., 191
Arbeli, Tzahi, 15
attachment, in homebuying, 93–94, 102
attractiveness, as advantage, 77
attrition bias, 107, 118, 223

backward induction, 129–31, 133, 223
bait-and-switch marketing phenomenon,
95, 223
bankruptcy, 83
bartering, 170
Bayesian inference, 181, 224
Bear Stearns, 17
beauty contest game, 63–64
Becker, Gary, 150, 209
Bed-Stuy (Brooklyn neighborhood), 88
beliefs, higher-order, 169, 180, 226, 227,
232, 233
Benson, Alan, 70
Bertrand, Marianne, 142
Beyoncé. *See* Knowles, Beyoncé
biases held by recruiters, 81. *See also types
of bias*
bidding wars, 93, 95–96, 100, 207
Big Brother (game show), 31–32, 35
Big Tech, xvi, 165
birds: blue jays, 58; bowerbirds, 72–73,
79; Clark's nutcracker, 187; foraging
behavior of, 114; Gouldian finch,
104–6, 115; grey teal, 197; northern
jacana, 65; peacocks, 173; storing
seeds, 187–88, 190

254 INDEX

bluffing, 168, 175–79
board games, 25, 78; strategic, 129; trivial, 131. *See also* Catan (board game); Monopoly (board game)
brinkmanship, 146–47, 160, 224
Buddhism, 48–49
budgets: for housing, 89–91, 101–2; for renting, 90
bullying, 104–7, 114, 118–19
businesses, and social issues, 172

capitalism, 204, 215–16
car buying, 53, 57
career paths, 25
Carpenter, John, xvii
Catalysts for Local Control, 87
Catan (board game), 129–30
Charles, Kerwin, 28, 47, 174
cheating, 39–40
chess (game), 26–27, 29–31, 35, 46, 85, 171
Chestnut, Morris, 12–14, 148
chief economist salaries, 177, 179
childcare, 142–44
child rearing, 9, 142, 160; cost of, 154
children, as products, 150
class identity, 22
climate change, 105, 197
cognitive biases, 102
college admissions, 104
Collins, Susan, 219
commitment, benefits of, 146–48, 160
community, sense of, 185, 199–200, 214, 218
commuting, 92, 193–94
commuting-time paradox, 194, 224
company culture, 106. *See also* work culture
comparative advantage, 20, 22, 224. *See also* advantages and disadvantages
compensation, 177–79, 182; effect on work, 126; piece-rate, 126, 231
competition: effect on employee satisfaction, 126; in workplace, 126, 138
compromise, 12, 92, 144, 147, 219

confidence: role in negotiation, 2–3; in statistics, 31
conspicuous consumption, 173–75, 200, 224
corner solution, 186, 225
corporate hierarchies, 132
correlation, positive versus negative, 6, 149, 229, 231
cowardice, 115
Credit Karma, 89
Curious Case of Benjamin Button, The (film), 166–69

data cleaning, 78, 225
dating, probability of success in, 49
deception, 57–58
decision fatigue, 96, 225
decision-making, 7, 91, 93, 96, 98, 168, 208, 224, 230, 232
deflationary spiral, 189–90, 225
demand. *See* supply and demand
desire, 49
Destiny's Child, 54–58
detachment, 48–49
Diggs, Miles "Diggzy," 116–17
discrimination, 29, 37, 142, 158–60, 209–10; pregnancy, 152; statistical, 159, 232; taste-based, 209, 232, 233
diversification strategy, 65–66, 189, 191–92, 225
Donkey Kong, 1
dream job, 67–68
drug testing, occupational, 5–6, 218
Dubner, Stephen, xiv, xvi
Dungeons & Dragons, 199
dysgraphia, 74

economic knowledge, 6–7
economic mobility, 87
economics, xiv, xvi–xvii, 4, 8, 41, 50; behavioral, 3, 9, 50, 59, 84, 219; communication of, 193; models, 43–44, 48, 57, 126, 147, 150, 155, 192, 194, 209–10, 224, 225

economic surplus, 5–6, 23, 124, 225
economy, 7, 97, 189–92; free-market, 11, 209; rules of, 10, 213
educational attainment, genes for, 28
emergency savings, 102, 188–89, 191, 201
emotions, influence on decision-making, 93
empathy, 53, 169
employee satisfaction, 107–9, 133, 135, 219
employment relationship, 22
endgame, 129–30, 133
endogenous preference formation, 48, 225
endorsement deals, 151
endowment effect, 94, 168, 225
equity, 99
ESG (environmental, social, governance) index funds, 192, 226
expected utility theory, 100, 226
experience, 44, 46, 48, 51
experiments, 52, 54, 59, 72–73, 76, 94–95, 126, 158, 177, 197; on different ways of rewarding employees and productivity, 127; on effects of meritocratic promotions, 128
externality, 170, 226

Fair Housing Act of 1968, 210
Family and Medical Leave Act of 1993, 154
Farm Bill (2018), 218
favoritism, 209–10
fear of unknown, 52, 59–60, 178
Federal Reserve, 5, 189–90, 206, 226
Federal Reserve Bank of Boston, 4–5, 98, 179, 217–19
Felix, Allyson, 151–52
Fellows of the Econometric Society, 42
financial crisis, 17–18
financial security, 1, 4, 19, 83, 150, 216
Fincher, David, 166
flipping, in housing market, 205, 209–10
Floyd, George, 31, 172
foreclosure, 83, 98, 179, 203

Fox, Vivica A., 12, 14, 146, 148, 179–80
Freakonomics (Levitt and Dubner), xiii–xiv, xvi–xvii
Freddie Mac, 86
Friedman, Milton, 11, 188

games: cat-and-mouse, 111–12; of chance, 25; chicken, 147; choosing to play, 27, 45; commitment, 145–46, 148, 224; competitive, 103, 106, 108, 111, 118, 224; cooperative, 71, 103, 108, 118, 224; fair, 25; hawk–dove, 104, 112, 227; lottery, 45; negotiation, 2, 9, 12, 53, 57, 62, 144, 168, 174, 230; one-shot, 117, 230; playing multiple simultaneously, 141, 144; producer–scrounger, 114, 231; pursuit-evasion, 111, 119; repeated, 117–18, 232; ultimatum, 54; voting, 79–80, 233. *See also specific games*
game theory, xvii, 2, 6–8, 11, 50, 146, 169, 171, 181, 226, 234; behavioral compared to evolutionary, 7, 224; evolutionary, 105, 226
gaming the system, 126–27
gender bias, 110; and gap between promotions for men versus women, 122
gender differences, in occupation and industry, 142
gender diversity, in graduate school, 33
gender pay gap, 142, 226. *See also* women: earning less than men
genetics, producing unfairness in social ways, 29
Gen Z, 5
geographic mismatch, contributing to unemployment, 69
George, Henry, 213–14
Get Out (film), 130
Glassdoor, 60, 66
Goldberg, Matthew S., 209–10
graduate school, as alternative to finance lifestyle, 22
Great Depression, 18, 63
Great Recession, 4, 17

256 INDEX

groupthink, 80
guesses, educated versus uneducated, 62–63, 65–66

halo effect, 75–78, 81, 227; associated with beauty, 77
Hamermesh, Daniel, 77
Hannah, Daryl, 74
happiness, and money, 165, 185, 189, 200–201
Henson, Taraji P., 166–69, 172
herding behavior, 96–97, 100, 102, 227
Hokey Pokey, 45, 219
homebuyers, 195–97, 208; Black, 88, 209–10; first-time, 83, 86–87
homebuying: avoiding common mistakes in, 93–98; location versus size of homes, 92
homeless, housing-insecure, or unhoused people, 199, 215–16
homeowners, 4, 28, 95, 98, 198, 203, 207; first-generation, 87–88
homeownership, 83–84, 91
home prices, 87, 97, 204, 206–7, 211
home sellers, xvii, 206, 208–10
household production, 144, 149–50, 227
housing: affordable, 9–10, 87, 198, 200, 204; and inequality, 199, 209–10; shortage, in United States, 86–87
housing costs, 86, 90, 199
housing market, 189, 203–4, 206, 219; bubbles, 96; competitive, 14–15, 95, 100, 103; diversity and representation in, 208–9; relationship to broader economy, xvi–xvii, 17, 178–79
human capital, 46, 227
Hurst, Erik, 28, 174
Hustle & Flow (film), 166
hypothesis testing, 30, 227

imposter syndrome, 40, 80
incentives, 13, 117, 125
income: absolute versus relative, 165, 232; percentage of spent on housing, 88;

required to afford a midprice home in America, 86; top 1%, 3; top 10% compared to bottom 10%, 1
income histories, of job applicants, 177
income stability, 149
index funds, 191–92, 201, 227
inequality, 199, 209–10
infighting, 105–6
inflation, 189–90, 228
information: asymmetry, 53, 56–57, 61, 114, 223; importance of when playing games, 8; strategically shared, 72
information-gathering, 62
infrastructure, 214–15
integration, opposition to, 87
interest rates, 99, 206, 226
intergenerational living, 85–86
internships, 17–20, 22, 73
intuition, 44
investing, 65, 185–91, 200–201

job-candidate evaluations, 80
job interviews: onsite, 76–77, 79; preparing for, 75–76
job market, 28, 69–70, 182; weak, 18, 48, 103, 109
jobs: application process for, 8, 175; approach to finding, 67
job satisfaction, after giving birth, 163–64
job stress, effect on health and productivity, 21
job tenure, 136
JPMorgan Chase, 17
jury trials, and strategic voting, 79
justice, 55

Kahn, Lisa B., 22
Kahneman, Daniel, 95
Kamenica, Emir, 142
kingmakers, 130, 133, 135, 137–38
Knetsch, Jack, 94
Knowles, Beyoncé, xvii, 54–57, 107, 116–17, 124–25, 182

INDEX   257

Knowles, Mathew, 54–58, 107
Krueger, Alan B., 56

labor market. *See* job market
landlords, 97, 213, 215
landowners, 213–16
land values, 204, 211, 214–16, 228
law of diminishing marginal returns, 63,
    165, 228
law of large numbers, 30, 46, 228
Lazear, Edward, 47, 95, 126
laziness, 21
leadership principle, 77
Lean In, 2–3
learning, 45–46
Lehman Brothers, 17
leisure, 21, 228
Levitt, Steven, xiii–xiv, xvi–xvii, 25, 41–
    43, 47–48, 196
list price. *See* market value, versus list
    price
loss aversion, 168, 228
lottery, 45, 94, 106
luck, 30, 46, 139
Luckett, LeToya, 54–58, 107

Magie, Lizzie, 213
management-hierarchy theory, 132, 228
marginal benefit, and marginal cost, 37–
    40, 155, 229
market value, versus list price, 93, 95–96,
    100, 102
marriage, 9, 141–44, 160; and divorce,
    141, 144–46, 148; effect on men's
    earnings, 149; as financial strategy,
    148–50; as game, 144–46; as group
    project, 147; and occupations, 70–71;
    subsidized by tax code, 149
Marshall, Alfred, 165
maternity leave, 142, 150–57, 161, 164, 175,
    180; and health impacts, 154
meaning, and productivity, 193
medical leave, 158
meritocracy, 3, 121, 128, 136–37, 158, 229

Merrick, Walter, 87
Merrill Lynch, 17
microaggression, 61
micromanaging, 123
Millennials, 4–5
money, xiv, 21, 186–94, 200–201, 205,
    207, 224, 225, 228, 233, 234; in balanc-
    ing family and career, 144–45, 149–51,
    155; and happiness and self-worth,
    164–65, 167, 169–71, 174–75, 182, 185,
    215; and housing, 84–85, 88, 90, 98–
    99, 206, 208; made off of celebrities,
    116–17; redistributed, in Monopoly,
    214; in ultimatum game, 54–55
Monopoly (board game), 213–15
Morgan Stanley, 17, 19–20
mortgage interest deduction, 83, 205, 229
mortgages, 90, 99, 195, 206
motherhood, and career penalty, 150,
    152–54
motivation, 18, 193
Mullainathan, Sendhil, 186
music industry, 56
Muthoo, Abhinay, 168

Nagel, Rosemarie, 64
Namsor, 74
narrative, importance of when describing
    data, 41
Nash equilibrium, 13, 229
National Bureau of Economic Research,
    75, 94, 154, 165, 176
negative reciprocity, 54, 229
negativity bias, 74, 81, 229
negging, 181, 183, 229
negotiating power, 12, 15, 23, 57, 168, 176,
    194, 229; in job market, 16–17
negotiation, 8, 11–14, 23, 146, 148, 167–
    69, 172; of salary or raise, 61, 172, 174–
    76, 178; under uncertainty, 60–62. *See
    also* games: negotiation
nepotism, 209–10
Never Split the Difference, 2
Nike, 151–52

258 INDEX

NIMBY (not in my backyard), 87, 204, 215, 230
null hypothesis, 30–31, 112, 230

occupations, geographically dispersed versus concentrated, 70
odds, 59
opportunity cost, 20, 40, 230
optical illusions, 72–73
optimal environmental strategy, 45
optimal foraging theory, 45, 230
optimism bias, 98, 230
options: inside, 60, 71, 86, 124, 144, 163–66, 176, 181, 228; inside versus outside, 12–17, 20, 23, 32, 53–54, 68, 81, 148, 163, 167, 181, 228; limited, 186; outside, 21–22, 55, 69, 145, 152, 166–69, 173–76, 180–82, 192, 229–30
organizational structure, 132
Oster, Emily, 150
overthinking, 62–63
overtime, 106–9, 114

Pan, Jessica, 142
pandemic (2020), 100, 194–96, 198, 206
paparazzi, 116–17
paradox of choice, 194, 230
Peele, Jordan, xvii
penalties for misconduct differing by gender, 111
Penguin Random House, 56
perfectionism, 60, 69
performance criteria, 122, 128, 133, 138
performance evaluations, 9, 156–59
permanent-income hypothesis, 188, 231
Perry, Tyler, 167–69
PhDs in economics, granted to Black people, 33
phone screenings, 75
popularity, 56
postpartum depression, 154
poverty, 187
power, role in economy, 11. *See also* negotiating power

pregnancy, and work, 151–55
prenuptial agreement, 146
present bias, 94, 231
principal-agent problem, 123–25, 231
private space, 195
probability, 30–31, 44
productivity, 21, 46, 106, 111, 118, 127–28, 134, 136, 193
projection bias, 145–46, 231
promotions, 9, 45, 121–22, 125–28, 131–39, 164–66, 182, 185; correlated with higher turnover, 131
property values, 84, 87
public good, 214, 231
public land, 215
public services, 193, 214
p-value, 112, 230

quality of life, 199, 201
quitting, compared to being laid off, 16

racism, 37, 172, 209
randomization, 107
Rea, Brynn, 14
recency bias, 157, 231
recession, 48, 98, 100, 190, 194. *See also* Great Recession
recession graduates, 18–19, 22
Redfin, xvi, 14–15, 86, 92, 100, 175–80, 189, 193–95, 197, 200, 206–7, 211, 219
reference points, 166–69, 172, 175–77, 182–83, 232
references, curating for job applications, 78–79, 81
relationship objectives, 146–47, 160. *See also* dating, probability of success in
relationships: cooperative, 71; romantic, 8; romantic, as negotiation games, 12–14, 22–23
remote work, 69, 100
rent-burdened households, 88
renting, 84, 90, 98; versus buying, 90
reputation, 111, 119
resale value of homes, 97

research on gender pay gap, 142
resistance to change, 87
résumés, 71–75, 81; fake, 75; names on, 74; with spelling errors, 73–74, 81
rewards, 45; external versus internal, 185, 226, 228
reward systems, 125, 127
risk, 191, 197; known versus unknown, 59; tolerance for, 188, 233
Roberson, LaTavia, 54–58, 107
romantic advances, unwanted, 36
roulette, 46
Roussanov, Nikolai, 174
Rowland, Kelly, 54, 107
rules, in games, 29–31, 44, 216

S&P 500, 191
salary: ideal level, 165; negotiating, 2
Sandberg, Sheryl, 3
San Diego, 86
saving, 10, 102, 185–89, 192, 200–201; mortgage payments as, 83, 91
scarcity, 186–87, 195, 200, 215, 232; in games, 103, 116
Seattle, 90–91, 99, 195–96, 198–99, 204, 206–7, 215–16
second homes, 195, 205–6
selection bias, 107–8, 136, 232
self-esteem, 180–81
self-worth, 163, 183
sexism, 37, 110
Shafir, Eldar, 186
signaling, 116–18, 173–74, 232
skills, 35, 51; versus luck, 26–29. See also luck
skin color, and discrimination, 29
Sklarek, Norma Merrick, xiv–xv
slacking off, 123
social responsibility, 43, 193
sour grapes phenomenon, 48–49
speculation bubbles, 96–97
spending, 10, 185–86, 188–90, 200
spousal income, correlation of, 149
starting conditions, in games, 29–32, 51, 232

statistics, 3, 30–31, 44
status quo bias, 52, 196, 198, 232
stay-at-home parents, 142, 150
stereotypes, in workplace, 109–11, 159–60
stereotyping, 169, 171–72, 174
stock market, 64–65, 84, 191; bubbles, 96
strategy, 1–2, 7, 39, 43, 131
Strawberry, Darryl, 74
stress, 21, 35, 99, 187, 196, 200
student loans, 5
study groups, in graduate school, 34–36
subprime mortgage crisis (2008), 96
sundown town, 210
sunk-cost fallacy, 84, 86, 101, 166, 233
supply and demand, 15, 86, 225, 233
survivorship bias, 3–4, 233

tax benefits, of homeownership, 83, 99, 205–6
taxes, 205–7, 214–16, 228, 231, 232
tempo, in gaming, 26–27, 41, 68, 171, 179, 233
Thaler, Richard, 47
time inconsistency, 145, 233
tournament, 126, 233
turnover, 164
Tversky, Amos, 95
Two Can Play That Game (film), 12, 146, 148, 180

ultimatums, 53–55, 234
uncertainty aversion, 59, 61, 76
unconscious bias, 155–59, 210
undifferentiated product, 67, 234
unemployment rate, in United States, 18
University of Chicago, Economics Department, 33, 41, 43–44, 134
US Census Bureau, 153
utility function, 44, 49, 234

values: held by companies, 77; personal, 218–19
value systems, 48, 50
Veblen, Thorstein, 173

wage gaps, 29

wealth: accumulation, 56, 83; accumulation through homeownership, 88, 203; elite levels of, 3, 56; generational, 27–28, 83, 86; individual, and genetic markers, 28; redistributed, 216

West Seattle, 92–93

wildfire smoke, 196–98

willingness to pay, 170–72, 175, 234

winner's curse, 101, 234

women: earning less than men, 109–10, 137, 142; in economics, 42, 136; impact of having a child on earnings of, 153–56, 161; in leadership positions, 137; leaving workforce after childbirth, 153; outearning men, 144; penalized for expressing anger in workplace, 111; perceived by men to have lower academic abilities, 34; underrepresented in careers where brilliance is valued, 110

work, as exchange of time for money, 192

work culture, 68, 108, 118; competitive, 78; toxic, 76. *See also* company culture; competition: in workplace

workers, lower-wage compared to higher-wage, 16–17, 166

workhorse, 61–62, 68

work-life balance, 10

workplace conflict, 9

workplace stress, effect on health and productivity, 21

zugzwang (compulsion to move), 171–72, 174, 234